What's Wrong with Ayn Rand's Objectivist Ethics

AriArmstrong.com

What's Wrong with Ayn Rand's Objectivist Ethics

Ari Armstrong

Eversol Press
Denver, Colorado

Eversol Press
Denver, Colorado

Armstrong, Ari
What's Wrong with Ayn Rand's Objectivist Ethics
Includes Index
Ethics, Political Philosophy

Designed by Jennifer Armstrong

ISBN: 978-0-9818030-3-6

Notes on the Text

In some cases I use parenthetical notes to cut down on the number of footnotes. I use the prefix TOE to refer to Ayn Rand's "The Objectivist Ethics," in *The Virtue of Selfishness* (New York: Signet, 1964), also published (with different pagination) by the Ayn Rand Institute at https://campus.aynrand.org/works/1961/01/01/the -objectivist-ethics/. I use the prefix AS to refer to Ayn Rand's *Atlas Shrugged* (New York: Dutton, 1992); this is the hardback 35th Anniversary Edition of the novel originally published in 1957. Note that, whereas Rand often uses italics, usually I omit such emphasis in these sources throughout.

For other citations, in the print edition I use footnotes with complete publication information so that readers do not have to flip to multiple pages to hunt down a citation, except I use "ibid." only when a citation repeats on the same page. In the ebook edition, I include complete citations in hyperlinked endnotes. The exception (in both versions) is that I use abbreviated citations for this work: Allan Gotthelf and Gregory Salmieri, eds., *A Companion to Ayn Rand*, part of the Blackwell Companions to Philosophy series (Chichester, UK: John Wiley & Sons, 2016).

Usually when referring to a generic or hypothetical person, I use the terms "he," "him," and "his" in a gender-neutral sense. Uses of the singular "they" and of "oneself" and the like can be esthetically unpleasant and distracting, and "he or she" and comparable formulations are clunky and apparently inadequate anyway. A writer can't win, but he (and "he" need not be male!) can try to get by as best he can.

In the ebook edition, I include page references in subscripted brackets that correspond with the physical pages of the print version; obviously in a free-flowing ebook these numbers may appear anywhere on the screen.

Finally, I note that writing this text has given me ample opportunity to reflect on my own moral failings in life, which I deeply regret.

Acknowledgements

Jennifer Armstrong designed the cover and print book and helped proofread the text.

Roger Bissell, Tobin Spratte, Dave Walden, Stephen Bourque, and three anonymous reviewers provided useful comments on a draft of this work (and of course are not responsible if problems or disagreements remain).

Staff at the Denver Public Library, the Auraria Library, and the Jefferson County Public Library (of Colorado) helped me track down some of the essays discussed in this work.

The online *Ayn Rand Lexicon*, published by the Ayn Rand Institute at http://aynrandlexicon.com (accessed at different times in 2017 and 2018), was a helpful source for locating some of the quotations that I reference in this work. The *Lexicon* originally was published in print as edited by Harry Binswanger (New York: New American Library, 1988).

Contents

1. Ayn Rand's Selfishness

AYN RAND'S CORE SURVIVAL-ORIENTED, egoistic moral theory—her metaethics—is wrong, as I will argue. But, before I get into the details of why her theory is wrong, I want to offer some context about Rand's cultural influence, her life, and her distinctive understanding of selfishness.

Rand obviously has dramatically influenced American intellectual and political culture, but why?

Rand's influence cannot be explained mainly by the number of her books sold. At around twenty-seven million copies, Rand's sales remain impressive by usual standards, yet Rand does not make Wikipedia's lengthy "list of best-selling fiction authors" of all time.[1] By contrast, J. R. R. Tolkien, Zane Grey, and John Grisham each has sold upwards of a quarter of a billion books; J. K. Rowling around half a billion; and Agatha Christie two to four billion. Yet, with few exceptions, we rarely find the authors on Wikipedia's list discussed in popular articles about culture, politics, and the news of the day,

---

1 The estimate of the number of Ayn Rand's books sold is from "About Ayn Rand," Ayn Rand Institute, https://www.aynrand.org/about/about-ayn-rand (accessed September 27, 2017); this figure includes both fiction and nonfiction works, but the bulk of sales are of Rand's two major novels. The Wikipedia list of best-selling fiction authors is at https://en.wikipedia.org/wiki/List_of_best-selling_fiction_authors (accessed September 27, 2017).

whereas we routinely find such discussion about Ayn Rand. This is so even though Rand's most famous work, *Atlas Shrugged*, came out in 1957, and Rand died in 1982, before over half of today's global population was born.[2] What explains Rand's relevance is that her books are about big ideas that appeal to a substantial subset of the population especially in the United States, Rand's adopted country, where Rand's advocacy of individualism and capitalism resonates among millions.

Rand's two major novels can be intimidating; *The Fountainhead* (1943) spans nearly eight-hundred pages, while *Atlas Shrugged* runs several hundred pages longer and features lengthy speeches rich in philosophic content. Light reading these books are not. So people who read Rand's novels tend to be interested in philosophy and the deep questions about human existence. These novels typically challenge people's long-held assumptions and often change people's thinking and way of life.

People who like Rand's work are drawn to it for various reasons. Some artists love Rand's story of Howard Roark (*The Fountainhead*), an architect with the will to make real his innovative vision. Neil Peart, the drummer and lyricist for the hall-of-fame rock band Rush, saw in Rand's work "an affirmation that it's all right to totally believe in something and live for it and not compromise."[3] Some business leaders find inspiration in the great industrialists of *Atlas Shrugged*. John Allison, who as head of the financial services corporation BB&T shepherded the company's growth in assets from $4.5 billion to $152

---

2 The United Nations puts the median age of the world's population at thirty; see *World Population Prospects: The 2017 Revision, Key Findings & Advance Tables*, United Nations Department of Economic and Social Affairs, 2017, https://esa .un.org/unpd/wpp/Publications/Files/WPP2017_KeyFindings.pdf, p. 1.

3 Andy Greene, "Q&A: Neil Peart On Rush's New LP and Being a 'Bleeding Heart Libertarian,'" *Rolling Stone*, June 12, 2012, http://www.rollingstone .com/music/news/q-a-neil-peart-on-rushs-new-lp-and-being-a-bleeding-heart -libertarian-20120612. In this interview Peart also says he came to disagree with Rand and evolve into a "bleeding heart Libertarian." Peart and many others appear on Wikipedia's "List of People Influenced by Ayn Rand," https://en.wikipedia.org /wiki/List_of_people_influenced_by_Ayn_Rand (accessed September 27, 2017). Incidentally, Jimmy Wales, co-founder of Wikipedia, joins that list.

billion, calls the ideas that Rand endorses "fundamental to business success and to personal happiness."[4] Various intellectuals from many fields—and we can stretch the category to include bookish politicians[5]—also find Rand's ideas compelling or at least interesting. Those who take Rand's ideas most seriously have formed an evolving cadre of intellectuals to promote Rand's philosophy of Objectivism. Following the publication of *Atlas Shrugged*, Rand turned to writing essays and delivering talks about her ideas and their application to culture and politics; many of these essays and talks are anthologized in a series of books.[6] Meanwhile, Nathaniel Branden, a close associate of Rand prior to their messy (and romance-related) break, developed seminars to advance Rand's ideas. Eventually it fell primarily to philosopher Leonard Peikoff to take up Rand's mantle. In 1985 Peikoff joined the newly formed Ayn Rand Institute (ARI);[7] in 1991 Penguin published Peikoff's *Objectivism: The Philosophy of Ayn Rand*, widely regarded as the definitive statement of Rand's philosophy.[8]

Since then, philosophers and other intellectuals associated with ARI have written or contributed to numerous other academic books and articles devoted to Rand's philosophy, including the

---

4   John Allison, "Introduction," in *Why Businessmen Need Philosophy*, ed. Debi Ghate and Richard E. Ralston (New York: New American Library, 2011), pp. ix, xii.

5   For example, see Craig Biddle, "Ted Cruz for President," *Objective Standard*, April   2,   2016,   https://www.theobjectivestandard.com/2016/04/ted-cruz-for -president/; and Ari Armstrong, "Paul Ryan Rejects Ayn Rand's Ideas—In Word and Deed," *Objective Standard*, August 12, 2012, https://www.theobjectivestandard .com/2012/08/paul-ryan-rejects-ayn-rands-ideas-in-word-and-deed/.

6   The Ayn Rand Institute lists Rand's works at https://www.aynrand.org/novels (accessed September 27, 2017).

7   "Announcements," *Objectivist Forum*, December 1984, vol. 5, no. 6, p. 13–14, in the bound *Volume 1–Volume 8: 1980–1987*, ed. Harry Binswanger and Leonard Peikoff (New York: TOF Publications, 1993).

8   Leonard Peikoff discusses the history of his book in *Objectivism: The Philosophy of Ayn Rand* (New York: Dutton, 1991), pp. xiv–xv. Rand said that Peikoff's lectures on which the book was based were "fully accurate," but she died before Peikoff completed his book, so she did not see or approve "the new wording and organization" of the book.

2016 Blackwell *A Companion to Ayn Rand*. As of 2018, ARI directly employs three full-time credentialed philosophers and several others with advanced degrees.[9] ARI's board consists mainly of academics and business leaders and includes chair Yaron Brook, who writes books and articles, podcasts, and travels the globe advocating Rand's ideas.[10] The Institute hosts conferences and online courses, distributes Rand's books to schools, organizes essay contests based on Rand's work, and runs an academic center to train "future Objectivist intellectuals."[11] Outside ARI's sphere, various academics engage with Rand's ideas with varying degrees of agreement.

Even some intellectuals who largely reject Rand's philosophy find her inspiring. Philosopher Roderick Long writes, "[I]t was Rand's works which first opened up to me the world of philosophy."[12] Robert Nozick found Rand's "two major novels exciting, powerful, illuminating, and thought-provoking."[13] Will Wilkinson of the Niskanen Center says that reading and discussing Rand's works was how he was "inducted into the tradition of classical liberal thought." He adds, "Rand encourages us to be excellent, to apply our powers to their limit, to make our lives adventures. . . . I simply would not have done what little I have done without this impetus to be better,

---

9   The Ayn Rand Institute lists its staff at https://ari.aynrand.org/about-ari/board -and-staff#aristaff (accessed February 1, 2018).

10   For an account of one of Brook's tours, see "Around the World in 44 Days," Ayn Rand Institute, July 19, 2017, https://ari.aynrand.org/blog/2017/07/19 /around-the-world-in-44-days. The Institute offers a biography of Brook at https:// ari.aynrand.org/experts/yaron-brook (accessed September 27, 2017).

11   "Programs & Initiatives," Ayn Rand Institute, https://ari.aynrand.org/about -ari/programs#objectivistacademiccenter-1 (accessed September 27, 2017).

12   Roderick T. Long, "Reason and Value: Aristotle versus Rand," in *Objectivist Studies* 3, ed. William Thomas (Poughkeepsie, NY: Objectivist Center, 2000), https://atlassociety.org/sites/default/files/Reason_Value.pdf, p. 5.

13   Robert Nozick, "On the Randian Argument," in *Reading Nozick*, ed. Jeffrey Paul (Totowa, NJ: Rowman and Littlefield, 1981), p. 222, n. 1.

to push myself harder, to expect more from life."[14] Philosopher Matt Zwolinski says that "without Ayn Rand," he never would have thought of "seriously studying philosophy, let alone making a career of it."[15] Economist Bryan Caplan reports that his interest in ideas "began with Ayn Rand, as it proverbially does." He writes, "I probably wouldn't be a professor if it weren't for her, and even if I were, I doubt I would be having a fraction of the fun."[16]

Another surprising example of the influence of Rand's fiction may be found at the free-market oriented Francisco Marroquín University in Guatemala, which features a sculpture and plaque commemorating Rand's work.[17] The plaque quotes from John Galt's speech in *Atlas Shrugged*:

> Do not lose your knowledge that man's proper estate is an upright posture, an intransigent mind and a step that travels unlimited roads. Do not let your fire go out, spark by irreplaceable spark, in the hopeless swamps of the approximate, the not-quite, the not-yet, the not-at-all. Do not let the hero in

---

14 Will Wilkinson, "First Letter to a Young Objectivist," *Fly Bottle*, August 12, 2004, http://www.willwilkinson.net/flybottle/2004/08/12/first-letter-to-a-young-objectivist/; Will Wilkinson, "Third Letter to a Young Objectivist: Ethics," *Fly Bottle*, March 2, 2005, http://www.willwilkinson.net/flybottle/2005/03/02/third-letter-to-a-young-objectivist-ethics/.

15 Matt Zwolinski, "A Critique of Ayn Rand's Theory of Rights," comments for a 2014 meeting of the Pacific Division Meeting of the American Philosophical Association, http://bleedingheartlibertarians.com/wp-content/uploads/2014/04/A-Critique-of-Ayn-Rands-Theory-of-Rights.pdf.

16 Bryan Caplan, "Intellectual Autobiography of Bryan Caplan," http://econfaculty.gmu.edu/bcaplan/autobio.htm (accessed October 10, 2017); Bryan Caplan, "Join the Party: Why You Should Celebrate Rand's 100th," *Library of Economics and Liberty*, February 2, 2005, http://econlog.econlib.org/archives/2005/02/join_the_party.html. The first line refers to Jerome Tuccile, *It Usually Begins with Ayn Rand* (New York: Stein and Day, 1971).

17 The piece is mentioned by Marla Dickerson, "Leftist Thinking Left Off the Syllabus," *Los Angeles Times*, June 6, 2008, http://www.latimes.com/world/mexico-americas/la-fi-guatemala6-2008jun06-story.html. Philosopher Stephen Hicks shows photos of the sculpture and plaque at "An Inspiring University Points to the Future," April 13, 2009, http://www.stephenhicks.org/2009/04/13/an-inspiring-university-points-to-the-future/.

your soul perish, in lonely frustration for the life you deserved, but have never been able to reach. Check your road and the nature of your battle. The world you desired can be won, it exists, it is real, it is possible, it's yours. (AS 1069)[18]

Rand's vision of a heroic and meaningful life filled with values and joy is the basic cause of her continued cultural relevance.

Rand advances a number of related ideas that many people find compelling. She advocates observation-based reason and personal happiness and rejects religion with its logical absurdities, appeals to authority, and pointless guilt. (That said, a surprising number of Christians embrace aspects of Rand's philosophy and try to meld the two traditions, as I did in my older teens.) She upholds objective moral truth and rejects moral subjectivism and cultural relativism. She glorifies productive achievement and opposes old-world aristocracy as well as modern cronyism and welfare-statism. She epitomizes the American tradition of industry; some of her language is reminiscent of that of Calvin Coolidge, who said "the chief business of the American people is business" and "the man who builds a factory builds a temple."[19]

Although Rand's works reach a wide international audience, Rand, an immigrant with a thick Russian accent, is a quintessentially American writer and intellectual.

Rand's Critics

Despite the fact that millions of people find inspiration in Ayn Rand's novels and ideas—or rather partly because of that fact—Rand regularly is subjected to vicious attacks in the popular media, even decades after her death. She continues to earn plenty of positive press, too, but the bad generally outweighs the good.

---

18   As noted in "Notes on the Text," when citing Ayn Rand's *Atlas Shrugged* (New York: Dutton, 1992), I'll use parenthetical notes with the prefix AS.

19   See Robert Sobel, "Coolidge and American Business," Calvin Coolidge Presidential Foundation, 1988, https://coolidgefoundation.org/resources/essays -papers-addresses-35/.

The main reasons for the widespread antipathy toward Rand are obvious. People on the Progressive left tend to dislike Rand because she advocates unregulated capitalism and the abolition of the welfare state. People on the conservative right tend to dislike her because she vocally advocates atheism and denounces all forms of religious faith. Both groups on the whole hate Rand because she advocates selfishness, which conflicts with Progressive collectivism and egalitarianism as well as with Christian self-sacrifice and service.

Consider some of the representative slights:

"[Rand's philosophy] makes a religious fetish of selfishness and disposes of altruism and compassion as character flaws. . . . Objectivism is basically autism rebranded." —Sam Harris[20]

"Rand . . . has been a key in the intellectual justification of the narcissism epidemic that has been growing in the United States during the last two to three decades." —Matthieu Ricard[21]

"From almost any page of *Atlas Shrugged*, a voice can be heard, from painful necessity, commanding: 'To a gas chamber—go!'" —Whittaker Chambers (*National Review*)[22]

"If Objectivism seems familiar, it is because most people know it under another name: adolescence. . . . Rand's achievement

---

20 Sam Harris, "How to Lose Readers (Without Even Trying)," August 24, 2011, https://www.samharris.org/blog/item/how-to-lose-readers-without-even-trying.

21 Matthieu Ricard, "Ayn Rand: Is This the Right Model for a Great Nation?," July 26, 2017, https://www.linkedin.com/pulse/ayn-rand-right-model-great-nation-matthieu-ricard.

22 Whittaker Chambers, "Big Sister Is Watching You," *National Review*, January 5, 2005 (originally published December 28, 1957), http://www.nationalreview.com/article/213298/big-sister-watching-you-whittaker-chambers.   For   Leonard Peikoff's reply, which *National Review* never published, see his "Reply to Whittaker Chambers," in *Essays on Ayn Rand's* Atlas Shrugged, ed. Robert Mayhew (Lanham, MD: Lexington Books, 2009), pp. 145–147.

was to turn a phase into a philosophy, as attractive as an outbreak of acne." —Michael Gerson (*Washington Post*)[23]

"Ayn Rand . . . [advocates] a world in which we're only thinking about ourselves and not thinking about anybody else, in which we're considering the entire project of developing ourselves as more important than our relationships to other people and making sure that everybody else has opportunity[, in which we're] all isolated and looking out only for ourselves."—Barack Obama[24]

"Rand's ruthless supremacism . . . —her stark division of humankind into 'makers and takers'—leads inexorably to a society like the one that staged 'The Hunger Games.'" —Judith Thurman (*New Yorker*)[25]

"Ayn Rand's philosophy actually says it is not only bad for society, but morally wrong to help other people because it makes them 'dependent.' Rand's philosophy says that altruism is evil, and that democracy (which they call 'collectivism') is the ultimate expression of this evil because

---

23 Michael Gerson, "Ayn Rand's Adult-Onset Adolescence," *Washington Post*, April 21, 2011, https://www.washingtonpost.com/opinions/ayn-rands-adult-onset -adolescence/2011/04/21/AFv2JyKE_story.html.

24 Douglas Brinkley, "Obama and the Road Ahead: The Rolling Stone Interview," *Rolling Stone*, November 8, 2012, https://www.rollingstone .com/politics/politics-news/obama-and-the-road-ahead-the-rolling-stone -interview-123468/. For my reply to Obama's remarks, see Ari Armstrong, "Obama, Unsurprisingly, Gets Ayn Rand Wrong," *Objective Standard*, October 25, 2012, https://www.theobjectivestandard.com/2012/10/obama -unsurprisingly-gets-ayn-rand-wrong/.

25 Judith Thurman, "A Libertarian House on the Prairie," *New Yorker*, August 16, 2012, https://www.newyorker.com/books/page-turner/a-libertarian-house-on-the -prairie.

it brings about a society in which government works to make people's lives better." —Dave Johnson (*Salon*)[26]

Never mind that almost all of the substantive claims about Rand in the quotes above and in comparable remarks elsewhere are based on wild misrepresentations of her ideas.

Many critics smear Rand's character as they dismiss her ideas. This is convenient, for surely (goes the thinking) the fact that Rand was a bad person helps explain why she promoted bad ideas. As rhetoric professor James Arnt Aune puts the point, "the particulars of [Rand's] private life call into question the validity of her moral philosophy."[27] What should we make of such claims?

Ayn Rand certainly was not perfect. She had a sexual relationship with Nathaniel Branden while married to another man (she did tell her husband in advance), a relationship that ended disastrously; she smoked cigarettes and took probably unhealthy amounts of prescription amphetamines (this *was* the mid-twentieth century);

---

26 Dave Johnson, "6 Reasons There's No Such Thing as Compassionate Conservatism," *Salon*, December 12, 2013, https://www.salon.com/2013/12/12/6 _reasons_theres_no_such_thing_as_compassionate_conservatism_partner/. For my reply, see Ari Armstrong, "Why Does Salon Lie about Ayn Rand's Ideas?," *Objective Standard*, December 18, 2013, https://www.theobjectivestandard.com/2013/12 /why-does-salon-lie-about-ayn-rands-ideas/. For more examples of spurious attacks on Rand, see Carrie-Ann Biondi's review essay of *A Companion to Ayn Rand* in *Reason Papers*, Winter 2017, vol. 39, no. 1, https://reasonpapers.com/wp-content /uploads/2017/09/rp_391_9rev.pdf, p. 124, n. 1.

27 James Arnt Aune, "Rhetorical Incorrectness?," *Journal of Ayn Rand Studies*, Fall 2002, vol. 4, no. 1, pp. 233–234. Some who conduct an internet search for Aune might regard his comments about Rand as ironic.

she could be short-tempered and alienating; she said troubling things about homosexuals, Native Americans, and others.[28]

Yet no one would fare well in an inquisition that listed all of a person's negative traits and bad relationships and ignored the positive ones. So let's glance at the other side of the ledger. Ayn Rand truly was a heroic figure on the order of the protagonists of her novels. She left her home in Russia to start over in a foreign land, then went on to write two highly successful—now classic—novels (along with various other works) in her adopted tongue. Her literature and philosophic work regularly appear in university curriculums. She continues to inspire artists, business leaders, political activists, scholars, and other readers around the world. And, if Rand could be imperial and mean, she could also be generous and show people "immense warmth," as philosopher Allan Gotthelf reflects about the time he spent with Rand when he was a student.[29]

"Rand the monster" is a convenient fiction for those who wish to reject Rand's ideas without the bother of critically evaluating them. Rand deserves better, and her ideas deserve a fair hearing. Let's start down that path by considering what Rand actually means by selfishness and related concepts.

---

28   Among the sources to discuss such things is Jennifer Burns, *Goddess of the Market: Ayn Rand and the American Right* (Oxford University Press, 2009), esp. pp. 85, 148, 156, 236, 238–239, 266. Michael Shermer goes so far as to liken Rand's early movement to a cult; see his "The Unlikeliest Cult," in *Why People Believe Weird Things* (New York: MJF Books, 1997), pp. 114–124, republished online at https://www.skeptic.com/reading_room/the-unlikeliest-cult-in-history/. James S. Valliant warns that some negative claims about Rand's personal life derive from the questionable memoirs of Nathaniel Branden and his one-time wife Barbara Branden—hardly unbiased observers; see Valliant's *The Passion of Ayn Rand's Critics: The Case Against the Brandens* (Dallas, TX: Durban House, 2005). For additional criticism of the Brandens' biographical works, see Shoshana Milgram, "The Life of Ayn Rand," in *A Companion to Ayn Rand*, pp. 36–37. As noted in "Notes on the Text," for the *Companion* I provide abbreviated citations in the notes.

29   Gotthelf and many others reflect on Rand in interviews compiled in Scott McConnell, *100 Voices: An Oral History of Ayn Rand* (New York: New American Library, 2010); Gotthelf's quote appears on p. 331.

Rand's Selfishness in Context

People who claim that Rand rejects such things as collaboration, friendship, compassion, and charity simply don't know what they're talking about.

We can see clearly that Rand does care about such things, for example, in the relationship of Howard Roark and Steven Mallory in *The Fountainhead*. Mallory is a struggling and misunderstood sculptor whose work is genius but who suffers a profound crisis of self-confidence. Roark visits Mallory in his squalid apartment and talks with the desperate young man for hours. During Roark's first meeting with Mallory, after the two men get to know each other, Roark expresses admiration for Mallory's work and asks him to talk about what matters to him. "Then [Roark] sat for hours, listening, while Mallory spoke of his work, of the thoughts behind his work, of the thoughts that shaped his life, spoke gluttonously, like a drowning man flung out to shore, getting drunk on huge, clean snatches of air."[30]

As for friendship, consider a scene where Roark, Mallory, Dominique Francon (Roark's love interest and a model for Mallory's work), and Mike Donnigan (a construction worker) gather after work on a job site:

> They did not speak about their work. Mallory told outrageous stories and Dominique laughed like a child. They talked about nothing in particular, sentences that had meaning only in the sound of the voices, in the warm gaiety, in the ease of complete relaxation. They were simply four people who liked being there together.[31]

What about charity? True, Rand was not too concerned about it. Yet, when Mallory falls on hard times, Roark "paid Mallory's rent and he paid for most of their frequent meals together." True enough, Roark couches his charity in selfish terms. He tells Mallory, "I'm not

---

30 Ayn Rand, *The Fountainhead*, centennial edition, (New York: Penguin Group, 2005), p. 339.
31 Ibid., p. 345.

doing it for you. At a time like this I owe myself a few luxuries. So I'm simply buying the most valuable thing that can be bought—your time" to work. He later says that his motive is not to "relieve the pain" of others, yet obviously such relief can result from the sort of charity that Rand endorses.[32]

Rand summarizes her view of charity this way:

> My views on charity are very simple. I do not consider it a major virtue and, above all, I do not consider it a moral duty. There is nothing wrong in helping other people, if and when they are worthy of the help and you can afford to help them. I regard charity as a marginal issue. What I am fighting is the idea that charity is a moral duty and a primary virtue.[33]

As for her personal life, "Rand was often extremely generous" toward others, point out Neera Badhwar and Roderick Long. They point out, for example, that Rand rescued "her first English teacher and her mother's close friend, Maria Strakhow, from a Displaced Persons' camp in Austria, paying for her passage and putting her up in her own home for a year."[34] In a letter, Rand assured her friend that she would be pleased to pay for her "passage to America." "Do not consider it as any kind of an imposition on me," Rand wrote to her friend, "but rather as a favor that you would do me, if you say that you care to come." In another letter, Rand urged her attorney to help the woman come to America, writing, "I would like very much to bring her to the United States, and would, of course, assume responsibility for her support."[35]

---

32 Ayn Rand, *The Fountainhead*, centennial edition, (New York: Penguin Group, 2005), pp. 399–400.

33 Alvin Toffler, "Playboy Interview: Ayn Rand," *Playboy*, March 1964, reproduced as *50 Years of the Playboy Interview: Ayn Rand* (Playboy Enterprises, 2012).

34 Neera K. Badhwar and Roderick T. Long, "Ayn Rand," *Stanford Encyclopedia of Philosophy*, September 19, 2016, https://plato.stanford.edu/entries/ayn-rand/ (including n. 7 at https://plato.stanford.edu/entries/ayn-rand/notes.html#note-7).

35 Michael S. Berliner, ed., *Letters of Ayn Rand* (New York: Dutton, 1995), pp. 302, 360. The letters in question are dated August 8, 1946 and January 29, 1947; several other letters in the volume also discuss the matter.

Although I think Rand leaves too little theoretical room for charity (as I'll explore in more detail in a future chapter) and that relieving the suffering of others can be a perfectly good motive for charitable giving, clearly it is a mistake to claim that Rand opposes charity.

Many people especially on the left seem to think that Rand's relative disinterest in charity, coupled with her opposition to the welfare state, implies that Rand is fine with people starving in the streets. What Rand actually thinks is that untrammeled capitalism—which she calls the "unknown ideal"—would lead to near-universal prosperity such that little charity would be necessary. (Rand's "ideal" capitalism contrasts with today's mixture of freedom and controls.)[36]

To be sure, Rand does not advocate capitalism fundamentally to alleviate poverty or for any other social goal. Rand is an individualist, and her basic argument for capitalism is that it leaves individuals free to act on their judgment to better their lives. Yet Rand would point out that what is good for each individual (in terms of broad principles) is good for individuals generally.[37] And Rand certainly thinks that capitalism is best for individuals.

What does Rand mean by capitalism, and what does she think it implies? Although this is not the place to defend Rand's political and economic views, we can at least get an idea of what Rand thought about such matters and review some of the basic facts that lend Rand's views initial plausibility. It is one thing to disagree with Rand about capitalism; it is another to distort what she thought about it.

Capitalism, Rand holds, is the political-economic system that results when government consistently protects the rights of individuals

---

36   See Ayn Rand, "What Is Capitalism?," in *Capitalism: The Unknown Ideal* (New York: Signet, 1967), p. 31.

37   Rand writes that "'good' and 'value' pertain only to . . . an individual living organism," not to a group. She grants that "the common good" has meaning as "the sum of the good of all the individual men involved." See Ayn Rand, "What Is Capitalism?," in *Capitalism: The Unknown Ideal* (New York: Signet, 1967), p. 20 (emphasis omitted).

to be free from the coercion of others (TOE 32–33).[38] Government, then, properly organizes the police, the military, and the courts, Rand holds. Obviously this is a radically different conception of capitalism than what Marxists, Progressives, and various others hold. For Rand, capitalism means that government consistently upholds people's rights—fundamentally their rights to life and property—so in such a system people interact by voluntary consent. The economic consequence is a vibrant, dynamic, and ever-growing economy in which, yes, some people earn spectacular wealth, and in which anyone who works purposefully for success can find it at some level.

Rand writes in her introduction to *Capitalism: The Unknown Ideal*, "No politico-economic system in history has ever proved its value so eloquently or has benefited mankind so greatly as capitalism— and none has ever been attacked so savagely, viciously, and blindly."[39] Here Rand is talking about the dominantly capitalistic societies that have existed since the dawn of the Industrial Revolution, not a consistent capitalism that she thinks would lead to vastly greater and more widespread prosperity.

In Rand's view, "human poverty and suffering" persist mainly to the degree that capitalism has not taken hold. "[C]apitalism," she writes, "is the only system that enables men to produce abundance."[40] In a world of abundance made possible by universal capitalism, opportunities would be widespread, good jobs would be plentiful, and economic progress would lead to ever-growing real wages. In such a world, few people would need charity, and the vast majority of

---

38 As noted in "Notes on the Text," when citing Ayn Rand's "The Objectivist Ethics," in *The Virtue of Selfishness* (New York: Signet, 1964), I'll use parenthetical notes with the prefix TOE.

39 Ayn Rand, "Introduction," in *Capitalism: The Unknown Ideal* (New York: Signet, 1967), p. vii.

40 Ayn Rand, "Requiem for Man," in *Capitalism: The Unknown Ideal* (New York: Signet, 1967), pp. 308–309.

people who did not need it easily could afford to voluntarily provide assistance to those few truly in need.[41]

Rand contrasts capitalism, based on individual rights, with all forms of collectivist statism, in which some individuals and their interests are sacrificed to an alleged "greater good." Bear in mind that Rand witnessed first-hand the rise of the Soviet empire. Communism was based on allegedly "rational" economic planning according to the Marxist dictum, "From each according to his ability, to each according to his need." The result was decades of mass slaughter, starvation, and economic stagnation. Today we see the remnants of Marxism in the totalitarian hellhole of North Korea and in the starving and oppressive Venezuela.

Meanwhile, the benefits of capitalism are hard to ignore by anyone open to evidence. Since the establishment of relatively free markets throughout much of the world, global population has skyrocketed even as the fraction of people—and, within the last few decades, even the absolute number of people—living in extreme poverty has plummeted.[42]

Unfortunately (by Rand's view), statist intervention in markets remains common throughout the world, even in relatively free regions, throttling economic growth and opportunities. To take just one example in the United States, occupational licensing frequently serves to squash competition to the (short-sighted) advantage of the politically connected and the harm of everyone else.[43]

Rand thoroughly studied the history and nature of capitalism. She was familiar with the works of great free-market economists such

41 Among those who discuss charity and welfare from the perspective of Rand's ideas are Yaron Brook and Don Watkins in *Free Market Revolution* (New York: Palgrave MacMillan, 2012), pp. 177–192; and Tara Smith in *Ayn Rand's Normative Ethics* (New York: Cambridge University Press, 2006), pp. 248–256.

42 See Max Roser and Esteban Ortiz-Ospina, "World Population Growth," *Our World in Data*, April 2017, https://ourworldindata.org/world-population-growth; and Max Roser and Esteban Ortiz-Ospina, "Global Extreme Poverty," *Our World in Data*, March 27, 2017, https://ourworldindata.org/extreme-poverty/.

43 For an example of this, see "Iowa Hair Braiding," Institute for Justice, http://ij.org/case/iowa-hair-braiding/ (accessed October 13, 2017).

as Ludwig von Mises.[44] Although Rand's views on economics are
controversial, they are part of a long intellectual tradition of (classical)
liberal political theory and economics, though (as she would put it)
more consistently developed.

Bryan Caplan recognizes the subtlety of Rand's thought in
the field:

> Rand was an insightful social scientist. A casual reading
> of *Atlas Shrugged* shows that she got the essence of general
> equilibrium theory. She loves to trace the indirect ripple effects
> of economic shocks, both positive (the invention of Rearden
> Metal) and negative (a new law forbidding people from owning
> multiple businesses). But a casual reading underestimates her
> contribution to social science. Rand's general equilibrium
> model encompasses *both* markets *and* politics. The invention of
> Rearden Metal does far more than change the economy; it also
> affects public opinion, which affects government policy, which
> in turn feeds back into the economy.[45]

Rand, then, is very much aware of the relationships between
her moral, political, and economic views. She sincerely thinks that
capitalism would lead to widespread prosperity and that poverty
would be a minor problem, easily handled by private charity. One
can argue that Rand is wrong about capitalism, that full capitalism
would in fact create widespread problems of destitution and misery,
and that only a robust welfare state combined with heavy regulation
of economic activity can solve such problems. But one cannot in

---

44 Rand recommended "the works of the great economist Ludwig von Mises,"
along with Henry Hazlitt's popular *Economics in One Lesson* and other works, in
a letter to Martin Larson dated July 15, 1960; see Michael S. Berliner, ed., *Letters
of Ayn Rand* (New York: Dutton, 1995), p. 582. Rand also criticized Mises's
philosophic ideas; see p. 260 of the same work.

45 Bryan Caplan, "Join the Party: Why You Should Celebrate Rand's 100th," *Library
of Economics and Liberty*, February 2, 2005, http://econlog.econlib.org/archives/2005/02
/join_the_party.html. It is worth noting here that Caplan disagrees with Rand's moral
theory; see Bryan Caplan, "Intellectual Autobiography of Bryan Caplan," http://
econfaculty.gmu.edu/bcaplan/autobio.htm (accessed September 29, 2017).

fairness claim that Rand thinks that capitalism entails the problems that Marxists or Progressives think it does.

Let us turn from Rand's selfish politics and economics to see what she means by designating selfishness a virtue.

In her 1964 five-page introduction to *The Virtue of Selfishness*—a nice summary of some of her main ideas in ethics—Rand defines selfishness as "concern with one's own interests."[46] But what are one's interests? The usual problem, Rand explains, is that people often confuse whatever someone wants to do with the person's interests. So, for example, if someone feels like robbing a bank or raping someone or murdering a foe, a person has an "interest" in doing such things, goes the usual line of thinking. But that's totally wrong, in Rand's view; rather, a person's interests must be defined by the objective requirements of human life. She writes:

> The Objectivist ethics holds that the actor must always be the beneficiary of his actions and that man must act for his own *rational* self-interest. But his right to do so is derived from his nature as man and from the function of moral values in human life—and, therefore, is applicable *only* in the context of a rational, objectively demonstrated and validated code of moral principles which define and determine his actual self-interest. It is not a license "to do as he pleases" and it is not applicable to the altruists' image of a "selfish" brute nor to any man motivated by irrational emotions, feelings, urges, wishes or whims.

Rand's goal is to wrest the concept of selfishness from those who abuse it. The wrong conception of selfishness offers a "package-deal" of brutes who "selfishly" abuse others and of rational and productive individuals who respect others' rights and interact with others by mutual consent. By the false view of selfishness, continues Rand, "An industrialist who produces a fortune, and a gangster who robs a bank

---

46 This quote and, until otherwise noted, subsequent quotes are from Ayn Rand, "Introduction," in *The Virtue of Selfishness* (New York: Signet, 1964), p. vii–xi (some emphasis omitted).

are regarded as equally immoral, since they both sought wealth for their own 'selfish' benefit."

Rand endorses selfish egoism as she condemns selfless altruism. By altruism, Rand does not mean being nice to others, befriending them, cooperating with them, or helping them. For Rand, a parent taking care of his child, someone helping a friend through a difficult time, and someone donating time or money to a worthy cause can be perfectly selfish acts. Rand's use of the term altruism comports with its original, philosophic meaning: dutiful self-sacrifice for others.[47] In Rand's view, "Altruism holds that man has no right to exist for his own sake, that service to others is the only justification of his existence, and that *self-sacrifice* is his highest moral duty, virtue, and value."[48] People often criticize Rand for her rejection of altruism without grasping what Rand meant by the term.

In Rand's view, abusing others or violating their rights cannot be in one's interests.[49] In "The Objectivist Ethics," she writes, "every living human being is an end in himself, not the means to the ends or the welfare of others." The implication, Rand continues, is that every person "must live for his own sake, neither sacrificing himself to others nor sacrificing others to himself" (TOE 27).

Further, Rand believes that benevolence can exist only to the degree that rational egoists live free from coercion: "Benevolence is incompatible with fear. It is only when a man knows that his

---

47 See George H. Smith, "Ayn Rand and Altruism, Part 1," Libertarianism.org (Cato Institute), October 23, 2012, https://www.libertarianism.org/publications /essays/excursions/ayn-rand-altruism-part-1.

48 Ayn Rand, "Conservatism: An Obituary," in *Capitalism: The Unknown Ideal* (New York: Signet, 1967), p. 195. The article (and original talk) are published by the Ayn Rand Institute, with different pagination, at https://campus.aynrand.org /works/1962/01/01/conservatism-an-obituary (accessed May 22, 2018).

49 We examine possible emergency-condition exceptions in a later chapter.

neighbors have no power forcibly to interfere with his life, that he can feel benevolence toward them, and they toward him."[50]

Of course people may dispute Rand's claim that her theory of ethics, in its logical implications, precludes abusive or rights-violating behavior. Perhaps Rand is wrong about what a survival- and interest-based moral theory implies. Yet it is important to distinguish how Rand thinks her theory works out from how critics think it works out. Philosopher Jason Brennan, who thinks egoism is basically wrong, aptly draws the relevant distinction:

> I acknowledge . . . that Rand in fact believes human beings have rights and that she believes that ethical egoism forbids us from sacrificing one another in order to promote our own interests. . . . More strongly, I acknowledge . . . that Rand thinks it's pretty much impossible for us to promote our own objective interests by preying upon other people. . . . However, I claim that Rand is mistaken about what ethical egoism implies. Her moral theory has horrific implications, implications which she thankfully does not endorse.[51]

As Brennan grants, Rand believes her moral theory entails consistently rights-respecting and just behavior toward others. I would go further than Brennan and say that very few of Rand's critics grasp the subtlety and strength of her arguments regarding such matters.

For good reason millions of people find inspiration in Rand's fiction and many thousands (at least) study her ideas intently. If this

50 Ayn Rand, "A Nation's Unity: Part II," *Ayn Rand Letter*, October 23, 1972, vol. 2, no. 2, in the bound *Volumes 1–4: 1971–1976* (Gaylordsville, CT: Second Renaissance, 1999) on p. 127. On this point, see also Nathaniel Branden, "Benevolence Versus Altruism," *Objectivist Newsletter*, July 1962, vol. 1, no. 7, p. 27, in the bound *Volumes 1–4: 1962–1965* (Gaylordsville, CT: Second Renaissance, 1990). George H. Smith refers to both works in his "Ayn Rand and Altruism, Part 5," Libertarianism.org (Cato Institute), November 20, 2012, https://www.libertarianism.org/publications/essays/excursions/ayn-rand-altruism-part-5.

51 Jason Brennan, "Rand, Egoism, and Rights: To Be Clear," *Bleeding Heart Libertarians*, July 24, 2014, http://bleedingheartlibertarians.com/2014/07/egoism-and-rights/.

seems perplexing to some of Rand's critics, perhaps that is because they deeply misunderstand—or grossly misrepresent—Rand's positions and basically fail to engage her ideas.

If such critics would take Rand's work more seriously, they might find, as I have, reasons to think that she is on the wrong track in important ways. They might also find, as I have, that Rand offers many important insights not only about metaethics but about metaphysics, epistemology, virtue theory, psychology, politics, economics, and other fields.

Looking Ahead

Rand was one of the most important thinkers of the twentieth century, and she deserves respectful engagement of her strongest arguments. This is important to bear in mind as we proceed, as most of the rest of this book is concerned with where Rand goes wrong in her thinking on ethics.

Here is what is to come. Chapter 2 offers a brief summary of Rand's basic moral case, her metaethics. Chapter 3 explains the essential flaws with Rand's metaethics.

Most of the rest of the book explains why particular aspects of Rand's moral philosophy fail the tests of evidence or plausibility. Chapter 4 shows that Rand's basic claims about biology, which hold that an organism's values normally orient to its personal survival, are mistaken. Chapter 5 shows that normal human values often deviate from Rand's survivalism (as we can sensibly call it). Chapter 6 deals with Rand's thought experiment about an indestructible robot, with her refined moral standard of man's life "qua man," and with the role that the choice to live plays in her theory. In each of these matters, Rand's moral philosophy succumbs to additional problems.

Chapter 7 explores the possibility of a rights-respecting egoist and finds that, although Rand's arguments on such matters are stronger than usually presumed, they still are not strong enough to save her theory from troubling implications. Chapter 8 reviews the problems that Rand's theory has in dealing with free riders and with charity.

Chapter 9 offers an alternate way to conceive of a person's ultimate end, one that avoids the problems of Rand's survival-oriented egoism while retaining a sort of Aristotelian flourishing similar to what Rand's theory also embraces. Then an extended appendix reviews important works about Rand's ethics.

The next step is to review the basic structure of Rand's moral theory.

2. Reviewing the Objectivist Ethics

WHEN I FIRST READ AYN RAND'S MORAL THEORY in high school (in the late 1980s), it seemed unassailable to me. Morality is not about obedience to some divine or earthly authority figure, Rand writes, nor about subjective feelings. Rather, morality is about objective right and wrong, based on whether a person, in fact, acts to maintain his life. An action is good and right and moral if it helps to advance your life (by reasonable expectation); it is bad and wrong and immoral if it undercuts your life.

To me, someone raised a devout Protestant and taught that morality is what God teaches us through the Bible, Rand's theory was revolutionary and liberating. Although ultimately I came to see crucial flaws in Rand's theory, I was and remain deeply influenced by it.

Rand's ideas about ethics are interesting and illuminating even when wrong, so they are worth learning. And we cannot understand what is wrong with the theory until we understand what the theory is.

Two of Rand's works are especially important in understanding her moral theory. The first, *Atlas Shrugged*, was published in 1957, when Rand was 52 years old. This novel—her last work of fiction[52]—expresses her mature philosophic views. Although in many cases gleaning a writer's views from a novel can be difficult given the complexities of plot and character, in *Atlas Shrugged* Rand unequivocally offers her own philosophic views, mainly in the form of a lengthy speech by John Galt, Rand's "ideal man."[53]

Following the publication of *Atlas Shrugged*, Rand turned to writing nonfiction and to giving speeches to spread her ideas. The second key work about her ethics is a ten-thousand-word paper she delivered in 1961 for a symposium at the University of Wisconsin.[54] This paper, "The Objectivist Ethics," is reprinted in *The Virtue of Selfishness*. Unsurprisingly, in "The Objectivist Ethics" Rand draws on Galt's speech for key parts of her argument.

In presenting her case, Rand says that the concept of value "presupposes an entity capable of acting to achieve a goal in the face of an alternative" (TOE 15). Then (after restating the point) Rand quotes a key passage from Galt's speech about the foundations of ethics:

> There is only one fundamental alternative in the universe: existence or nonexistence—and it pertains to a single class of entities: to living organisms. The existence of inanimate

---

52 Rand's 1934 play *Night of January 16* (originally *Penthouse Legend*) was published in 1968; for the history see the Plume edition (New York: 1987), pp. 1–16. Rand also revised her 1936 novel *We the Living* for republication in 1959; see Robert Mayhew, "*We the Living*: '36 & '59," in *Essays on Ayn Rand's We the Living*, second edition, ed. Robert Mayhew (Lanham, MD: Lexington Books, 2012), p. 209. Some of Rand's earlier fiction was published after her death in *The Early Ayn Rand*, ed. Leonard Peikoff (New York: New American Library, 1984); *Three Plays* (New York: Signet, 2005); and *Ideal* (New York: New American Library, 2015). Rand did develop a few pages of notes for a new novel that she never finished, *To Lorne Dieterling*; see David Harriman, ed., *Journals of Ayn Rand* (New York: Plume, 1999), pp. 704–716.

53 Rand describes Galt as her "ideal man" in biographical interviews archived by the Ayn Rand Institute; see Shoshana Milgram, "Who *Was* John Galt?," in *Essays on Ayn Rand's Atlas Shrugged*, ed. Robert Mayhew (Lanham, MD: Lexington Books, 2009), p. 73.

54 Some "twelve hundred students, faculty members and visitors" attended Rand's address; see Nathaniel Branden's preface for his *Who Is Ayn Rand?* (New York: Paperback Library, 1964), p. 5.

matter is unconditional, the existence of life is not: it depends on a specific course of action. Matter is indestructible, it changes its forms, but it cannot cease to exist. It is only a living organism that faces a constant alternative: the issue of life or death. Life is a process of self-sustaining and self-generated action. If an organism fails in that action, it dies; its chemical elements remain, but its life goes out of existence. It is only the concept of "Life" that makes the concept of "Value" possible. It is only to a living entity that things can be good or evil. (TOE 15–16)

That is a very rich statement, so let us unpack it.

First we need to get a handle on Rand's distinction between living and nonliving things. It is obviously true that a living thing can stop living and die. But then, doesn't the organism merely change forms like anything else can? All the same chemicals are there; they just stop functioning as they did before. How is that different from an ice cube ceasing to exist by melting and then turning into vapor? Such an objection misses the thrust of Rand's point.

Rand begins her comments with a discussion of values. (Rand uses similar language in *Atlas Shrugged*; see AS 1012). She is talking about an alternative with respect to the outcome of value pursuits—which only living things engage in—and, in her view, the main alternative an organism faces is life or death.

Philosopher Tara Smith, whose defense of Rand's moral theory is among the best in offer, draws our attention to the term "faces," which implies an active and goal-directed process. Organisms face alternatives, including the alternative of life and death, but ice cubes, rocks, planets, and other nonliving things do not *face* alternatives. Nonliving things may change form, but the change makes no difference to them. As Smith puts the point, "Live organisms . . . have something at stake: their lives."[55]

---

55   Tara Smith, *Viable Values* (Lanham, MD: Rowman & Littlefield, 2000), pp. 83, 86, 90.

Organisms face alternatives in that they might do one thing over another—say, chase food versus try to stay warm—and in that they might succeed or fail in pursuing any goal. A lion might catch a gazelle and eat it, or, alternately, miss the gazelle and go hungry. Rand says that an organism's fundamental alternative is to remain alive or to die. At least at first glance, that sounds plausible—we can easily think of many things that organisms do to keep themselves alive (such as eat food, seek shelter, and avoid dangers), and organisms cannot pursue any goals after they die.

Rand's claims about the relationship of values to life form the foundation of her moral theory. Clearly Rand does not wish to claim merely that an organism must stay alive in order to pursue values. Anyone with any moral theory would grant that. For example, one must stay alive to advocate egalitarianism or to wage genocidal war. Rand wants to press the much stronger claim that an organism normally pursues values and, in the case of human beings, should pursue values, exclusively for the ultimate aim of staying alive. The purpose of moral principles, Rand argues, is to guide people's actions toward that end.

How does Rand reach her far-reaching conclusions about the relationship between values and life? The key is her understanding of life: "Life is a process of self-sustaining and self-generated action." Rand here refers to the life of an individual organism (as opposed to the process of evolution). Life is not something static; it is not an end state to be achieved at a given moment. Life is a characteristic of an organism from the moment it is conceived to the moment it dies; it is essentially the process of the organism functioning and taking actions—pursuing values—to stay alive.[56] Normally (Rand believes) the ultimate aim of an organism's actions is self-sustenance.

Rand's remarks about the relationship between the concepts of life and of value flow from her analysis of life. Life involves action that is self-sustaining, so value—"that which one acts to gain and/or keep" (TOE 15)—normally relates to the sustenance of the

---

56   On this point, see Harry Binswanger, *The Biological Basis of Teleological Concepts* (Los Angeles, CA: Ayn Rand Institute Press, 1990), pp. 64–65.

organism. Rand's argument is that, if you understand life correctly, you understand that a value is something normally pursued ultimately for the sake of sustaining life.

Rand's approach here might strike some readers as odd. She seems to present the basics of an enormously rich theory integrating biology and ethics in just a few lines of text. What is going on here?

A key to grasping Rand's case is to realize that Rand overwhelmingly is an inductive thinker. Her aim is to look out at the world and report back the general principles implied by what she observes. With respect to ethics, she aims to draw our attention to the nature of living things. Rand thinks that if you observe living things and think carefully about their nature, you will see that life entails a process of action by the organism, action generated by the organism and directed toward sustaining its life. For example, you can observe that a plant grows leaves to convert solar radiation to usable energy, that it grows roots to absorb nutrients, and that these actions in turn help to sustain the plant's life. You can observe that a hawk hunts and eats small animals and that this provides nutrients that help keep the hawk alive. Look at living things out in the world and observe how they operate, Rand implies, and you will see the evidence for her case.

Leonard Peikoff, a philosopher who worked closely with Rand for many years, emphasizes that the proof for the principle that life is the standard of value is based on inductive evidence. Ultimately, he says about such matters:

> [T]he proofs are inherent in the percepts. . . . So what is the proof of life as the standard? . . . [T]he proof is: "Look, there are things. Those are living entities. That's it." There is no

other proof. All that analysis [offered on top of that] is just a way of conceptualizing what is there in the data.[57]

When we turn to criticizing Rand's theory, we too will look out at living things and observe them. As I will argue, the relationship between values and life is not what Rand thinks it is. But for now let us continue with Rand's theory.

Rand expands her idea that life versus death is an organism's fundamental alternative by stating the implication that an organism's life is its ultimate value. Then she follows up with a restatement of the relationship of the concepts of life and value:

> An ultimate value is that final goal or end to which all lesser goals are the means—and it sets the standard by which all lesser goals are evaluated. An organism's life is its standard of value: that which furthers its life is the good, that which threatens it is the evil.

Without an ultimate goal or end, there can be no lesser goals or means: a series of means going off into an infinite progression toward a nonexistent end is a metaphysical and epistemological impossibility. It is only an ultimate goal, an end in itself, that makes the existence of values possible. Metaphysically, life is the only phenomenon that is an end in itself: a value gained and kept by a constant process of action. Epistemologically, the concept of "value" is genetically dependent upon and derived from the antecedent concept of "life." To speak of "value" as apart from "life" is worse

---

57 Leonard Peikoff, *Understanding Objectivism*, ed. Michael S. Berliner (New York: New American Library, 2012), p. 63. Peikoff's style here is informal because the published text derives from a set of oral presentations. Harry Binswanger also makes the point that Rand's case is fundamentally inductive; see "Harry Binswanger's 1977 Letter to Robert Nozick," *Check Your Premises*, January 31, 2016, http:// www.checkyourpremises.org/harry-binswangers-1977-letter-to-robert-nozick/. And Chris Matthew Sciabarra notes that Rand's "arguments for [the] internal relationship" between life and value "are inductive"; see his *Ayn Rand: The Russian Radical* (Pennsylvania State University Press, 1995), p. 242.

than a contradiction in terms. "It is only the concept of 'Life' that makes the concept of 'Value' possible." (TOE 17)

Rand's Aristotle-inspired claim about an ultimate end implies that values are hierarchical, with lower-order values helping to support higher-order ones, and with life as the highest-order value. (Of course only people are aware of this hierarchy.) Hence, Rand sees all values except life as a means to some other value. (We could say that the value of life is a means to itself.) This relationship of values to life is what supports Rand's claims about the relationship between the concepts of value and life. By Rand's lights, we properly conceive of value as a means, ultimately, to life. If we do not think of values as holding this means-ends relationship, then we're just confused. (I deal with the Objectivist take on ends in themselves and on constitutive values in later chapters.)

Rand's point is not that every action that every organism takes necessarily furthers its own life, without exception. Rand grants that an organism can exist "for a while in a crippled, disabled, or diseased condition" (TOE 16), whether because of misfortune or because the organism's actions are misaligned with its life. If a deer freezes in front of a set of headlights rather than runs for cover, it may be struck and killed (see TOE 19). Rand offers the example of children born without the capacity to feel pain (TOE 18); such children often cut, burn, and otherwise harm themselves. An American girl with the condition, lacking normal pain responses, was more likely to eat scalding food, injure herself as a result of risky climbs, and so on.[58]

How does Rand deal with human choice? People often choose values that harm rather than further their lives (see TOE 19–20). Some people abuse drugs and engage in risky sex, for example. At the extreme, someone might strap on a bomb and blow himself up to advance a religious cause.

Rand's point is that normally when an organism pursues a value it thereby furthers its life, and, when this is not the case, we have cause

---

58 "Rare Disease Makes Girl Unable to Feel Pain," Associated Press, November 1, 2004, http://www.nbcnews.com/id/6379795/ns/health-childrens_health/t/rare-disease-makes-girl-unable-to-feel-pain/.

to say that something has gone wrong. Either a challenge is beyond an organism's capabilities, or the organism suffers an injury or a genetic glitch, or, in the case of humans, a person acts wrongly or in error. The fact that an organism can do something that does not further its life or that harms its life does not undercut the general relationship between life and values. After all, it is only because values normally sustain life that an organism is even alive to do something that undercuts its survival. The failures are the exceptions that prove the rule.

We can look at the heart as an example.[59] Normally a heart pumps to circulate blood, which is necessary to keep an organism alive. The heart evolved to do this. That doesn't mean that every beat of a heart circulates blood. Due to malformity or injury, a heart can beat without pumping blood, or it can develop an arrhythmia and pump blood poorly. Just because a heart can pump without circulating blood does not mean that we should doubt that a heart normally pumps to circulate blood. If hearts did not normally pump to circulate blood for survival-related functions, we'd have no cause to say that a heart that stops beating or that performs in some other way has failed. Similarly, by Rand's account, we can say that something has gone wrong when an organism takes an action that fails to support its life only because life-sustaining action is the norm.

If valid, Rand's theory profoundly disrupts competing moral theories. Any other purported moral standard, Rand argues, rests on some confusion about the nature of life and of values. A theorist who thinks that the standard of value is something other than the individual's life simply does not understand what value is. So if someone says that the standard of value instead is (for example) God's will, Kantian duty, or the greatest good for the greatest number, then, by Rand's lights, the person literally does not know what he is talking about. He is not attending to the relevant details about the nature of life and its relationship to values. And he is using the concept of

---

59   Eric Mack also uses the heart as an example to illustrate the meaning of Rand's moral claims; see his "The Fundamental Moral Elements of Rand's Theory of Rights," in *The Philosophic Thought of Ayn Rand*, ed. Douglas J. Den Uyl and Douglas B. Rasmussen (University of Illinois Press, 1984), pp. 127–129.

value in a way that rips it from the context in which it is formed (its relationship to life); he is stealing the concept.[60]

If Rand's theory is true, then why do more people not recognize it as true? One problem is that the relationship between the values that we pursue and their impact on our lives often is complex and hard to suss out. For example, why do we enjoy fine food (as opposed to basic rations) or listen to music? Why should we live virtuously rather than lie, cheat, and steal when we can get away with it? It may seem as though many of our values have nothing to do with staying alive and that many actions that would further our lives clash with basic moral tenets. Rand would respond that many seemingly frivolous values really do further one's life and that actions that really are immoral cannot ultimately further one's life—because life is the basis by which we establish a human action as moral or immoral. Consider these points in more detail.

Life's small enjoyments are crucial motivators to go on living in a robust way, Tara Smith argues. "Many of life's 'dispensable' embellishments—friends, music, movies, sports, stylish writing, good cooking—stoke a person's enthusiasm for life," she writes.[61] Regarding art, Rand writes, "Art *is* inextricably tied to man's survival—not to his physical survival, but to that on which his physical survival depends: to the preservation and survival of his consciousness." The function of art, Rand argues, is to represent broad philosophic abstractions in concrete, perceptual form.[62]

As for virtue, Rand argues that a person can achieve life-sustaining values through the years only by acting virtuously. A rational person's

---

60   What Rand calls the "stolen concept" fallacy is described in an editorial note as "the fallacy of using a concept while denying the validity of its genetic roots, i.e., of an earlier concept(s) on which it logically depends," in Ayn Rand, "Philosophical Detection," in *Philosophy: Who Needs It* (New York: Signet, 1984), p. 22. The note in turn references Nathaniel Branden, "The Stolen Concept," *Objectivist Newsletter*, January 1963, vol. 2, no. 1, pp. 2, 4, in the bound *Volumes 1–4: 1962–1965* (Gaylordsville, CT: Second Renaissance, 1990).

61   Tara Smith, *Viable Values* (Lanham, MD: Rowman & Littlefield, 2000), p. 138.

62   Ayn Rand, "The Pscyho-Epistemology of Art," in *The Romantic Manifesto*, revised edition (New York: Signet, 1975), pp. 17, 20.

"three cardinal values" are reason, purpose, and self-esteem, Rand argues, and he can achieve these values only by embracing the virtues of rationality, productiveness, and pride, with the latter understood as "moral ambitiousness" (TOE 25, 27). In short, Rand says that, to live successfully, a person needs to think rationally about the world and how to navigate it, produce the values on which life depends, and take seriously his life and its requirements.

Rand's conception of moral virtues is central to her moral theory as well as to her theory of rights.[63] She argues that a virtuous person—one who is rational, honest, independent, productive—advances his life in a social context by productively collaborating with others by mutual consent rather than through force or fraud (see TOE 27). And a person without virtue will sabotage his life, including by violating the rights of others.

Critics can argue that Rand's egoistic ethics logically leads to or permits immoral behavior, but critics who are knowledgeable about Rand's views and honest when discussing them will grant that Rand makes some sophisticated arguments that rational egoism entails moral virtue. Rand is deeply committed to virtue ethics and to individual rights, as both her nonfiction works and her novels reveal.

What of happiness? Some people think that Rand's theory amounts to obsessing about staying alive at the cost of happiness. But to Rand the rational pursuit of one's life is at the same time the pursuit of happiness. "Existentially, the activity of pursuing rational goals is the activity of maintaining one's life; psychologically, its result, reward and concomitant is an emotional state of happiness," she writes (TOE 29). Rand's novels illustrate in great detail her views about the relationship between happiness and life-sustaining action. We can reasonably wonder whether Rand has taken a full account of happiness, but we should acknowledge at least that Rand develops a robust theory of how happiness fits into her ethics.

Much more can be said about Rand's moral theory—many essays and books have been written about it—and I will discuss details in the

---

63 The most substantive work on Rand's theory of virtue is Tara Smith's *Ayn Rand's Normative Ethics* (New York: Cambridge University Press, 2006).

chapters that follow. But, for our purposes, the description above should suffice to convey the essential features of the case that Rand lays out.

Whatever else might be said about Ayn Rand or her moral theory, clearly she thought deeply about ethics and cared deeply about formulating a true moral theory that lays out how people may flourish by acting virtuously. Even if Rand's core theory ultimately fails, as I think it does, it is an impressive achievement. Rand came close to a correct metaethical framework (or so I'll argue), and, even though she got the foundations wrong, many of her observations about ethics remain true.

In the next chapter we explore the main problems with Rand's metaethics.

3. The Essential Fallacies
of Rand's Ethics

BEFORE TURNING IN FUTURE CHAPTERS to finer-grained criticisms of Rand's moral theory, I want to offer a broad overview of its essential problems.

Rand holds that a value is something that a living thing acts to gain or keep and that the concept of value presupposes that a value is such to a particular organism and for some purpose. "The concept 'value' . . . presupposes an answer to the question: of value to whom and for what?" (TOE 15). This view is partly right, partly wrong.

I do not dispute Rand's claim that things that are valuable are such to particular living things, a view typically referred to as the agent relativity of values (a term that, to my knowledge, Rand never used).

Other people do dispute that claim. Philosopher Michael Huemer describes an opposing view: "The absolutist view is that it is possible for some things to be good, simply, or in an absolute sense; whereas agent-relativists think that things can only be good *for* or *relative to* certain individuals." An example of an absolutist view that Huemer gives is holding that "intelligent life existing on Earth has a certain property: goodness." Huemer continues, "Rand bases her ethics on the agent-relative position, but she offers no argument for it, only a bald assertion."[64] Rand would reply to Huemer, I think, by claiming that the evidence for agent relativity is implicit in every observation of value. If you look at values in the world—food, shelter, love, entertainment—you will see that a value is such to some living thing. Further, Rand would presumably reply, those who imagine values apart from valuers are "stealing" the concept of value. We develop the concept of value by observing agent relative values, so it is illegitimate to then apply the concept outside that context. As for examples of alleged "absolute" values, such as the goodness of intelligent life existing, perhaps Rand would reply (and anyway I would reply) that such claims implicitly depend on the point of view of someone to whom things could be a value, namely the person considering the matter. If you imagine a lifeless universe and then think about the value that life would bring to it, you will probably find it hard not to think of yourself as a god looking out at the expanse, a being to whom things matter.

A complex academic debate over "absolute" versus agent relative value is not very interesting for our purposes. I follow Rand in holding that values are agent relative, and I think those who hold otherwise face a serious challenge even to coherently explain what values are. So I take the agent relativity of values for granted for purposes of this book.

We do, however, need to sort out some of the confusing language about agent relative and absolute values. Certainly Rand does not think that morals are "relative" in the sense that they depend on individual or collective opinion or whim. She holds that a value is such in relation to a valuer, and that is the relationship to which the term "agent relativity" refers. Rand holds that ethics is an objective science and that moral principles apply universally. The sort of "absolute values" that Rand rejects are those taken to be values apart from valuers. There is no such "absolute value" in that sense, Rand

---

would say, and moreover the term misunderstands the concepts of absolute and of value.

I concede, then, that it makes sense to ask "to whom" something is of value (at least potentially); the problem comes with Rand's assumption that a value must be for something else. If it were true that every value must be of value for something else, then we would end up, as Rand argues, with a hierarchy of values in means-ends relationships, with some value serving as the final end. But Rand's assumption about the relationship of values is false.

If a person experiences anything as valuable for its own sake, as an end in itself, apart from its contribution to survival (whether or not the thing valued also furthers survival), then Rand's case is false. So, for example, if someone experiences, as valuable for its own sake and not for the further end of survival, listening to a piece of fine music, watching his child develop, having sex with a loving partner, enjoying an exquisite meal, watching a beautiful sunset, playing a fun game, or reading a finely written work of philosophy, then that demonstrates conclusively that Rand is wrong about the relationship of values. And, as I think is obvious, such is the case.

Objectivists reply to this line of argument (about valuing things as ends in themselves) in a couple of main ways. First, they say, all of our legitimate values do contribute to our survival, even if it is not obvious how this is so. Second, they argue, if we try to develop a morality with values detached from survival, we inevitably end up with some sort of errant moral subjectivism or intrinsicism. I deal with these objections in detail in subsequent chapters. For now I will try only to pique the reader's common-sense understanding that we value some things as ends in themselves, not as means to survival, and it really is the case—it is objectively true—that we do so.

We need to avoid confusion here. Objectivists talk about experiencing certain things as ends in themselves and about certain values helping to constitute our lives, as opposed to purely serving as means to survival. For example, Objectivists say that the joy of art is in a sense an end in itself and that reason is not just a means to staying alive but an essential part of what it means to be human. However, it remains the case, within the Objectivist framework, that any value that we experience as an end in itself, and any value that helps to constitute our lives, can be pursued as a proper value only because and to the extent that it serves a person's life in terms of survival. As Objectivist scholars Allan Gotthelf and Gregory Salmieri put the point, "[V]irtues and values have the place they do in a successful human life only because each plays a crucial role in enabling a human being to survive."[65] Fundamental to Rand's approach is the ultimate value of life—as opposed to death. It remains the case, then, that, by the Objectivist ethics, every legitimate value must be a means to survival.

My position is that, contra the Objectivist ethics, our experience of certain things as ends in themselves (or valuable in their own right) does not necessarily dependent on whether our pursuit of such things furthers our survival. Further, values that properly help to constitute our lives do not necessarily further our survival. So, despite superficial similarities between Rand's views and my own regarding ends in themselves and constitutive values, the fundamental difference remains that Rand sees all proper values as means to survival, and I do not.

Even if we thought that all values were means to some ultimate value, Rand offers no good reason to think that an organism's life in terms of survival is that value.

Life in a meaningful sense is a process of "self-generated action" (TOE 15), no doubt. And life is to a large degree a process of self-sustaining action. But life is not only about the organism pursuing values to sustain its survival. Living things normally also take action for the sake of offspring and other relatives, as we'll see in more detail in the next chapter. This fact by itself does not, of course, suggest the proper course for human conduct, but it does reveal a basic problem with the way that Rand conceives of values.

What should we make of Rand's claim that, metaphysically, life "is an end in itself: a value gained and kept by a constant process of action" (TOE 17)? We should first note that we now invoke a very different sense of the term "end in itself" than what we previously considered. Normally an organism indeed pursues many values to

---

65   Allan Gotthelf and Gregory Salmieri, "The Morality of Life," in *A Companion to Ayn Rand*, p. 81. In later sections I discuss in more detail values as ends in themselves and as constituents of life.

keep itself alive, and surviving is the process of an organism pursuing values to survive. I grant that life is a self-sustaining cycle in this sense, but this does not prove that every value aims at survival. If an organism pursued some value that was not aimed at its survival, its survival (as a result of its survival-oriented activities) still would be an end in itself in the sense of a self-sustaining cycle. So Rand makes an interesting point about the nature of survival, but she does not demonstrate that all values do or should aim at survival.

My basic argument, then, is that what fundamentally matters are things that we experience as ends in themselves, not survival as a self-perpetuating cycle. To begin to see why, imagine that we could step out of ourselves and observe our lives. We would see that many of the actions that we take further our survival and that our survival is a self-perpetuating cycle, a metaphysical end in itself. Why would we care about that? Unless we have some reason to care about our lives—unless we experience some things as ends in themselves—the observations about survival have no bearing on our concerns or actions. And if we have a basis to care about our lives, then there is no reason to assume that we can or should care only about values aimed at survival. Even if it were the case—by fantastic coincidence—that the only things that we experienced as ends in themselves were things that, by attaining them, best furthered our survival, still the normative primary would be the experience of things as ends in themselves.

Because we can experience certain things as ends in themselves, we have good reason to care about our continued survival, at least in most contexts, as a means to those ends. So Rand is correct that many of the values that we pursue are means to survival. But she gets the fundamental relationship wrong. Life in terms of survival is not the end to which all other values are means; survival is the end of many values (such as nutritious food) and in turn a means to things that we value as ends in themselves.

Rand, then, makes the crucial observations that survival is necessary for the pursuit of values and that survival is the goal of many of our values. But Rand does not establish that life in terms of survival is the "final goal or end to which all lesser goals are the means."

Rand's main remaining argument is this: "Without an ultimate goal or end, there can be no lesser goals or means: a series of means going off into an infinite progression toward a nonexistent end is a metaphysical and epistemological impossibility" (TOE 17). Is this argument sound, and, if so, what does it imply?

J. Charles King does not accept Rand's argument:

If I am to reach rational decisions, I will need to have some kind of ranking order between values; but from the fact that something is an end in itself, it does not follow that it cannot be more or less valued than another thing that is also an end in itself. Thus, the organization of a code of values, while it may depend upon the existence of ends in themselves, does not depend upon the existence of an ultimate value. The claim that there must be an ultimate value, if there is to be any value at all, is therefore mistaken.[66]

This seems troublesome. If there can be multiple ends in themselves, how are we to rank and prioritize them? "For a ranking to exist, there must also exist a standard," Paul St. F. Blair notes in his reply to King.[67]

We seem to be stuck in a conundrum. We seem to experience multiple things as ends in themselves, but we also seem to need some sort of ultimate end to guide our actions. Rand's survival-based standard seems a ready solution, but it does not survive scrutiny.

My solution, as I outline in more detail in Chapter 9, is that things that we experience as ends in themselves can also help to constitute a broader ultimate end. So it is not the case, as Rand has it, that every value is a means to the ultimate end; instead, every value is either a means to or a constituent of the ultimate end. To preview my approach

---

66   J. Charles King, "Life and the Theory of Value," in *The Philosophic Thought of Ayn Rand*, ed. Douglas J. Den Uyl and Douglas B. Rasmussen (University of Illinois Press, 1984), p. 108.

67   Paul St. F. Blair, "The Randian Argument Reconsidered: A Reply to Charles King," *Reason Papers*, Spring 1985, no. 10, https://reasonpapers.com/pdf/10/rp_10_7.pdf, p. 92.

in Chapter 9, I think the ultimate end properly conceived is a person's life of integrated values, rather than his life in terms of survival.

This chapter has been highly abstract, and readers may wish to return to it in light of the more-detailed discussions to follow. Hopefully the material here serves as an overview of the problems with Rand's approach.

In the next chapter, we consider values in the context of living things generally and the problems with Rand's claims about biology as they pertain to her metaethical theory.

4. The Error in Rand's Biology

THE RELATIONSHIP THAT RAND THINKS EXISTS between life and values does not hold. It is not the case that living things normally act only to sustain their own lives.

As we've seen, Rand thinks that organisms normally take actions ultimately only to further their own lives and that the very meaning of value depends on the supportive relationship of values to life. Human beings can pursue values that do not aid their survival or that even actively undermine their survival, but, Rand argues, such actions properly are evaluated as bad by the standard of life.

Rand's biology is wrong. Living things very often take actions that undermine their survival, and that is perfectly normal. This fact undercuts Rand's claims about the relationship between life and values—values do not, in fact, solely support an organism's life. Life is not just a process of self-sustaining action; it is partly that, but it is also more than that. Normally organisms act not only to advance their own lives but to advance the reproduction of their genes by aiding offspring or close relatives.

Let us retrace Rand's views on the matter. Rand says of the biological functions of organisms:

> On the physical level, the functions of all living organisms, from the simplest to the most complex—from the nutritive function in the single cell of an amoeba to the blood circulation in the body of a man—are actions generated

by the organism itself and directed to a single goal: the maintenance of the organism's life. (TOE 16)

What is true of physical functions is also true of the actions of all nonhuman living things, Rand argues. "[T]here is no alternative in a plant's function," she writes; "it acts automatically to further its life, it cannot act for its own destruction" (TOE 18). Regarding animals guided by sensation, Rand writes: "Its life is the standard of value directing its actions. Within the range of action possible to it, it acts automatically to further its life and cannot act for its own destruction" (TOE 19). Any animal with the power of perception also has "an automatic knowledge of what is good for it or evil, what benefits or endangers its life"; "it cannot ignore its own good, it cannot decide to choose the evil and act as its own destroyer" (TOE 19).

Others who embrace Rand's philosophy make comparable claims. Leonard Peikoff writes that "within the limits of their ability, [organisms] act necessarily to attain those objects that sustain their existence. They can be destroyed, but they cannot pursue their own destruction."[68] Tara Smith writes, "Plants and lower animals are genetically coded to act automatically in self-sustaining ways."[69] (Although Smith does not here say that organisms act only in this way, she describes life in terms of survival as the only possible source of values.) Allan Gotthelf and Gregory Salmieri write, "Every non-human organism is programmed by its nature to act in just those ways that will bring about certain items and conditions without which it could not survive."[70]

We can see clearly that Rand's view of biology is wrong by looking at what living things do. A vivid example is the matriphagous—"mother eating"—spider. Biologist Sarah Blaffer Hrdy explains:

---

68 Leonard Peikoff, *Objectivism: The Philosophy of Ayn Rand* (New York: Dutton, 1991), p. 213.

69 Tara Smith, *Ayn Rand's Normative Ethics* (New York: Cambridge University Press, 2006), p. 22.

70 Allan Gotthelf and Gregory Salmieri, "The Morality of Life," in *A Companion to Ayn Rand*, p. 63.

After laying her eggs, an Australian social spider (*Diaea ergandros*) continues to store nutrients in a new batch of eggs—odd, oversized eggs, far too large to pass through her oviducts, and lacking genetic instructions. Since she breeds only once, what are they for?

These eggs are for eating, not for laying. But to be eaten by whom? As the spiderlings mature and begin to mill about, the mother becomes strangely subdued. She starts to turn mushy. . . . As her tissue melts, her ravenous young literally suck her up, starting with her legs and eventually devouring the protein-rich eggs dissolving within her.[71]

This is hardly a case of the mother's physical functions directed to the maintenance of her life.

The case of the matriphagous spider is dramatic, but nature offers many other examples of organisms functioning or acting to further their genes rather than their personal survival. Most salmon and members of various other semelparous species reproduce only once and then die; at some point the reproduction of their genes takes precedence over their own survival. The male praying mantis often loses his life during reproduction as his partner bites off his head during sex and then eats him after. Worker honeybees will sacrifice their own lives by stinging an enemy, something usually fatal to the bee. Some parent birds will feign injury to draw a predator away from a nest, behavior that increases the odds that the bird's offspring will live but that puts the parent's life at profound risk.[72]

Organisms undercut their personal survival not only by risking or sacrificing their lives for their existing offspring or for close relatives: Members of various species also divert resources from their personal survival to winning the battle to mate. Hrdy describes her shock when, as a student in the late 1960s, she learned that male

---

71 Sarah Blaffer Hrdy, *Mother Nature* (New York: Pantheon Books, 1999), p. 43.

72 The examples of the mantis, the bee, and the bird come from Richard Dawkins, *The Selfish Gene*, new edition, (Oxford University Press, 1989), pp. 5–6.

langur monkeys "would grab infants from their mothers and bite them to death." Obviously such behavior does not help the male langur survive, so what's going on? "After the male killed her infant, the langur mother mated with him," Hrdy discovered.[73] Infanticide in this case is about helping the male reproduce, not about helping the male stay alive.

We can also observe sexual display traits, which divert resources from keeping the individual alive to helping the individual reproduce by attracting the attention of mates or by fighting off rivals. These traits include antlers and the colorful feathers of the male peacock. BBC Earth has video of a type of puffer fish that labors for days creating intricate (and apparently sexy) sea-floor art out of sand.[74] Various male beetles develop ornate weaponry to challenge sexual rivals.[75]

We need look no further than our own species to see that many people spend extraordinary amounts of energy for sex. Huge industries are devoted to little else, and a substantial amount of violent crime is due to jealous rivalries and the like.

In sum, the physical functions and actions of organisms are not oriented toward the "single goal" of maintaining "the organism's life." Generally, evolution tends to program individual organisms to optimize the survival of their genes, not their personal survival. As Richard Dawkins puts it, organisms are their genes' "survival machines."[76] They are built (by evolutionary processes) fundamentally to serve the survival of the genes; generally organisms serve their personal survival only insofar as doing so furthers the survival of their genes. Often the organism's survival furthers the survival of its genes, but not always.

---

73 Sarah Blaffer Hrdy, *Mother Nature* (New York: Pantheon Books, 1999), pp. xv–xvi.

74 Jerry A. Coyne, "'If This Doesn't Get Him Noticed, Nothing Will': The Marvels of Sexual Selection," *Why Evolution Is True*, April 15, 2017, https:// whyevolutionistrue.wordpress.com/2017/04/15/if-this-doesnt-get-him-noticed -nothing-will-the-marvels-of-sexual-selection/.

75 Nicholas Wade, "Extravagant Results of Nature's Arms Race," *New York Times*, March 23, 2009, http://www.nytimes.com/2009/03/24/science/24armo.html.

76 Richard Dawkins, *The Selfish Gene*, new edition, (Oxford University Press, 1989), p. v.

To put the point in different terms, the biological goal of action is not individual survival but "everflowing life," to borrow a phrase from the Greek poet Nonnos[77]—the continuous cycle of living things reproducing themselves.

Other critics of Rand have pointed to the biological problems behind Rand's ethics (although a surprising number of works about Rand's ethics omit discussion of the issue). In his critique, Robert Nozick points out:

> [T]here are natural selection arguments that innate preferences for behavior which is reproductive behavior, and for behavior after reproduction which enhances the chances of the progeny's survival, even to destroying oneself to guard one's young, will be selected for in the evolutionary process. So beings may be preprogrammed or predisposed to do things which lessen their *individual* chances of survival.[78]

Michael Huemer similarly notes that traits are selected via evolution for "producing more copies of one's genes," so "if anything is the ultimate 'value' for living things, it would be gene-reproduction (technically, 'inclusive fitness')," not just individual survival.[79] Will Wilkinson notes, "Survival can be instrumental to inclusive fitness,

---

77   Nonnos, *Dionysiaca: Books 1–15*, trans. H. W. D. Rouse (Harvard University Press, 1940), Loeb Classical Library no. 344, book 7. Incidentally, I learned of this work because of the speculation that the term semelparous (meaning to give birth only once) may derive from the mythological figure of Semele of Nonnos's work; see Stephen B. Heard, "The 'One Thing I Teach that Nobody Ever Forgets' May Be Wrong!," *Scientist Sees Squirrel*, October 20, 2015, https://scientistseessquirrel.wordpress.com/2015/10/20/the-one-thing-i-teach-that-nobody-ever-forgets-may-be-wrong/.

78   Robert Nozick, "On the Randian Argument," in *Reading Nozick*, ed. Jeffrey Paul (Totowa, NJ: Rowman and Littlefield, 1981), pp. 222–223, n. 2.

79   Michael Huemer, "Critique of 'The Objectivist Ethics,'" http://www.owl232.net/rand5.htm (accessed February 2, 2017). Huemer also notes that "nature is not teleological," but that is not the sense in which Harry Binswanger or I use the term teleology below. An organism's functions and actions can be end-directed due to evolutionary pressures rather than due to some supposed purpose of nature.

but it is not necessarily so."[80] Neera Badhwar and Roderick Long summarize the point:

> The biological premise that survival is the ultimate goal of all living things is mistaken. Animals of many species risk their own death for the sake of reproduction, or for protecting their young or even their group. But even if survival were the ultimate goal of other species, it need not be ours.[81]

Given the centrality of reproduction to living things, consider the oddity of Leonard Peikoff's offhand dismissal of it: "Leaving aside reproduction, to which every organism owes its existence, [*self*-preservation] is the goal of all automatic biological processes and actions."[82] We would indeed have to leave aside reproduction for Rand's metaethical arguments to work. But the implications of Peikoff's brief admission are the opposite of what he suggests. That "every organism owes its existence" to reproduction shows that organisms often do things directed at ends other than their own survival. Hence, the relationship between values and survival on which Rand bases her metaethics proves to be a mirage.

The core of Rand's moral theory is that values are inherently related to an organism's survival. In terms of the biology at least of nonhuman species, organisms normally pursue values for the survival of their genes. These biological facts undercut Rand's arguments about an organism's life being its ultimate value and about the genetic

---

80   Will Wilkinson, "Third Letter to a Young Objectivist: Ethics," *Fly Bottle*, March 2, 2005, http://www.willwilkinson.net/flybottle/2005/03/02/third-letter-to-a-young-objectivist-ethics/.

81   Neera K. Badhwar and Roderick T. Long, "Ayn Rand," *Stanford Encyclopedia of Philosophy*, September 19, 2016, https://plato.stanford.edu/entries/ayn-rand/. Badhwar and Long cite these points about biology, among other points, to dismiss as not "plausible" the "survivalist view" of Rand's moral theory. Instead, they argue, Rand endorses "surviving qua human being" or "living a life proper to a human being," not just survival, as the point of morality. I agree that Rand's survivalism is not ultimately plausible, but her explicit theory definitely is survivalist in the relevant sense.

82   Leonard Peikoff, *Objectivism: The Philosophy of Ayn Rand* (New York: Dutton, 1991), p. 231.

dependency of the concept of value on the concept of life, with life understood here to refer to the survival of an individual organism. In short, the foundations of Rand's moral theory crumble under the pressure of today's standard biology.

Binswanger's Rebuttal

Recall that Rand's *Atlas Shrugged* came out in 1957, and Rand delivered "The Objectivist Ethics" at a conference in 1961. Rand was born in 1905, less than half a century after the publication of Darwin's *On the Origin of Species* and decades before the discovery of the evolutionary role of DNA. Richard Dawkins's influential *The Selfish Gene* was not published until 1976, a couple decades after Rand had formulated her moral theory.

So Rand in her early years would have been exposed to the basics of Darwinian evolution, but a great deal of scientific research and popularizing has gone on in the field since Rand's days as a student. Anyway, Rand never studied evolutionary theory in any detail. She wrote in 1973, "I am not a student of the theory of evolution and, therefore, I am neither its supporter nor its opponent."[83] Although I am not a biologist, I have access to good popular works about evolution that were not available to Rand as she developed her theory.

Rand's lack of familiarity with evolutionary theory, of course, does not by itself imply that her biological claims are wrong. But the facts show her to be wrong.

Harry Binswanger, someone with an extensive knowledge of evolutionary theory and a philosopher who long has advocated Rand's

---

83 Ayn Rand, "The Missing Link," in *Philosophy: Who Needs It* (New York: Signet, 1984), p. 45. Rand also told Nathaniel Branden that she was "not prepared to say" whether living things evolved; see Branden's "The Benefits and Hazards of the Philosophy of Ayn Rand: A Personal Statement," *Journal of Humanistic Psychology*, Fall 1984, vol. 24, no. 4, p. 49. Note that the Ayn Rand Institute enthusiastically embraces the theory of evolution. For example, Keith Lockitch, who works for the Institute, delivered a lecture about the development of evolutionary theory—see his "Darwin and the Discovery of Evolution," Ayn Rand Institute, March 18, 2008, https://ari.aynrand.org/issues/science-and-industrialization/scientific-and-technological-progress/Darwin-and-the-Discovery-of-Evolution.

ideas, argues that Rand's biology is correct. Binswanger is fully aware of the challenges to Rand's biology and moral framework presented by such cases as the predator-diverting parent bird. Binswanger presents his case in *The Biological Basis of Teleological Concepts*, based on the doctoral dissertation he wrote from 1969 through 1973.[84] Although Binswanger makes a valiant effort to reconcile Rand's theory with modern biology, ultimately his effort fails, for reasons we'll see.

I agree with Binswanger's central thesis: "The actions of living organisms, even of non-conscious organisms such as plants, are goal-directed."[85] But I disagree with him (and with Rand) that the ultimate goal of those actions generally is the maintenance of the organism's life; it is instead the furtherance of the organism's genes.

Binswanger aims largely to elaborate a claim that Rand makes in a footnote to "The Objectivist Ethics":

> When applied to physical phenomena, such as the automatic functions of an organism, the term "goal-directed" is not to be taken to mean "purposive" (a concept applicable only to the actions of a consciousness) and is not to imply the existence of any teleological principle operating in insentient nature. I use the term "goal-directed," in this context, to designate the fact that the automatic functions of living organisms are actions whose nature is such that they *result* in the preservation of an organism's life. (TOE 16)

Binswanger grants that fostering offspring generally takes resources from the parents' personal survival and sometimes costs the parents their lives. He writes that, "since the parents must expend considerable energy and take large risks in mating and reproducing, the consequences to the prospective parents' survival are negative: they would be vastly better off if they were able to refrain from reproductive behavior." But, continues Binswanger, if an organism were not the

---

84   Harry Binswanger, *The Biological Basis of Teleological Concepts* (Los Angeles, CA: Ayn Rand Institute Press, 1990), p. i.

85   Ibid., p. 1. The term "goal-directed" here does not imply that nature itself has goals or anything of the sort; see Binswanger p. 117 for a further description of the term.

sort of creature that reproduced, then the organism would not exist, for its parents would not have produced it. "Barring mutations that eliminate the gene complexes for reproduction," Binswanger writes, "there is no way for a given organism to obtain the benefits of past acts of reproduction without having to repeat those acts upon their own maturity." Hence, he writes, even "the diversionary behavior of mother birds" to draw predators away from their young "serves their lives," in that the mother bird probably never would have been born but for the diversionary behavior prevalent in the species.[86]

Binswanger extends this line of thought even to maladaptive traits that obviously hinder the survival of an organism. For example, even if an animal's "pleasure-pain mechanism" were "'mis-wired,' as it were, causing an animal to be triggered into purposeful behavior which has no survival value, or which is definitely harmful, . . . such purposeful behavior is still goal-directed in that the existence of the pleasure-pain mechanism *as such* is explainable by its survival value."[87] To apply Binswanger's analysis, we could say that a plant that grew leaves without chlorophyll (and lacking any other life-serving purpose) would be acting on a mechanism—leaf growing—that "is explainable by its survival value."

Binswanger's approach is creative, but it is strained as an explanation of biology, and it does not rescue Rand's egoistic moral theory.

Binswanger wants to preclude the very possibility of self-sacrificial behavior by organisms. When a male praying mantis mates with a voraciously hungry female, when a bee stings an enemy of the hive, when a parent bird draws the attention of a fox, when a spider reproduces and ends up consumed by her offspring, these are not really examples of self-sacrificial behavior, suggests Binswanger; they are cases of individuals doing the sorts of things that made their existence and hence their survival possible. But the salient fact is that the individual organisms end up dead because of their functions or actions. The mantis loses its head, the bee loses its vital organs,

---

86   Harry Binswanger, *The Biological Basis of Teleological Concepts* (Los Angeles, CA: Ayn Rand Institute Press, 1990), pp. 156–157.
87   Ibid., p. 172.

the bird gets munched by the fox, the spider becomes food for her babies. An organism does not serve its survival by doing something that causes it to die.

The straightforward way to describe the biology is to say that, due to evolutionary pressures, individual organisms tend to take actions that best further the survival of their genes. Such is the basis of the teleological nature of animate functions and actions. Often organisms promote their genes by taking actions that sustain their own survival, and sometimes they promote their genes by risking or sacrificing their own survival for the sake of the survival of genetically related organisms.

What about cases of severe maladaptation, as with our beast with faulty pleasure-pain wiring and our plant that makes chlorophyll-free leaves? Evolutionarily speaking, severe maladaptations make little difference, because usually organisms with them quickly die, yet the cases shed light on the relationship between actions and life. It makes sense to say that the ability to experience pleasure and pain or to grow leaves generally serves the relevant sort of creature's survival and reproduction, but, in cases of severe maladaptation, the related functions or actions do not actually serve any further goal. We can say that actions and physical functions of living things normally serve an ultimate goal while granting the occasional exception. This is not a case of "a series of means going off into an infinite progression toward a nonexistent end" (TOE 17); rather, it is the case of a goal terminating in itself. If an animal chews off its own limbs because doing so gives it a twisted pleasure, that action is not a means to anything else.

Objectivist philosopher Gregory Salmieri seeks to prop up Binswanger's case, but he runs into additional problems. Salmieri summarizes Binswanger as saying that, when an organism acts for reproductive success rather than its own survival, "all such actions can be understood as required for the individual organism's life, since its life depends on other members of its species engaging in the actions."[88] This does not answer the obvious objection, already mentioned, that the organism still risks or sacrifices its own life for the sake of other, closely related organisms.

Salmieri immediately offers a very different argument: "[F]or species whose actions are selected by deterministic mechanisms, there are sometimes ambiguities about whether the individual organism or the species (or family) is the unit of life."[89] This remark concedes the entire case.

Here Salmieri is commenting on the statement by Allan Gotthelf and him: "Life, as Rand understands it, is a full-time activity: *all* of an organism's actions must contribute directly or indirectly to sustaining itself."[90] If we might interpret "an organism" and "itself" here to refer to an entire species or to a family, as Salmieri suggests in his note, then the basis of Rand's metaethics falls away. For Rand, the relevant "unit of life" pertaining to value obviously is the individual organism, not some grouping of organisms such as a family, a hive, a herd, or a species.

If Salmieri were to reply that some organisms (including humans) pursue values only for personal survival while others do not, then his claim would be wrong on factual grounds: Members of every species frequently act for the survival of others. If Salmieri were to reply that people uniquely should act exclusively for their own survival, then he would have to do so without the aid of Rand's metaethics.

Sensing the problem, Salmieri continues:

> Such ambiguities do not arise in the case of human life (on Rand's view, at least), because human action is directed by the faculty of reason, which is an attribute of the individual and functions by free will. If a human being reproduces or assists others, he does so

---

88 Allan Gotthelf and Gregory Salmieri, "The Morality of Life," in *A Companion to Ayn Rand*, p. 99, n. 16. The article officially is by Gotthelf and "completed by" Salmieri after Gotthelf's death; the note in question was written by Salmieri alone; see p. 98, n. 1 for more details. Salmieri imprecisely refers to an organism's actions as potentially for "the survival of its species (or its genes)"; generally relevant to an organism's actions are its close relatives, not its species as a whole.

89 Ibid., p. 99, n. 16.

90 Ibid., p. 77.

by *choice*; and Rand holds that he should only make this choice when he has egoistic reasons for doing so.[91]

Salmieri's argument cannot succeed. The entire point of Rand's metaethics is to establish a necessary supportive relationship between an organism's values and its life in terms of survival. If Salmieri concedes that organisms can pursue values for ends other than their own survival, then the relationship that Rand thinks she has discovered does not hold. And if that is the case, then Objectivists cannot just presume that humans should act egoistically, each for his own survival, or that the "faculty of reason" requires such. Salmieri leaves Rand's egoism floating without a metaethical base, and he (inadvertently) further weakens Binswanger's case.

Although Binswanger offers important insights into the biological basis of values, he does not show that organisms always act for their own survival, nor does he shore up the biological foundations of Rand's moral theory.

Rand sees a connection between biology, by which (she believes) all of an organism's functions and actions normally support its own life, and ethics, by which all of a human being's conscious actions should support his own life. The fact that organisms normally act self-sacrificially (with respect to their own survival) toward offspring or other closely related relatives, then, shatters the base of Rand's strictly egoistic ethics.

Rand's basic approach to ethics is wrong. Morality is not fundamentally about people pursuing their own survival (nor about them reproducing their genes).[92] In trying to tie values to survival, Rand misses a great deal of what is important about human values.

Next we consider cases of normal and important human values that clearly are not just about survival.

---

91 Allan Gotthelf and Gregory Salmieri, "The Morality of Life," in *A Companion to Ayn Rand*, p. 99, n. 16.

92 As Steven Pinker humorously observes, if people acted fundamentally to reproduce their genes, "men would line up outside sperm banks and women would pay to have their eggs harvested and given away to infertile couples"—see his *The Blank Slate* (New York: Viking, 2002), pp 53–54. I picked up this reference from Sam Harris, *The Moral Landscape* (New York: Free Press, 2010), p. 13.

5. Values, Life, and Death

LIVING THINGS OTHER THAN PEOPLE tend to function and act so as to maximize the survival of their genes, not to maximize their personal survival. Objectivists might reply that people should pursue their individual survival as their ultimate end because they are able to do so. Yet, aside from the fact that Rand's version of egoism is then left without its metaethical moorings, it is wildly implausible that people should treat every value as a means to their survival. People just do not normally act that way, and most of us would think it bizarre if they did. (Note that, whenever I refer to what most people do, I am not suggesting that ethics is somehow a matter of consensus; I am instead opening to question some of Rand's claims by suggesting that they are implausible.)

What I offer in this chapter, and in the next three chapters, are reasons to doubt the plausibility and structural integrity of Rand's survivalist metaethics. That Rand cannot plausibly account for normal values gives rise to much of the skepticism surrounding Rand's moral claims. Surely it is not the case that everything we do is or should be, ultimately, about keeping ourselves alive.

Keep in mind here that Rand is not saying that life (as opposed to death) is an important value among others; she is saying that survival is one's (proper) ultimate value, which every other value properly serves. It is not enough, within Rand's moral framework, merely to refrain from taking obviously self-destructive actions; morality demands that a person further his survival with every action. So if you take an action that does not serve your life (in the sense of survival), you thereby forfeit an opportunity to do so. In this sense, an action either supports one's survival or fails to do so. As Tara Smith puts the point, "No action is sealed off from the progress of a person's life."[93] Recall that, for Rand, life in terms of survival is the "final goal or end to which all lesser goals are the means" (TOE 17)—not some, all. So the question is whether values really work that way.

Values and Motivation

Obviously our survival consumes much of our time and energy. Everything we do for the sake of our health, from brushing our teeth to buying a comfortable mattress to eating nutritious foods to getting doctor-recommended surgeries, aids our survival. Many other values have indirect impacts on our survival; for example, maintaining social ties and (responsibly) enjoying physical pleasures contribute to mental health and the will to live. Undeniably our survival is important to all of our other values, for once we die we can no longer pursue any value. Survival is hugely important, and Rand deserves credit for emphasizing its moral importance.

But is survival all that ultimately matters? If we can locate legitimate values that do not serve survival, or that do not only do so, then the existence of such disproves Rand's moral theory. Of course, by Rand's lights, the legitimacy of values is determined by their relationship to survival; if something does not advance survival, then it just is not a proper value. But if it looks like a value, acts like a value, and for all the world seems like a value worth pursuing, then we should seriously consider its candidacy as a bona fide value. If the apparent value clashes with theory, then maybe we should question the theory and not just the value.

The disconnect between values and personal survival is perhaps most obvious in the context of the (normal) relationship between parent and child. If you ask parents why they had children, normally their answer will not be to sustain their own survival. Indeed, the

---

93 Tara Smith, *Viable Values* (Lanham, MD: Rowman & Littlefield, 2000), pp. 112–113.

suggestion that the moral purpose of having a child is to further the parent's survival would understandably strike most people as fantastic. In most cases having a child imposes physical, emotional, and financial costs, resources that otherwise could go directly toward the parents' survival.[94] Although maternal mortality rates have plummeted with the improvement of medicine, women still face a small risk of dying from complications of pregnancy or childbirth.[95] Recall Harry Binswanger's admission that living things generally "would be vastly better off if they were able to refrain from reproductive behavior."[96]

Rand's theory also has trouble explaining why people pursue careers that are risky (logger, firefighter, astronaut, soldier) or probably low-paying (artist, writer, park ranger, philosopher).[97] Shouldn't people concerned fundamentally with their own survival seek work that is safe and high paying?

Moreover, we enjoy a great many pleasures that are not obviously tied to our survival. We eat to live, of course, yet people also often live to eat. An optimally nutritious meal may not be an optimally

---

94 The typical financial cost of raising a child in the United States is over $230,000; see Mark Lino, "The Cost of Raising a Child," U.S. Department of Agriculture, January 13, 2017, https://www.usda.gov/media/blog/2017/01/13/cost-raising-child.

95 Nina Martin and Renee Montagne, "Focus On Infants During Childbirth Leaves U.S. Moms In Danger," NPR, May 12, 2017, http://www.npr.org/2017/05/12/527806002/focus-on-infants-during-childbirth-leaves-u-s-moms-in-danger. Incidentally, my wife developed severe preeclampsia prior to giving birth; see my "The Expectant Parent's Guerrilla Guide to Preeclampsia," August 26, 2015, http://ariarmstrong.com/2015/08/the-expectant-parents-guerrilla-guide-to-preeclampsia/.

96 Harry Binswanger, The Biological Basis of Teleological Concepts (Los Angeles, CA: Ayn Rand Institute Press, 1990), p. 156.

97 Neera K. Badhwar mentions such examples in "Is Virtue Only a Means to Happiness?," in Objectivist Studies 4, ed. William Thomas (Poughkeepsie, NY: Objectivist Center, 2001), p. 6.

enjoyable meal. Sex can bring profound physical benefits,[98] yet surely people do not normally have sex solely because of its survival value. And presumably puffing a cigar, say while sipping a Scotch and playing a round of Texas Hold'Em, would be out on strictly survivalist grounds.

Hardly anyone thinks he pursues all values ultimately to further his survival. Are the vast majority of people deluded about why they do or should pursue values—or is something off about Rand's moral theory?

Consider how Rand's theory might deal with such difficulties. As we saw previously, Tara Smith finds survivalist implications for many values through a theory of motivation. Enjoyment of life's pleasures helps us survive, Smith argues. Because we need, psychologically, to stay motivated to survive, Smith writes, "the will to live is crucial to satisfying life's requirements." How do we keep ourselves at difficult tasks over many months or years? Smith writes, "When success in some endeavor is neither in sight nor certain, it is easy to lose the conviction of its possibility. This is why enjoyment becomes valuable." Many seemingly slight values such as music and sports "stoke a person's enthusiasm for life." She continues, "While 'frills' enhancing the enjoyment of life may seem to carry more impact on flourishing than on sustenance, their contribution to survival is vital."[99] Smith is not saying that some values contribute to flourishing over and above survival; she is saying that flourishing and survival are one and the same goal, that flourishing is robust survival or "life that is prospering or in good condition."[100]

---

98   For example, frequent sex seems to reduce risks to men of prostate cancer and heart disease; see J. R. Rider et al., "Ejaculation Frequency and Risk of Prostate Cancer: Updated Results with an Additional Decade of Follow-up," *European Eurology*, December 2016, vol. 70, no. 6, via PubMed at https://www.ncbi.nlm.nih.gov/pubmed/27033442; and Hui-Fang Yang et al., "Does Serum Homocysteine Explain the Connection Between Sexual Frequency and Cardiovascular Risk?," *Journal of Sexual Medicine*, July 2017, vol. 14, no. 7, http://www.jsm.jsexmed.org/article/S1743-6095(17)31193-1/fulltext.

99   Tara Smith, *Viable Values* (Lanham, MD: Rowman & Littlefield, 2000), pp. 137–139.

100   Ibid., p. 126.

Smith continues the point: "By cultivating his taste for jazz or his skill at bowling, a person may make himself better able to relax after work or to keep his problems in perspective or to enjoy his life and thus have a stronger motivation to take good care of himself in other respects."[101]

Smith follows earlier claims by Rand and her associates. Nathaniel Branden writes that pleasure is "a profound psychological need." It is "at once an emotional payment for successful action and an incentive to continue acting."[102] Rand states the inverse of the point: "A chronic lack of pleasure, of any enjoyable, rewarding or stimulating experiences, produces a slow, gradual, day-by-day erosion of a man's emotional vitality, . . . until the day when his inner motor stops."[103] Harry Binswanger writes, "Even such actions as play and the pursuit of esthetic enjoyment can be seen as contributing to survival, insofar as they help maintain the individual's mental health."[104]

How does the claim about the importance of a value's motivating force hold up? Let us consider the strongest arguments before turning up the criticism.

Start with children. Rand and her supporters can make an initially plausible case that having children, for people who want them, really does support the parents' survival. To be granted entry into "Galt's Gulch" in *Atlas Shrugged*, people must (among other things) pledge, "I swear by my life and my love of it that I will never live for the sake of another man, nor ask another man to live for mine" (AS 731). This does not bar parents; a mother of two "open, joyous, friendly" boys takes the oath and lives in the gulch (AS 785).

How could having children possibly be consistent with holding one's own life (in terms of survival) as the highest moral aim?

---

101   Tara Smith, *Ayn Rand's Normative Ethics* (New York: Cambridge University Press, 2006), p. 21.

102   Nathaniel Branden, "The Psychology of Pleasure," in *The Virtue of Selfishness* (New York: Signet, 1964), p. 61.

103   Ayn Rand, "Our Cultural Value-Deprivation," in *The Voice of Reason*, ed. Leonard Peikoff (New York: NAL Books, 1989), p. 104.

104   Harry Binswanger, *The Biological Basis of Teleological Concepts* (Los Angeles, CA: Ayn Rand Institute Press, 1990), p. 203.

Although some children help with parents' work and as adults take care of parents with health problems, that sort of material gain is not what Rand has in mind. The rewards of parenthood include the intense and joyous relationship with the child and the inspiration of watching a child learn to navigate the world. Watching a child develop his abilities is comparable to appreciating a great work of art—it can be profoundly moving.

So Rand sees rewards not only in material terms but in spiritual terms. "Love, friendship, respect, admiration," Rand writes, are "the spiritual payment given in exchange for the personal, selfish pleasure which one man derives from the virtues of another man's character" (TOE 31). This idea can be expanded to encompass a parent's love for a child as the child develops. Rand also describes raising children, if done well, as a sort of career, with most of the same rewards (save remuneration) as other forms of productive work.[105]

What about taking a low-paying or dangerous job? Presumably Rand would answer that, to live successfully, a person has to do work that he loves. *The Fountainhead* is largely about the hero pursing his passion, architecture, and for a time he lives in poverty doing that. A person who hates his job is less likely to advance in his career and less able to gain the motivation from work to succeed in other areas of life. People who love fighting fires or teaching philosophy (or whatever) will better pursue their survival overall by pursuing those careers, rather than by picking a safer, higher-paying career they don't much like.

Regarding the simple pleasures of life—fine food, drink, games, sex, a long shower—no doubt sensibly indulging in such pleasures furthers survival by keeping a person away from depression and oriented to robust value pursuits.

Yet do people really have children, pursue an enjoyable career, and pursue the pleasures of life ultimately only in order to survive better? Should they?

---

105 Alvin Toffler, "Playboy Interview: Ayn Rand," *Playboy*, March 1964, reproduced as *50 Years of the Playboy Interview: Ayn Rand* (Playboy Enterprises, 2012).

Smith's case (as applied to our examples) is implausible. Before the advent of modern medicine, pregnancy and childbirth were extremely dangerous for women. Would Smith say that, for women who nevertheless wanted to have children, the motivational value of having them (in terms of survival) outweighed risks to life? Or would she say that intentionally having children prior to modern medicine was immoral because it obviously threatened the woman's survival? Either reply is troublesome.

Even today, the idea that the survival value of having children outweighs the costs in terms of risks and treasure strains credulity. The simple fact that most parents would take a bullet for their children, or in whatever way necessary risk or sacrifice their own lives to save their children, undercuts the claim that raising children is fundamentally about personal survival (a theme we'll explore in more detail later). Simply put, people do not normally have children to further their survival; far more often they consciously trade off some robustness of personal survival for the sake of their children.

Similarly, people do not normally take dangerous or low-paying jobs to maximize their survival. True, people tend to enjoy what they're good at, but what that implies for the consistent survivalist is that he'd try to become competent doing something relatively safe and high-paying (granting that there can be trade-offs between risk and pay). Furthering their survival is definitely a major factor in most people's choice of jobs, but it is hardly the only factor.

No doubt simple pleasures, sensibly pursued, can feed a person's drive to live. But is that really the only reason, ultimately, why we enjoy such pleasures? Most people regard the link between pleasures and survival, where it exists, as a happy coincidence. Hardly anyone would say that he pursues pleasures in order to stay alive; most people would say that they live partly in order to enjoy themselves, and that seems like a sensible stance. If someone learned that he had a condition whereby he shortened his life by a minute every time he had sex, he'd probably still have a lot of sex (if marginally less). Although the example is unrealistic, it points to the real and widespread phenomenon of people accepting hits to the robustness of their survival for the sake of other values.

With respect to pursuing art and music, Rand does not offer a strictly motivational account based on its pleasures; rather, she argues that art also serves a psychological need of conceptual creatures (as we've seen). I think Rand is on to something important in terms of art's relation to our conceptual capacity, but it is not plausible that our capacity to enjoy (say) music evolved to help us survive or ultimately serves to do only that. Far more likely, I think, is that our capacity to enjoy music is largely an epiphenomenon of our evolved social and cognitive capacities, and we enjoy it not just because it helps keep us alive.

Claims that having children, taking a risky job, pursuing life's pleasures, and enjoying art ultimately serve a person's survival usually become just-so stories. The effect is to insulate Rand's theory from objections. If a pursuit is obviously and pointlessly self-destructive, then Objectivists join everyone else in declaring such pursuits immoral. But, within the realm of pursuits that on their face seem sensible, there is no value that an Objectivist cannot defend as "really" about survival, however surprising that may seem to everyone else.

Consider the best-case scenario for Objectivists. Even if, by conscious intent or happy coincidence, all of a person's choices and pleasures in life maximized his survival, that would not demonstrate that his survival is his proper ultimate value. The metaethics still would have to be established on other grounds. In practice, strained claims about the survival value of life's joys and pleasures serve to patch Rand's shaky metaethics and make it seem more plausible.

Next we turn to related problems for the Objectivist ethics regarding the nature of happiness.

The Disconnect between Happiness and Survival

We saw earlier that Rand believes that happiness is the emotional consequence of pursuing one's life in the sense she means. Although Rand makes some interesting observations about the nature of happiness, she does not show that happiness follows specifically from rationally pursuing survival.

Let us back up and review Rand's theory of emotions. Here is Rand's central passage on the matter in "The Objectivist Ethics":

In psychological terms, the issue of man's survival does not confront his consciousness as an issue of "life or death," but as an issue of "happiness or suffering." Happiness is the successful state of life, suffering is the warning signal of failure, of death. Just as the pleasure-pain mechanism of man's body is an automatic indicator of his body's welfare or injury, a barometer of its basic alternative, life or death—so the emotional mechanism of man's consciousness is geared to perform the same function, as a barometer that registers the same alternative by means of two basic emotions: joy or suffering. Emotions are the automatic results of man's value judgments integrated by his subconscious; emotions are estimates of that which furthers man's values or threatens them, that which is for him or against him—lightning calculators giving him the sum of his profit or loss. (TOE 27)

The claim that emotions are "automatic results of man's value judgments" often is true. For example, it seems that we have an innate fear of things like spiders and snakes (a point against Rand's theory), but a person can enjoy handling spiders and snakes deemed safe and even feel friendly toward the creatures. Some American Christians, drawing inspiration from certain Biblical passages (see Mark 16:18 and Luke 10:19), intentionally handle dangerous snakes as a sign of their faith. (Their faith hasn't stopped a number of them from dying from snake bites.)[106] To take another example, the image of Hitler invokes in most people feelings of revulsion and anger but in some people feelings of racial pride. In turn, most people (justifiably!) feel revulsion or disgust toward those who view Hitler positively.

Yet emotions are not only a result of a person's value judgments. Some people feel depressed or generally unhappy, or alternately manically enthusiastic, because of their brain physiology, owing to some past trauma or current problem (such as a tumor or hormonal

---

106   Joshua Rhett Miller, "Snake Handling Puts Religious Freedom, Public Safety in Spotlight after Kentucky Death," Fox News, February 26, 2014, http://www .foxnews.com/us/2014/02/26/snake-handling-puts-religious-freedom-public -safety-in-spotlight-after-kentucky.html.

malfunction). Sometimes in such cases medication, surgery, or therapy can help. People who feel depressed due to some chemical imbalance probably view their lives as not going very well. In such cases the causation runs largely the opposite way of what Rand has in mind: The emotion gives rise to the value judgment. Still, we can grant that usually our value judgments give rise (via our physiology) to our emotions.

What should we make of Rand's grander claim that happiness is the result of the judgment that we are surviving in a robust way? No doubt we will likely feel fearful and unhappy if we believe our survival is threatened and safe if it is not. But that hardly means that our happiness is related exclusively to our surviving well, and Rand offers no evidence that it is.

By contrast, we can find ample evidence that happiness is about more than our survival. For example, a woman who wants to get pregnant and does so probably will feel extremely happy about that, even if she (reasonably) believes the pregnancy will not further her survival. And if the pregnancy fails, she probably will feel very sad about that for reasons that have nothing to do with her survival, which might actually be enhanced by an early termination.

Rand presents a stark choice: One can either pursue one's survival as an ultimate end and thereby achieve happiness—or fail (at least to a substantial degree) to achieve either. In Rand's view, people who pursue their survival can achieve the "state of non-contradictory joy" which is happiness; a joy possible only to the person "who desires nothing but rational goals, seeks nothing but rational values and finds his joy in nothing but rational actions" (TOE 29)—with "rational" understood here to pertain to the pursuit of one's survival. But we do not face a binary choice between joyfully pursuing our survival as our ultimate end and miserably drifting toward death. We can happily pursue many values that do not serve (or that do not only serve) our survival.

Rand does not present independent evidence that happiness results only from pursuing survival. Rather, she seeks to make plausible the idea that happiness results exclusively from pursuing one's survival rather than (as most people think) partly from pursuing values that do not necessarily or only serve survival. If Rand is wrong about her metaethics, then there is no reason to think that she is right about the source of happiness.

Ends in Themselves

Rand does talk about certain experiences as ends in themselves. In "The Objectivist Ethics," Rand talks about the experience of "pure happiness" as an "end in itself." Such an experience makes a person think, "*This* is worth living for," Rand writes (TOE 29). Regarding her hobby of stamp collecting, Rand writes: "In the course of a career, every achievement is an end in itself and, simultaneously, a step toward further achievements. In collecting, every new stamp is an event, a pleasure in itself and, simultaneously, a step toward the growth of one's collection."[107] Rand writes about art:

> One of the distinguishing characteristics of a work of art (including literature) is that it serves no practical, material end, but is an end in itself; it serves no purpose other than contemplation—and the pleasure of that contemplation is so intense, so deeply personal that a man experiences it as a self-sufficient, self-justifying primary. . . .[108]

Leonard Peikoff discusses sex as an end in itself. He describes happiness as a sort of "metaphysical pleasure" and sex as "a form of feeling happiness" that serves a "spiritual need." He continues, "Sex is moral, it is an exalted pleasure, it is a profound value. Like happiness, therefore, sex is an end in itself; it is not necessarily a means to any further end, such as procreation."[109]

---

107 Ayn Rand, "Why I Like Stamp Collecting," in *The Ayn Rand Column*, revised second edition (New Milford, CT: Second Renaissance Books, 1998), p. 125. The article originally was published in *Minkus Stamp Journal*, 1971, vol. 6, no. 2.

108 Ayn Rand, "The Pscyho-Epistemology of Art," in *The Romantic Manifesto*, revised edition (New York: Signet, 1975), p. 16.

109 Leonard Peikoff, *Objectivism: The Philosophy of Ayn Rand* (New York: Dutton, 1991), pp. 344, 346 (emphasis omitted). "Spiritual" here means pertaining to human consciousness.

How do such comments fit with Rand's basic moral theory that life is the ultimate value that all other values serve? As Peikoff summarizes the point, "Objectivism says that remaining alive is the goal of values and of all proper action."[110] But isn't Peikoff saying that sex, as an end in itself, does not have the further goal of remaining alive? How do we make sense of this?

Rand uses the term "end in itself" in two distinct senses. When she refers to life as an end in itself, she means that it is the ultimate value that all other values help support. Rand does not in this context refer mainly to our emotional experience of living; she refers to life as a self-sustaining process. The sense in which life is an end in itself has direct bearing on her moral theory.

When Rand refers to a joyful experience or to happiness broadly as an end in itself, she means that the experience does not have a direct tangible benefit. Rand is not saying that an experience of meaning or pleasure or happiness is valuable apart from its relationship to survival; she is saying that such an experience can reflect the pursuit of life-furthering values and can serve to motivate the pursuit of survival. Recall that Rand says that art is an end in itself but also that it is "inextricably tied to man's survival." Earlier we saw from Tara Smith's work that pleasures can serve as motivation to pursue life. None of this changes the fact that, for Rand, in terms of metaethics, only life is the ultimate value and an end in itself in that sense.

Rand would reject the notion that something that does not serve survival can be an end in itself; that would be the error of intrinsicism, in her view. It would be improper to interpret Rand's statements about ends in themselves apart from her survival-oriented metaethics.

But, again, Rand's explanations of how experiences of meaning, pleasure, and happiness fit in to her survival-based moral theory are not plausible. Most people who reflected on the matter would not say that enjoying art, hobbies, and sex, or that experiencing happiness, is just an emotional consequence of pursuing survival or else a means

---

110 Leonard Peikoff, *Objectivism: The Philosophy of Ayn Rand* (New York: Dutton, 1991), p. 213 (emphasis omitted).

to pursuing survival. Rather, most people would say that such things are valuable in themselves, even apart from their relationship to survival, and that we pursue survival largely to achieve them. Such is the view that passes the plausibility test.

Risk of Life and Suicide

Earlier I mentioned Objectivist just-so stories about how various values "really" ultimately support survival, even though it seems they do not (only) do so. Perhaps the oddest just-so story in Rand's moral theory is how risking one's life for others, or even committing suicide, can be in service of one's own survival. The claim strains credulity (to understate the point).

One sort of case involves risking one's life for a friend or loved one. In *Atlas Shrugged*, not long after giving his speech advocating selfish survival, John Galt threatens to kill himself rather than watch his lover be tortured. As Galt is about to be taken into custody by the villains, he tells his lover:

> [I]f they get the slightest suspicion of what we are to each other, they will have you on a torture rack—I mean, physical torture—before my eyes, in less than a week. I am not going to wait for that. At the first mention of a threat to you, I will kill myself and stop them right there . . . .
>
> I don't have to tell you . . . that if I do it, it won't be an act of self-sacrifice. I do not care to live on their terms, I do not care to obey them and I do not care to see you enduring a drawn-out murder. There will be no values for me to seek after that—and I do not care to exist without values. (AS 1091)

Another sort of case involves suicide in the face of terminal illness or extreme oppression. Leonard Peikoff writes:

> Suicide is justified when man's life, owing to circumstances outside of a person's control, is no longer possible; an example might be a person with a painful terminal illness, or a prisoner in a concentration camp who sees no chance of escape. In cases such as these, suicide is not necessarily a

philosophic rejection of life or of reality. On the contrary, it may very well be their tragic reaffirmation. Self-destruction in such contexts may amount to the tortured cry: "Man's life means so much to me that I will not settle for anything less. I will not accept a living death as a substitute."[111]

In *Atlas Shrugged*, after Cherryl Taggart discovers that the man she married is a vicious fraud, and she faces the overwhelming terror that a life of values is not possible to her, she flings herself into a river to her death. She runs toward the river with "the power of a creature running for its life" and "with full consciousness of acting in self-preservation" (AS 908). Although we as readers may think that Cherryl is making a tragic mistake—that her future prospects are not as grim as she thinks—we should not, Rand suggests (and I agree), regard her as immoral.

Yet another sort of case involves dying for an ideological cause. Alvin Toffler asks Rand if that would be permissible, and she says it would be:

> [A] man has to live for, and when necessary, fight for, his values—because the whole process of living consists of the achievement of values. Man does not survive automatically. He must live like a rational being and accept nothing less. . . . All values have to be gained and kept by man, and, if they are threatened, he has to be willing to fight and die, if necessary, for his right to live like a rational being. You ask me, would I be willing to die for Objectivism? I would. But what is more important, I am willing to *live* for it—which is much more difficult.[112]

What are we to make of such cases? Considering first the cases involving Galt and people facing extreme distress, certainly I think

---

111 Leonard Peikoff, *Objectivism: The Philosophy of Ayn Rand* (New York: Dutton, 1991), pp. 247–248 (emphasis omitted). Tara Smith offers similar arguments in *Viable Values* (Lanham, MD: Rowman & Littlefield, 2000), pp. 143–145.

112 Alvin Toffler, "Playboy Interview: Ayn Rand," *Playboy*, March 1964, reproduced as *50 Years of the Playboy Interview: Ayn Rand* (Playboy Enterprises, 2012).

that Galt and Peikoff are justified in their approach. But their views on the matter of self-risk and suicide are not compatible with arguments that Rand offers in "The Objectivist Ethics" for holding one's own survival as the ultimate moral value. Rather, the implication of what Galt and Peikoff say is that one's survival is not the ultimate end; rather, survival of a particular sort is. But then the theoretical base of Rand's moral theory crumbles away, and we need a different sort of moral theory to justify what Galt and Peikoff advocate.

The strongest case we can offer for what Galt and Peikoff advocate, from the perspective of "The Objectivist Ethics," is that there can come a point where it is literally impossible to act to pursue one's survival, so then suicide is justifiable. (Cherryl thought she had reached that point but was mistaken.) But the claim is implausible, and anyway it would justify inaction as much as suicide.

If Galt literally were unable to take action to further his survival following the horror of watching his loved one tortured to death, then, strictly on a survival-based ethic, Galt should be indifferent between killing himself and letting himself die. Or perhaps he should have a slight preference for dying in agony over time, because then at least his bare survival would be extended somewhat.

But Galt cares about more than his survival, and we would be horrified if he did not. That Galt would rather kill himself than witness his lover's pain, would rather die that his lover might live, would rather die than endure unspeakable agony, demonstrates that he ultimately cares about more than his continued existence. If life is his standard of value here, it is not in the sense that he discusses in his speech or that Rand describes in the first few pages of "The Objectivist Ethics."

We can see a similar tension between Rand's metaethical arguments and her sanction of self-risk in the context of emergency aid. Rand writes:

> If the person to be saved is a stranger, it is morally proper to save him only when the danger to one's own life is minimal. . . . If the person to be saved is not a stranger, then the risk one should be willing to take is greater in proportion to the greatness of that person's value to oneself. If it is the man or woman one loves, then one can be willing to give one's

own life to save him or her—for the selfish reason that life
without the loved person could be unbearable.[113]

A similar criticism as before applies here: Rand seems to be
saying that the bearableness of life matters over and above survival.
Anyway, how Rand describes heroism is hardly how most people see
it: If a man saves his wife's life at the cost of his own, his last thought
probably is not that his own life would be unbearable if he were to
live and his wife die; it is probably only that he really wants his wife
to live. Such a hero normally is not operating on a moral standard
based on his own survival.

There is another problem. On a survival-based ethics, why should
one endure even a minimal risk for a complete stranger? In normal
circumstances, the chances that the death of a random stranger
could negatively impact one's life are so close to zero that any risk of
personal death would count against intervention. Of course in real
life people often do take substantial risks to save complete strangers,
and generally people think well of such heroes.

None of this is to deny Rand's point that a sensible person takes
on greater risk to save a loved one than to save a stranger. But Rand's
remarks about saving a stranger seem implausible, and her remarks
about saving a loved one clash with her survival-based ethics.

Rand's endorsement of dying for a cause also seems at odds with
her survivalist ethics, at least in most cases. The only scenario I can
think of in which a consistent egoist plausibly might risk his life for
a cause is if he lives under a tyrannical regime that imposes extreme
risks to his survival and from which he cannot realistically hope to
hide or flee. But usually when we think of people risking their lives
for a cause we think of them enduring great risks to their survival
for the sake of an improved quality of life for themselves and others.
Certainly the American Revolutionaries did not put their survival
first in fighting the crown, which was arguably less oppressive (by
Objectivist standards) than modern American government. There is

---

113 Ayn Rand, "The Ethics of Emergencies," in *The Virtue of Selfishness* (New York:
Signet, 1964), pp. 45–46.

also the question of whether the egoist would lead the charge or let others do it (a matter we consider in more detail in Chapter 8). Perhaps there are psychological reasons to think that sometimes our values may lead us to risk or surrender our lives. Eyal Mozes argues that we need to strongly embrace values in order to live in a robust way. We become emotionally attached to our central values, and on rare occasions this attachment may lead us to risk our lives. He writes:

> [F]orming strongly held values might, in some rare cases, lead one to take actions leading to death; but in general, such strong values are much more likely to greatly *enhance* one's chances of survival, both by consistently guiding one's actions towards goals that help one's survival, and through their contribution to self-esteem and to happiness.[114]

Mozes's case is implausible. He is basically saying that once we embrace values in order to survive, we have to pursue those values even when doing so results in our death. Yet people fundamentally concerned with their survival should be able to modify their values in such cases. Psychology is not as strong a force here as Mozes supposes—and even if it were the sensible move for a survivalist would be to seek a cure for this psychological defect (as it would have to be regarded) or an escape from it. As Roderick Long points out in his reply to Mozes, "[I]f Galt's only reason for committing suicide is to avoid unbearable psychological suffering, then he ought to jump at the chance to let Dagny be tortured if he were to be offered an amnesia pill; but that hardly seems plausible."[115]

---

114   Eyal Mozes, "Flourishing and Survival in Ayn Rand," commentary on Roderick T. Long, "Reason and Value: Aristotle versus Rand," in *Objectivist Studies* 3, ed. William Thomas (Poughkeepsie, NY: Objectivist Center, 2000), https://atlassociety.org/sites/default/files/Reason_Value.pdf, p. 96.

115   Roderick T. Long, "Foundations and Flourishing: A Reply to Miller and Mozes," in Long's "Reason and Value: Aristotle versus Rand," in *Objectivist Studies* 3, ed. William Thomas (Poughkeepsie, NY: Objectivist Center, 2000), https://atlassociety.org/sites/default/files/Reason_Value.pdf, p. 110.

Nathaniel Branden addresses self-risk in a 1970 essay (written after his break with Rand), and his remarks also are hard to reconcile with Rand's survival-based metaethics. Branden first indicates that a person's main concern should not be "immediate, physical self-preservation"; to be consistent with Rand's metaethics, it should instead be robust and long-term self-preservation. Branden discusses risking one's life to escape a dictatorship, and doing so plausibly would offer better odds of surviving long-term. Branden also says that important values provide the "enjoyment [that] is the emotional fuel that keeps [a person] moving," and that once a person holds such values, "a man may have no desire to live without them." Branden says that a person should value "the *human* mode of life" and "love the thought, the effort, the struggle" of life.[116]

Branden's arguments here, which anticipate those of Tara Smith and Mozes, are less plausibly tied to life in terms of survival than to life of a certain quality. It is perfectly reasonable to say that it would be better to die than to live under certain conditions, but such a position does not flow from Rand's metaethical claims.

Far more plausible than the accounts of Peikoff, Mozes, and Branden is that people embrace some legitimate values for reasons other than to further their survival, so it is no great surprise when people risk or surrender their lives for the sake of those values.

At a certain point, efforts to contort things into a survivalist ethic such as dying for a loved one or committing suicide to avoid suffering begin to look like after-the-fact rationalizations, akin to religious apologetics.

In the next chapter, we look at some additional problems that Rand's moral theory has with making sense of normal values, starting with Rand's thought experiment about an indestructible robot.

---

116 Nathaniel Branden, "Rational Egoism: A Reply to Professor Emmons," *Personalist*, Spring 1970, vol. 51, no. 2, p. 204–205.

6. Robots, Man Qua Man, and the Choice to Live

IN THIS CHAPTER, WE EXPLORE three areas of Rand's moral theory that scholars have debated for decades. In each of these areas Rand's theory runs into trouble, providing further evidence that something is wrong with the theory.

Death and Robots

To illustrate her claim about the relationship between values and life, Rand raises a peculiar hypothetical about an indestructible robot. Rand believes that this example illustrates that values necessarily orient to survival; in fact, it illustrates the opposite. Here is how Rand presents the case:

> [I]magine an immortal, indestructible robot, an entity which moves and acts, but which cannot be affected by anything, which cannot be changed in any respect, which cannot be damaged, injured or destroyed. Such an entity would not be able to have any values; it would have nothing to gain or to lose; it could not regard anything as for or against it, as serving or threatening its welfare, as fulfilling or frustrating its interests. It could have no interests and no goals. (TOE 16)

Apparently Rand means to imply that the robot can be aware of the world and take action but that it cannot experience pleasure or pain and cannot have interests. In other words, it is similar to the robots we now have in the early decades of the twenty-first century, except it cannot be damaged. It operates by programming or chance, not by motives. Morally speaking, it is like any other nonliving thing. But then what is the purpose of the hypothetical in Rand's argument? Obviously something that "cannot be affected by anything" cannot have values. But why should we assume that a robot cannot be affected by anything because of its indestructibility? Why cannot an indestructible robot be affected by certain things— why can it not, say, enjoy watching a sunset or talking with a friend?

Rand seems to be claiming that, if something were indestructible, it necessarily could not be affected by anything. It could not experience pleasure or pain, happiness or sadness, joy or despair. This is how Leonard Peikoff takes Rand's example: "To an indestructible entity, no object can be a value. Only an entity capable of being destroyed and able to prevent it has a need, an interest (if the entity is conscious), a reason to act."[117]

The argumentative function of the robot example seems clear: If it is true that something that cannot be destroyed—that cannot die— therefore cannot have any values, then that bolsters Rand's claim that the only possible or coherent ultimate end of values is survival.

But there is no reason to think that Rand's claim is true. As Michael Huemer puts the point:

Assume the robot has feelings, desires, and/or moral beliefs. In that case, why wouldn't it have *values*? Why wouldn't it value the things that made it feel happy, for instance, or the things that it desired, or the things it believed to be morally good? In

---

117 Leonard Peikoff, *Objectivism: The Philosophy of Ayn Rand* (New York: Dutton, 1991), p. 211 (emphasis omitted).

this case, Rand appears to be giving a thought-experiment to refute her own view, rather than to support it.[118]

Before exploring Huemer's critique in more detail, we should step back and remind ourselves that Rand's hypothetical is impossible. No complex physical entity can be indestructible; anything that can be formed, created, or put together can also be destroyed. If we can imagine a robot that can survive a nuclear blast, a trip to the center of the Sun, or the forces of a black hole, then we can also imagine an even more formidable threat to the robot. So, as a practical matter, everything is at some risk, however remote, of destruction.

The purpose of the hypothetical, then, is to suss out the relationship of values to life. Is it true, as Rand argues, that the ultimate end of values is an organism's survival? Or, alternately, is it the case that we can morally pursue some values that do not sustain our lives? If it would be possible for an immortal robot to pursue values, then that would conclusively demonstrate that Rand's moral theory is wrong. And that is the case.

I don't know whether human beings ever will build robots capable of experiencing pleasure and pain and of caring about things, but it seems like it is theoretically possible. Why couldn't such a robot be in some respects like a human and enjoy, say, drawing? As humans we enjoy exercising our faculties (at least in some circumstances). As all mammalian young enjoy playing and wrestling, so human children enjoy learning how to use their minds and bodies. My son loves to draw. The evolutionary explanation for the enjoyment we take in exercising our faculties is obvious: By developing our faculties we become better at keeping ourselves alive and reproducing our

---

118   Michael Huemer, "Critique of 'The Objectivist Ethics,'" http://www. owl232.net/rand5.htm (accessed August 30, 2017). On this point see also Robert Nozick, "On the Randian Argument," in *Reading Nozick*, ed. Jeffrey Paul (Totowa, NJ: Rowman and Littlefield, 1981), pp. 208–209; Roderick T. Long, "Reason and Value: Aristotle versus Rand," in *Objectivist Studies* 3, ed. William Thomas (Poughkeepsie, NY: Objectivist Center, 2000), https://atlassociety.org/sites/default /files/Reason_Value.pdf, p. 41; and Ole Martin Moen, "Is Life the Ultimate Value? A Reassessment of Ayn Rand's Ethics," *Reason Papers*, October 2012, vol. 34, no. 2, https://reasonpapers.com/pdf/342/rp_342_9.pdf, p. 107.

genes. But there is no reason to think that, if humans could design a robot that could enjoy drawing, that this capacity would depend on the robot's destructibility. Although drawing, for my son, probably has some remote connection to his survival (in that it improves his manual dexterity and the like), a conscious, feeling robot should be able to enjoy drawing a picture, or looking at sunsets, or reading a novel, or doing any of a multitude of other things, without it contributing to its survival.

Besides robots, we can also imagine such possibilities as a genetically engineered or modified human whose body does not age and who self-repairs extremely well. The *X-Men* comics give us the science-fiction example of Wolverine, who practically is indestructible, at least until he becomes ill from his metal body parts as in the film *Logan* (2017). Notably, once Wolverine does become ill, there is apparently no action he can take to save himself, and everything he does before his death is for the sake of something other than his survival. In criticizing Rand's example of the robot, J. Charles King imagines a person made indestructible who still enjoys such things as sex, food, friendship, and philosophizing.[119]

In attempting to prop up Rand's take on the immortal robot, Peikoff points out that the robot would not have to eat, go to the dentist, or come out of the rain. Sure, but the robot would not have to have all of the same values as people to undercut Rand's point, just some values.

Peikoff then says that without "the alternative of life or death," there can be no "need satisfaction or need frustration," and therefore no "pleasure and pain sensations, which accompany need satisfaction or frustration in conscious creatures." The robot, Peikoff continues, would not need to work, to rest, or to have friends. On this last point, Peikoff writes, "Friends are men who share the same values; in order to have a friend, one must first hold some values."[120] In

---

119   J. Charles King, "Life and the Theory of Value," in *The Philosophic Thought of Ayn Rand*, ed. Douglas J. Den Uyl and Douglas B. Rasmussen (University of Illinois Press, 1984), p. 109.

120   Leonard Peikoff, *Objectivism: The Philosophy of Ayn Rand* (New York: Dutton, 1991), pp. 210–211.

making such claims, Peikoff presumes that values can exist only for the sake of survival, then concludes that, since the robot cannot die, it cannot have values. But human beings enjoy learning about the world, talking with friends, observing art and pretty landscapes, and so on, not just because those things advance our survival, but because we are biologically suited to do so. A robot could be similarly suited to enjoy certain things.

As a simplified example, imagine a sexual robot. For conscious organisms that have it, sex normally is extremely pleasurable. (As we've seen, evolutionarily speaking sex is primarily about the reproduction of genes, not the survival of the organism.) If a genie sprang from a lamp and granted us the wish of immortality, that would not make our biological capacity for sexual pleasure go away. It just is not the case that the only reason human beings have (or should have) sex is to further their survival, and neither is it the case that a robot could enjoy sex only if it were mortal. If we could wire up a robot to enjoy sex, whether sex advanced the robot's survival would be, to the robot, largely beside the point.

We can take the example of the sexual robot further and imagine that sexual pleasure is the only sort of pleasure the robot is capable of experiencing. It does not like drawing, looking at sunsets, contemplating art, reading novels, or any of other things that people normally like. But it loves having sex. In this case, if the robot were immortal, its immortality would not interfere with its ability to enjoy sex. If the robot were mortal, it would then have a reason to treat its survival as a valuable means to the end of experiencing sexual pleasure.

Tara Smith raises the interesting argument that a literally immortal robot would have no reason to pursue a given value today as opposed to tomorrow or in a trillion years.[121] Our sexual robot example can illustrate Smith's point. If a robot experienced sexual pleasure, it would have no reason to have sex today; no matter how long it put off having sex, provided it had sex at any interval, it still would have an infinite amount of sex. But Smith's point holds only

---

121   Tara Smith, *Viable Values* (Lanham, MD: Rowman & Littlefield, 2000), pp. 88–89.

if we assume that the robot experiences no built up displeasure by delaying sex (displeasure that, I think it is safe to say, humans have). Presumably the robot's wiring would determine how often it wants to have sex. Anyway, we have to rein in hypotheticals dealing with infinity or they quickly lead to absurd results. The absurdity in this case shows the limitations of Rand's example, not the impossibility of values that do not further survival.

It is worth noting an odd implication regarding Rand's claims about an immortal robot. A person who accepts Rand's moral theory should turn down a (hypothetical) offer of immortality. The person should respond something like, "It is only because I face the alternative of life or death that I can have any values, so if I became immortal I would be unable to have any values. Therefore, I choose the certainty of death over the promise of immortality." If someone tried to impose immortality on an Objectivist, he should resist. That is, he should pursue eventual death as a value—something he acts to (eventually) gain—for the sake of his ability to pursue values prior to death. A survival-based moral theory that can hold death as a hypothetical value seems peculiar, to say the least.[122]

Smith offers another line of argument:

> [T]he general fact that life depends on certain conditions is what gives rise to pleasure and pain. Consequently, if we stripped away the possibility of death, we would be eliminating the very thing that makes pleasure and pain possible. Thus, we cannot suppose that an immortal being would continue to experience pleasure or pain.[123]

This is a faulty argument. Just because X is responsible for bringing about Y, does not mean that if X goes away that Y also will go away.[124] Sure, conscious creatures evolved the capacity to

---

122   Robert Nozick also raises this point in "On the Randian Argument," in *Reading Nozick*, ed. Jeffrey Paul (Totowa, NJ: Rowman and Littlefield, 1981), p. 210.

123   Tara Smith, *Viable Values* (Lanham, MD: Rowman & Littlefield, 2000), p. 89.

124   Eric Mack also makes this point in "Problematic Arguments in Randian Ethics," *Journal of Ayn Rand Studies*, Fall 2003, vol. 5, no. 1, p. 12.

experience pleasure and pain to spur them to take action to sustain their lives and to reproduce. But, given that we do have that capacity now, we would not automatically lose it if somehow we were able to become immortal. Similarly, if we become able to create robots with the capacity to experience pleasure and pain, that capacity could be entirely independent of the robot's survival.

Huemer is right: Once we consider the relevant details and implications, Rand's example of the robot undercuts her moral theory rather than supports it. What the example actually illustrates is that survival is a means to other values, not that all values are a means to survival.

Next we consider the role that Rand's conception of "man qua man" plays in her moral theory.

Man Qua Man

Does Rand's refined moral standard of life as "man qua man" make sense of the values we have considered? What does Rand mean by this phrase, and what are the implications for her moral theory?

Start by retracing Rand's steps. As we've seen, "the issue of life or death" is central to Rand's approach to ethics (TOE 15). Normally when Rand talks about life in the context of her moral theory, she means life as opposed to death, life as survival; she does not mean some other sort of life that includes values oriented to something other than survival.

For Rand, a standard of value is relevant to all living things. "An organism's life is its standard of value: that which furthers its life is the good, that which threatens it is the evil," Rand writes (TOE 17).

Rand transitions to a discussion about moral standards, which are the province of humanity, by quoting from Galt's speech: "Man has been called a rational being, but rationality is a matter of choice— and the alternative his nature offers him is: rational being or suicidal animal. . . . A code of values accepted by choice is a code of morality" (TOE 23).

This is the point at which Rand introduces the standard of value regarding human morality:

> The standard of value of the Objectivist ethics—the standard by which one judges what is good or evil—is man's life, or:

that which is required for man's survival qua man. Since reason is man's basic means of survival, that which is proper to the life of a rational being is the good; that which negates, opposes or destroys it is the evil. Since everything man needs has to be discovered by his own mind and produced by his own effort, the two essentials of the method of survival proper to a rational being are: thinking and productive work. (TOE 23)

So it is clear that, by "man qua man," Rand means man as a rational being. She is not saying that rationality lets people morally embrace values that do not further their survival; she is saying that the way that people achieve their survival is by using reason.

Rand clarifies:

Man cannot survive, like an animal, by acting on the range of the moment. . . . [T]hat which is required for man's survival qua man . . . does not mean a momentary or a merely physical survival. . . . It does not mean the momentary physical survival of a crawling aggregate of muscles who is willing to accept any terms, obey any thug and surrender any values, for the sake of what is known as "survival at any price," which may or may not last a week or a year. "Man's survival qua man" means the terms, methods, conditions and goals required for the survival of a rational being through the whole of his lifespan—in all those aspects of existence which are open to his choice.

Man cannot survive as anything but man. He can abandon his means of survival, his mind, he can turn himself into a subhuman creature and he can turn his life into a brief span of agony. (TOE 24)

Some readers might be tempted to fixate on Rand's rejection of "survival at any price" and think that she is after survival of a particular quality or survival plus values apart from survival. But in context it is clear that Rand means that "survival at any price" cannot actually result in long-term, robust survival. The price that people must pay to survive long-range is to act by reason. So Rand definitely would not say that a person who happens to be alive thereby demonstrates that he is moral, because the person, through his actions, might have brought himself close to death (or closer than he needs to be) and made his survival precarious.

Rand is still building a survivalist standard—to be moral a person must strive to keep himself as far away from death as possible over the course of his lifespan. Rand does not here undermine the fundamental importance of survival in her moral theory; she explains what long-term survival requires. Remember that "reason is man's basic means of survival" for Rand: We should note well what is the means and what is the end. Survival remains the ultimate value that all other values support.

My reading of Rand on this point is consistent with the most authoritative interpretations of her. Leonard Peikoff puts the point this way: "The Objectivist standard of morality is not a momentary or a merely physical survival; it is the long-range survival of man—mind and body. The standard is not 'staying alive by any means,' because, once we speak in long-range terms, there is only one means of sustaining human life," reason.[125]

Tara Smith interprets Rand's remarks similarly: "[W]hen Rand claims that the standard of life is 'that which is required for man's survival qua man,' she is not raising the threshold of morality's demands, introducing some unwarranted, alien standard. . . . Rand is simply calling attention to the fact that only certain kinds of action will suffice to sustain a human life."[126]

Allan Gotthelf and Gregory Salmieri spend considerable effort explaining Rand's relevant passages, and they conclude: "The structure of Rand's argument makes it clear that she intended the

---

125 Leonard Peikoff, *Objectivism: The Philosophy of Ayn Rand* (New York: Dutton, 1991), p. 219.

126 Tara Smith, *Viable Values* (Lanham, MD: Rowman & Littlefield, 2000), p. 136 (emphasis omitted).

standard of value to include only content that could be derived from the requirements of man's literal survival."[127]

Still, it is easy to see why various critics think that Rand is pulling a fast one with her "man qua man" standard. In practice, it seems remarkably as though, by introducing the "man qua man" standard, Rand sneaks various values into her moral theory that do not actually have survival as their end. I think of this as the "survival-plus" standard—survival plus other values not aimed at survival.

Eric Mack describes this problem as "the Shuffle"—"when the real world counterexamples" to Rand's survivalism (such as cases of successful parasitism) "cannot be denied," Rand's defenders tend to "scamper" to a "man qua man" standard that is about more than survival (survival-plus), and when they need to focus on metaethical justification they return to strict (albeit robust and long-range) survivalism.[128]

Similarly, Michael Huemer points out that, on survivalist premises, "it would always be morally wrong to sacrifice your life for anything" (for example). Huemer surmises, "Rand does not want these results. Thus, she introduces the idea that the good is not merely life but life qua man." By Huemer's lights, "man qua man" effectively functions as a fudge term, letting Objectivists have their survivalism and eat it too.[129]

Certainly Rand does not intentionally introduce dueling moral standards. As we've seen, Rand and her defenders can come up with arguments about how various values that do not seem to support survival "really" do so, if we squint hard enough. I just don't think those arguments are usually convincing. So, in effect, the "man qua

127   Allan Gotthelf and Gregory Salmieri, "The Morality of Life," in *A Companion to Ayn Rand*, p. 79.

128   Eric Mack, "Problematic Arguments in Randian Ethics," *Journal of Ayn Rand Studies*, Fall 2003, vol. 5, no. 1, p. 22.

129   Michael Huemer, "Critique of 'The Objectivist Ethics,'" http://www.owl232. net/rand5.htm (emphasis omitted; accessed February 10, 2018). Huemer uses the language about fudge; the bit about having something and eating it too is my play on Galt's line about cake (see AS 1016).

man" standard does serve to introduce values into Rand's moral system that do not fundamentally support survival.

Next we consider the role that the premoral choice to live plays in Rand's theory and the problems with that construct.

The Choice to Live

Rand's survivalism has a basic problem of getting the normative ball rolling. Even if (counterfactually) it were true that, in the nonhuman world, living things normally pursued their own survival through their every function and action, Rand would then have to make the case for survivalism for people, who can choose what to do. Should people choose to do something rather than nothing? Should they choose to pursue only their survival rather than their survival plus other values not oriented to survival?

In answering such questions, Rand wants to avoid all hints of intrinsicism and moral duty. So she does not want to say that somehow life is good in itself, apart from a person's choices, or that a person somehow has a moral duty to survive. Rand also wants to avoid all hints of subjectivism and moral arbitrariness. And she needs to do all of this without falling into the is-ought bog.

To solve these problems, Rand proposes that a person's premoral (but non-arbitrary) choice to live gets him started down the path of values, logically commits him to survivalism, and, combined with her point about the objective impact of values on survival, meets the is-ought challenge.

Rand's theory of the choice to live is vulnerable to criticism on several fronts, which is why it has been debated by critics and defenders of Rand's theory almost since it first saw print. Three main questions arise: 1) Is the choice to live subject to moral evaluation, and, if not, how can Rand criticize those who choose something other than survival as their ultimate end? 2) Is choosing to orient all of one's values to survival really the only viable alternative to death, as Rand suggests? 3) Does the choice to live describe how people actually behave, or is it a mere theoretical construct?

Toward answering such questions, let us first retrace Rand's position. In *Atlas Shrugged*, John Galt says, "To remain alive, [a person] must think. But to think is an act of choice" (AS 1012).

After discussing the "fundamental alternative" of life or death (AS 1012–1013), Galt points out that, unlike plants and animals, people act by choice. Not all people even have a "desire to live," Galt says, and even when they do such "does not give [them] the knowledge required for living" (AS 1013). He then says:

> Man has been called a rational being, but rationality is a matter of choice—and the alternative his nature offers him is: rational being or suicidal animal. Man has to be man—by choice; he has to hold his life as a value—by choice; he has to learn to sustain it—by choice; he has to discover the values it requires and practice his virtues—by choice. (AS 1013)

Galt continues: "Since life requires a specific course of action, any other course will destroy it. A being who does not hold his own life as the motive and goal of his actions, is acting on the motive and standard of death" (AS 1014). By Rand's lights, then, a person chooses to live by choosing to be rational, and the only alternative to choosing life and rationality is drifting toward death.

A bit later Galt continues: "No, you do not have to live; it is your basic act of choice" (AS 1015). He goes on to say that a person can succeed at living only by acting rationally toward that end.

So far it is unclear whether the basic choice to live is morally evaluable. Is someone who does not make the choice a moral monster, or would it make no more sense to condemn such a person than it would to condemn a stone?

A bit later Galt contrasts the basic choice to live, which is one and the same as the basic choice to think, with evasion. "Thinking is man's only basic virtue," Galt says, and a person's "basic vice, the source of all his evils, is . . . the act of blanking out, the willful suspension of one's consciousness, the refusal to think" (AS 1017). "Non-thinking is an act of annihilation," Galt continues: "When a man declares: 'Who am I to know?'—he is declaring: 'Who am I to live?'" (AS 1018)

This line of thinking seems to make the choice to live morally praiseworthy, because surely evasion is morally condemnatory. Rand lays out two basic paths: A person can choose to think and thereby choose to live, or a person can choose to evade and thereby drift toward death. We should keep this background in mind when Galt says (serving as Rand's voice): "My morality, the morality of reason, is contained in a single axiom: existence exists—and in a single choice: to live. The rest proceeds from these" (AS 1018).

Later (after discussing the virtues), Galt suggests that most everyone wishes to live unless they somehow (through error or evasion) suppress that wish. He says, "I am proud of my own value and of the fact that I wish to live. This wish—which you share, yet submerge as evil—is the only remnant of the good within you, but it is a wish one must learn to deserve" (AS 1021).

How does the wish to live relate to the choice to live? I think Rand is saying that normally people naturally wish to live, at least initially, but only some people choose to live by choosing to think; many others evade facts and thereby betray their wish to live.

Rand (through Galt) then proposes a complex psychological theory linking evasion, the use of force to loot wealth created by others, and a pathological fear of death. Galt explains that, by using retaliatory (defensive) force, he does not share the perpetrator's "evil or sink to his concept of morality." Galt continues, "I merely grant him his choice, destruction." Immediately after condemning the initiation of force, Galt says:

> You who are the worshippers of the zero—you have never discovered that achieving life is not the equivalent of avoiding death. . . . You seek escape from pain. We seek the achievement of happiness. . . . It is not death that we wish to avoid, but life that we wish to live. . . . [Y]ou do not wish to live, and only fear of death still holds you to the existence you have damned. (AS 1024)

The result of pervasive evasion, then, is that a person fails to think, fails to make the choice to live, negates his initial wish to live, seeks to avoid death by looting the values produced by those who do choose to think and live, and clings to a zombie-like life only out of a grotesque "fear of death." Galt returns to these themes through his speech.

In *Atlas Shrugged*, an archetype of a person who chooses not to live is James Taggart. Finally, when cheering on the torture of John

Galt, Taggart sees through his own evasions to his nihilistic, envious hatred of the virtuous who choose to live:

> The protective walls of emotion, of evasion, of pretense . . . had crashed in the span of one moment—the moment when he knew that he wanted Galt to die, knowing fully that his own death would follow. He was suddenly seeing the motive that had directed all the actions of his life. . . . [I]t was the lust to destroy whatever was living, for the sake of whatever was not. It was the urge to defy reality by the destruction of every living value. . . . [H]e knew that he had never wanted to survive, he knew that it was Galt's greatness he had wanted to torture and destroy. . . . In the moment when he, James Taggart, had found himself facing the ultimatum: to accept reality or die, it was death his emotions had chosen. (AS 1145)

Rand returns to the choice to live in "The Objectivist Ethics." For a conscious, perceptual-level animal, Rand writes, "its senses provide it with an automatic code of values, an automatic knowledge of what is good for it or evil, what benefits or endangers its life" (TOE 19). Human beings are not like other animals in this respect; as conceptual, volitional beings, we have "no automatic code of survival" (TOE 19). We need to learn how to survive by using reason. And to use reason we need to choose to activate our minds. Rand then again relates the choice to think to the choice to live: "Psychologically, the choice 'to think or not' is the choice 'to focus or not.' Existentially, the choice 'to focus or not' is the choice 'to be conscious or not.' Metaphysically, the choice 'to be conscious or not' is the choice of life or death" (TOE 21).

In the main two works in which she presents her moral theory (in 1957 and 1961), then, Rand suggests that the choice to live is morally evaluable and in no way arbitrary.

But how does Rand avoid falling into either intrinsicism or subjectivism?[130] If there is no inherent reason to choose to live, then the choice seems to be arbitrary, a mere subjective preference, placing an "objective" moral theory on a foundation of sand. If there is an inherent reason to choose to live, then choosing to live is not arbitrary, but it seems to become a sort of moral obligation, and a person can be morally condemned for not making that choice. Moreover, if there is an inherent reason to live, then whatever that reason is seems to be the moral primary, not life in terms of survival. Some critics of Rand think that her choice to live makes her ethics inherently subjectivist. Roderick Long writes:

> [Rand's] official doctrine, as I read it, is that moral considerations come into play only as a result of the choice to live. It is difficult to avoid the implication—though Rand clearly wishes to—that the choice to live is arbitrary, a groundless, subjective, existentialist commitment for or against which rationality has nothing to say.[131]

Such subjectivism is easy to read into Rand's 1970 essay "Causality Versus Duty": "Life or death is man's only fundamental alternative. To live is his basic act of choice. If he chooses to live, a rational ethics will tell him what principles of action are required to

---

130   Rand clearly had trouble with the issue of intrinsicism versus subjectivism early in her career. In the mid-1940s, in notes for "The Moral Basis of Individualism," a work that Rand never finished, Rand posits as an axiom: "I wish to survive—my survival is desirable." She continues, "If anyone now asks: But why do I have to hold my survival as desirable?—The answer is: You don't have to. It is an axiom, to be accepted as self-evident." This "axiom," though, seems to be either a moral obligation preceding choice or else a mere subjective preference. See David Harriman, ed., *Journals of Ayn Rand* (New York, Plume, 1999), p. 303. Darryl Wright discusses Rand's remarks in his "Ayn Rand's Ethics: From *The Fountainhead* to *Atlas Shrugged*," in *Essays on Ayn Rand's* Atlas Shrugged, ed. Robert Mayhew (Lanham, MD: Lexington Books, 2009), pp. 266–268.

131   Roderick T. Long, "Reason and Value: Aristotle versus Rand," in *Objectivist Studies* 3, ed. William Thomas (Poughkeepsie, NY: Objectivist Center, 2000), https://atlassociety.org/sites/default/files/Reason_Value.pdf, p. 34.

implement his choice. If he does not choose to live, nature will take its course."[132]

Douglas Rasmussen also worries about the apparent arbitrariness of the choice to live: "If all moral obligations are hypothetical in character, that is, if the determination of what we ought or ought not do is only possible if we have chosen to live, then the decision to either live or not to live would seem incapable of moral evaluation by Rand's ethics."[133]

Tara Smith seems to concede Rasmussen's point when she emphasizes that the choice to live is not morally evaluable: "[T]he choice to live is what gives rise to values. All 'shoulds' depend on purposes; whether to pursue one's life is the question of whether to adopt any purposes at all. What this means is that the choice to live is not subject to rational appraisal."[134]

Leonard Peikoff appears to argue both sides. He says that the choice to live in Rand's system "is not a moral choice; it precedes morality." Yet Peikoff complains of the criticisms of "philosophy professors" to the effect that the choice to live is arbitrary, whimsical, or groundless. There are grounds for making the choice to live, Peikoff writes: The "grounds are reality." He continues:

> A man who would throw away his life without cause, who would reject the universe on principle and embrace a zero for its own sake—such a man, according to Objectivism, would belong on the lowest rung of hell. His action would indicate so profound a hatred—of himself, of values, of reality—that he would have to be condemned by any *human* being as a monster.[135]

---

132   Ayn Rand, "Causality Versus Duty," *Philosophy: Who Needs It* (New York: Signet, 1984), p. 99. Note that this edition of the book incorrectly lists the original date of the essay as 1974.

133   Douglas B. Rasmussen, "Rand on Obligation of Value," *Journal of Ayn Rand Studies*, Fall 2002, vol. 4, no. 1, p. 71.

134   Tara Smith, *Viable Values* (Lanham, MD: Rowman & Littlefield, 2000), p. 107.

135   Leonard Peikoff, *Objectivism: The Philosophy of Ayn Rand* (New York: Dutton, 1991), pp. 245, 247–248.

How can we condemn someone as a monster for failing or declining to make a choice that "precedes morality"?

An elegant way to resolve the conundrum about whether the choice to live is morally evaluable, one that makes the best sense of Rand's writings on the matter, is to recognize a difference between not choosing to live and choosing not to live.[136] A person who never made the premoral choice to live, or who completely lost interest in life and stopped choosing to live, would have no reason to take any action; he would just drift toward death, as Rand describes in "Causality Versus Duty." That is different from the case of a person such as Taggart who is driven by evasion to an envious and destructive hatred. A person who passively fails to choose to live is not morally condemnable, but a person who through evasion proactively chooses not to live is condemnable.

Yet this distinction (between not choosing to live and choosing not to live) takes us only so far, for what explains the presumption of life that Taggart rejects? If Taggart's primary sin is evasion, as Rand suggests, then there must be something that he is evading.

Darryl Wright proposes that "it is possible to directly experience one's life as a value" and that "there are easily accessible nondeliberative grounds for making the choice to value one's life."[137]

Wright's approach is interesting, yet it immediately runs into various problems. If there are grounds to choose to live, then making the choice to live seems to become a sort of moral obligation, bringing Wright uncomfortably close to intrinsicism (although Wright denies that). And if there are "nondeliberative grounds" to choose to live, then why can there not be (as I believe) similar grounds to pursue values that do not (only or at all) serve survival? What's more, Wright plays both sides regarding whether Taggart's actions are morally evaluable: "There may be nothing that someone who does not value his life has a moral reason to do," yet there is "a real defect

---

136 Douglas B. Rasmussen makes this distinction in "Rand on Obligation and Value," *Journal of Ayn Rand Studies,* Fall 2002, vol. 4, no. 1, p. 78.

137 Citations in this paragraph and the next are from Darryl Wright, "Reasoning about Ends," in Allan Gotthelf and James G. Lennox, eds., *Metaethics, Egoism, and Virtue* (University of Pittsburgh Press, 2011), pp. 28–30, 32.

or corruption in that person traceable to a groundless rejection of life," he writes. Wright also has trouble deciding which comes first, the choice to live or the nondeliberative grounds to choose: "One comes to find life choiceworthy as a result of having sought out and achieved values within it," he writes. If one has to achieve values in order to "experience one's life as a value," then what are the grounds for pursuing the initial values?

Rand's choice to live is plausibly premoral and non-arbitrary only on the assumption that all values tie to survival. As we've seen, this is how Rand and her advocates cast the matter. Allan Gotthelf and Gregory Salmieri offer another clear statement of this:

> Rand held that the phenomenon of valuing only arises in the context of an organism's pursuit of its life as its ultimate value. At whatever times and to whatever extent a person is not engaged in this pursuit, he can have no values at all, and can act only in the joyless, destructive manner of James Taggart.[138]

Other of Rand's remarks tie the choice to live to the relationship of values and life. In a letter to John Hospers dated April 29, 1961, Rand reiterates that "only the requirements of an organism's life make the existence of values possible." Hence, "to choose any value, other than one's own life, as the ultimate purpose of one's actions is to be guilty of a contradiction and of the fallacy of the 'stolen concept.'" She continues, "one has already accepted" life as the ultimate value "by accepting the concept 'value,' because the concept 'value' has no other source, base, meaning or possibility of existing."[139] Here Rand suggests that a person has implicitly made the choice to live, at least to a degree, in asking about values, which is what gives rise to the contradiction if the person then denies the ultimate value of life.

---

138 Allan Gotthelf and Gregory Salmieri, "The Morality of Life," in *A Companion to Ayn Rand*, p. 67.

139 See Rand's letter in Michael S. Berliner, ed., *Letters of Ayn Rand* (New York: Dutton, 1995), p. 562 (emphasis omitted).

In 1962, while still working closely with Rand, Nathaniel
Branden similarly attempted to sail between the Scylla of intrinsicism
and the Charybdis of subjectivism:

> By identifying the genetic roots of "value" epistemologically,
> [Rand] demonstrates that not to hold man's life as one's
> standard of moral judgment is to be guilty of a logical
> contradiction. . . . [L]ife is the basic value that makes all
> other values possible; the value of life is not to be justified by
> a value beyond itself; to demand such justification—to ask:
> Why should man choose to live?—is to have dropped the
> meaning, context and source of one's concepts. "Should" is
> a concept that can have no intelligible meaning, if divorced
> from the concept and value of life.
>
> If life—existence—is not accepted as one's standard, then
> only one alternative standard remains: non-existence. . . .
> The man who does not wish to hold life as his goal and
> standard is free not to hold it; but he cannot claim the
> sanction of reason; he cannot claim that his choice is as valid
> as any other. It is not "arbitrary" . . . whether or not man
> accepts his nature as a living being. . . .[140]

If it is true that values can be understood only in relation to
survival, then we really do ultimately face a binary choice: life or
nothing. In that context, choosing life is not arbitrary, because there
is literally nothing else to choose.

But now Rand's theory about the choice to live faces another
serious problem: It is not plausible. Most people neither orient all
of their values to survival nor live joyless and destructive lives. The
obvious explanation for this is that not all of our legitimate values, in

---

140 Nathaniel Branden, "The Moral Revolution in *Atlas Shrugged*," in *Who Is Ayn Rand?* (New York: Paperback Library, 1964), pp. 26–27 (emphasis omitted); the work is copyright by Nathaniel Branden in 1962. Note that Branden later "repudiated" this book, "primarily" because of the biographical essay by Barbara Branden in it; see Michael Etchison, "Break Free! An Interview with Nathaniel Branden," *Reason*, October 1971, http://reason.com/archives/1971/10/01/break-free/8.

fact, orient to our survival. That we do not actually face the binary choice, survivalism or death, I think, is mainly what gives rise to the common complaint that Rand's choice to live becomes arbitrary. It just is not true that, if people do not choose to treat their survival as their ultimate value, that they thereby face the void of death. Therefore, it is arbitrary to say that a person must choose to live in Rand's survivalist sense, if he is to pursue values at all.

At one level, Rand's moral theory seems refreshingly simple and straightforward. Values are about life; choose to live! Why, then, does the theory get bound up in decades of arcane debates about immortal robots, the meaning of the phrase "man qua man," the nature of the choice to live, and so on? Of course part of the answer is that philosophers often love to carry on such discussions. (For many people in academia, the alternative of life or death is prior only to the alternative of publish or perish.)

But I think there is something deeper at work. It is hard to explain and justify a theory that is wrong. The earth-centered model of the solar system seems simple too—but it requires complex epicycles to explain observed facts. Rand's survival-centered model of values similarly seems simple at first glance and yet requires intellectual gyrations to deal with basic facts of human life.

In the next chapter, we explore the problems that Rand's moral theory has in coping with individual rights.

7. Egoism and Rights

RAND CERTAINLY BELIEVES THAT HER SURVIVAL-BASED, egoistic moral theory is compatible with rights-respecting behavior; indeed, she believes that such a moral theory is required for the firm establishment of rights.

Near the end of his speech in *Atlas Shrugged*, John Galt notes that America (in its essential principles of liberty) was founded on "the premise that man is an end in himself, not the means to the ends of others, that man's life, his freedom, his happiness are his by inalienable right." Galt continues, "Rights are conditions of existence required by man's nature for his proper survival. If man is to live on earth, it is right for him to use his mind, it is right to act on his own free judgment, it is right to work for his values and keep the product of his work" (AS 1061).

In Rand's view, egoism implies that each person properly pursues his own life-promoting values, and the principle of rights recognizes that fact in a social context. For Rand, egoism goes hand-in-hand with rights, and any moral sanction of the sacrificial use of people goes hand-in-hand with rights violations. So, for example, Communism holds that individuals should serve the (supposed) collective good, so Communism does not recognize the individual's right to his own life.

More broadly, any ethical system that sanctions an individual's self-sacrificial action for others, which Rand terms altruism, ultimately will be unable to support or sustain a political system based on individual rights, because the purpose of rights is to sanction self-interested action by individuals (granting that an individual often has an interest in other people doing well). Only a morality rooted in self-interest logically supports rights, in Rand's view.

In her 1963 essay "Man's Rights," Rand explains, "'Rights' are a moral concept . . . that provides a logical transition from the principles guiding an individual's actions to the principles guiding his relationship with others." She continues: Any variant "of the altruist-collectivist doctrine which subordinated the individual to some higher authority, either mystical or social," has fostered some variant of "statist tyranny." The alternative is a moral theory that holds "man as an end in himself, and society as a means to the peaceful, orderly, *voluntary* coexistence of individuals."[141] In short, egoism eschews the sacrifice of individuals and instead upholds their rights.

Challenges to Rand's Case for Rights

Does Rand's case hold? It is obvious why an egoist would want other people to respect and protect his rights. It is not obvious why an egoist would rationally want to consistently respect and protect the rights of others. Would not a sensible egoist strategically violate the rights of others in order to gain various values such as wealth, prestige, and pleasure? Further, would not a sensible egoist call for a society that protected the "rights" of some people—those who produce wealth and support themselves—and not others?

Michael Huemer argues that egoism is inherently incompatible with rights. He offers a hypothetical example to illustrate why:

> Suppose that I am in a hurry to get somewhere. I am walking to work, and if I am late, my boss gets mad at me. Furthermore, I like to get to work on time, because I have a lot of work that I want to get done. It is in my interests to get to work on time, but I am running a little bit late this morning. . . .

---

141 Ayn Rand, "Man's Rights," in *The Virtue of Selfishness* (New York: Signet, 1964), pp. 92–93.

Now as I walk down the street, there are a lot of people in my way, slowing me down. I just happen to have in my pocket a hand-held disintegrator ray, though. The gun will quickly disintegrate any person I aim it at. It is believed that victims of disintegration suffer brief but horrible agony while being disintegrated, but after that, no trace of them is left. I hold back on disintegrating the people in my path, though, because some of them might be potential clients for my business. But then I see this homeless guy ahead, just wandering down the street. He is not threatening me, and I could go around him, but that would take a second or two longer, and I'm in a hurry. So I pull out the gun and disintegrate him, and then continue on my way.

Assume that I live in a society in which homeless people are so little respected that my action is both legal and socially acceptable. . . . So I will not be punished for my action. Assume further that I dislike homeless people and don't like to see them on the street. So I do not feel bad about seeing the homeless guy disintegrated. In fact, it amuses me. Nor will my conscience bother me, because I am an ethical egoist, and so I believe that my action was morally virtuous. Therefore, after destroying the homeless guy, I should feel proud, not guilty.

The question is: Was my action morally right? If egoism is true, it was.[142]

Generalizing from Huemer's analysis, Jason Brennan argues:

Rand's theory does forbid human sacrifice, but only contingently. Ethical egoists are committed to the view that if raping, dismembering, and murdering some other person *were* slightly better for you than any alternative action, then

---

142   Michael Huemer, "Why I Am Not an Objectivist" (sec. 5.3.2), http://www.owl232.net/rand.htm (accessed October 23, 2017).

you'd be justified, indeed, obligated to rape, dismember, and murder some other person.[143]

Obviously if such criticisms find their mark, then Rand's theory of rights cannot hold up, and indeed her entire moral theory must be rejected. What should we make of such claims?

Virtue and Rights

Rand spends little effort explicitly explaining why individuals have an obligation to respect the rights of others. This is no oversight on her part; rather, Rand thinks she has established that point implicitly with her presentation of the virtues and of related points. It is impossible to understand Rand's case without following the logical progression of her argument.

Both in *Atlas Shrugged* and in "The Objectivist Ethics," Rand makes the same general sequence of arguments. After stating her basic metaethical views, Rand then proceeds to a discussion of the virtues, then talks about why human beings can and should interact by mutual consent (by trade), then explains why individuals should not initiate force against others.

Consider these points in more detail. After laying out her metaethical views in Galt's speech, Rand summarizes, "My morality, the morality of reason, is contained in a single axiom: existence exists—and in a single choice: to live. The rest proceeds from these." In the same paragraph, Rand notes that to live a person needs three "supreme and ruling values," reason, purpose, and self-esteem (which entails the view that one is "worthy of living"). Those values "imply and require all of man's virtues"; Rand lists the major ones as rationality, independence, integrity, honesty, justice, productiveness, and pride (AS 1018). With respect to a person's relations with others,

---

143   Jason Brennan, "Craig Biddle's Chart on Essential Moral Theories; Objectivist Strawmen," *Bleeding Heart Libertarians*, July 16, 2014, http:// bleedingheartlibertarians.com/2014/07/craig-biddles-chart-on-essential-moral -theories-objectivist-strawmen/.

the virtues of independence, honesty, justice, and productiveness are most relevant. Take these in turn.

Independence refers to "one's acceptance of the responsibility of forming one's own judgments and of living by the work of one's own mind" (TOE 26). The material aspect of this is closely related to productiveness. Using force to get values from others, without their consent, undermines one's independence.

Honesty entails the recognition "that neither love nor fame nor cash is a value if obtained by fraud." By saying the apparent value so acquired is not even a genuine value, Rand means that its attainment undermines the person's life rather than serves it. How? "[A]n attempt to gain a value by deceiving the mind of others," Galt says, "is an act of raising your victims to a position higher than reality, where you become a pawn of their blindness, a slave of their non-thinking and their evasions, while their intelligence, their rationality, their perceptiveness become the enemies you have to dread and flee" (AS 1019).

Justice means giving each person his due, both in spiritual and material realms. Rand ties justice to rationality in that it demands that people not seek to fake reality with respect to others (AS 1019–1020).

Productiveness entails one's "recognition of the fact that you choose to live—that productive work is the process by which man's consciousness controls his existence, a constant process of acquiring knowledge and shaping matter to fit one's purpose" (AS 1020).

Productiveness brings the obvious payoff of material wealth that one can use to advance and enjoy one's life. But material gain is not the only significance of the virtue. A person who mooches off of others, as opposed to one who creates wealth productively, puts his fate in the hands of those others. As Rand colorfully puts the point, "[T]he man who lets a leader prescribe his course is a wreck being towed to the scrap heap" (AS 1020). If the other people fail to provide the mooch with a living or refuse to provide one, the person's very life is then in peril. A person is left helpless, having never developed the habits and skills to produce wealth for himself.

Productiveness also brings profound psychological rewards. Rand says that "your work is the process of achieving your values, and to lose your ambition for values is to lose your ambition to live." A representative example is the unemployed layabout who dies of a drug overdose. A productive purpose is so central to a person's life, Rand writes, "that any value you might find outside your work, any other loyalty or love, can be only travelers" along life's journey (AS 1020).

After discussing the virtues and then briefly discussing the nature of happiness (and a few related topics), Rand (through Galt) goes on to discuss the implications of virtuous living in a social context. Rational people relate consensually by trade. "A trader is a man who earns what he gets and does not give or take the undeserved," Rand writes (AS 1022). Trade is possible among people precisely because they are able to produce values and to interact with others by reason; it is an outgrowth of human virtue.

The alternative to interacting with others by consent is interacting by force. For Rand, the moral impropriety of initiating force against others is closely related to the propriety of respecting others' rights. "A right cannot be violated except by physical force," she notes.[144] Rand refers to initiated force, not defensive force; so, for example, police arresting a murderer would count as a defensive use of force. Rand has a broad conception of what force entails; for example, breach of contract, fraud, and extortion involve an "indirect use of force" for "obtaining material values without their owner's consent."[145]

Rand, then, sees a straight line from virtues to rights. Once we understand the virtues, and also understand that people can interact through production and trade (which implies that life among people need not be a zero-sum game), then rights-respecting behavior readily follows. Rand says that we have a positive obligation to deal with other people (whenever we do) by use of reason (which implies consent) and a negative obligation not to deal with others by force:

Do you ask what moral obligation I owe to my fellow men? None—except the obligation I owe to myself, to material

---

144   Ayn Rand, "Textbook of Americanism," in *The Ayn Rand Column*, revised second edition, ed. Peter Schwartz (New Milford, CT: Second Renaissance Books, 1998), p. 85.

145   Ayn Rand, "The Nature of Government," in *The Virtue of Selfishness* (New York: Signet, 1964), p. 111.

objects and to all of existence: rationality. I deal with men as my nature and theirs demands: by means of reason. I seek or desire nothing from them except such relations as they care to enter of their own voluntary choice. . . .

Whatever may be open to disagreement, there is one act of evil that may not, the act that no man may commit against others and no man may sanction or forgive. So long as men desire to live together, no man may initiate . . . the use of physical force against others. (AS 1022–1023)

Rand then turns to a discussion that mainly focuses on why rights violations are bad for the victims. By this point clearly she believes that she has robustly established that individuals should not violate others' rights.

Practical Principles

Critics of Rand such as Huemer and Brennan are unlikely to be swayed by Rand's invocation of the virtues to endorse rights-respecting behavior. After all, they would likely reply, is not the central tenet of Rand's egoism that individuals should further their own survival? Then mustn't every virtue be subordinated to that primary goal? It just does not seem plausible (the critics will say) that being virtuous in the ways that Rand describes would always and without exception further one's survival.

Yet Rand's case is stronger than her critics typically allow.

Consider a simple example. You walk out of a store and into the parking lot and observe a shopper in front of you walking to his car. A wallet slips from the shopper's bag to the ground, yet he continues on without noticing this. The shopper seems to be tired or distracted or otherwise not at full alertness. You see him get into his car and drive off. Even at a distance, you can see that the wallet, which happens to be right next to your car, is stuffed with bills. It is a slow time of day, and you see no one else in the parking lot. It is not the sort of store with video surveillance of the lot. Anyway, if someone saw you pick up the wallet and confronted you, you could easily claim that you hadn't seen who dropped it and that you planned to return it later.

The authorities almost certainly would not prosecute you for picking up the wallet, although at least morally it is a sort of petty theft. So what should you do?

If you pick up the wallet, keep the cash, and later discard the rest, you could use the money to buy groceries, pay rent, buy a new pair of shoes, visit the doctor, or do any number of other things to benefit your life. On the other hand, if you yell after the shopper or return the intact wallet later, at best you'll get a measly reward and a thank-you, and at worst you'll be accused of taking the wallet in the first place.

It seems that, on a survivalist ethic, the obvious choice is to take the money. But, I think we can agree, that would be obviously immoral. How would Rand reply?

Rand, as amplified by her advocates, offers four main interrelated reasons (in addition to those given) why violating others' rights is bad for a person. It places a person's choices beyond reason and makes them arbitrary, it puts a person at profound risk of retribution and censure, it degrades a person's moral psychology, and it undermines a rights-respecting culture. Consider these points in turn.

Rand's main argument against violating rights—and against straying from principles generally—is that human beings need to guide their actions by principles to live successfully. This is essentially an epistemological argument; the claim is that people are unable to make good decisions without the guidance of principles, including the principles embodied in the virtues.

Leonard Peikoff points out, as an example, that it is illegitimate just to assume that money stolen is of equivalent value to money productively earned. Something obtained by violating moral principles is not a value at all in the context of a person's long-term needs, which only principles are capable of addressing.[146]

"A principle is a basic generalization," Peikoff writes, a person's "major form of using concepts . . . to reduce the complexity

---

146 Leonard Peikoff, *Objectivism: The Philosophy of Ayn Rand* (New York: Dutton, 1991), pp. 272–273.

facing him while retaining all the information that is essential for successful action."[147]

We know that producing wealth and trading with others on a consensual basis is a stable way to live successfully (barring accidents and the like). We know that violating people's rights puts a person at risk of getting caught and gaining a bad reputation, and it involves hiding from the truth. In a given case, it is simply impossible to rationally determine that violating someone's rights would be advantageous to a person's life, on net and in the long term. By contrast, although acting on principle does not guarantee success in any given endeavor, it is the only way to reliably achieve long-term success.

Tara Smith contrasts the principled Objectivist teleological (ends-oriented) theory of rights with any pragmatic consequentialist theory, arguing that consequentialism "offers no guidance" for determining when to respect rights and when to violate them in specific cases.[148]

As we have seen, embedded in Rand's discussion of the virtues is the idea that straying from virtue is impractical. The person who tries to gain values through deception places himself in a clash with others and faces constant risk of being found out and shunned by respectable people.

In his discussion of honesty, Peikoff works "through a standard example" involving why "a man [should] not execute a well-planned swindle," such as selling "stock in a fake gold mind." The swindler, of course, would have to concoct a bundle of lies to promote the fraud, and each challenge from others would require the creation of a new set of lies. Each of the swindler's lies "creates a risk of his detection and exposure by anyone with access to the facts." And the swindler makes himself dependent on the gullibility of others.[149] By violating

---

147   Leonard Peikoff, "Why Should One Act on Principle?," in *Why Businessmen Need Philosophy*, ed. Debi Ghate and Richard E. Ralston (New York: New American Library, 2011), p. 239.

148   Tara Smith, *Moral Rights & Political Freedom* (Lanham, MD: Rowman & Littlefield, 1995), p. 115.

149   Leonard Peikoff, *Objectivism: The Philosophy of Ayn Rand* (New York: Dutton, 1991), pp. 270–271.

the rights of others, a criminal risks not only direct retribution by private parties and government but the loss of reputation, thereby undercutting his ability to trade and engage with other decent people in the future.

Consider the inherent risks even of a rights violation as seemingly safe as taking the wallet of the shopper considered above. If you take the wallet, you cannot be certain that no one else saw you, perhaps someone sitting unnoticed in another car or someone observing a video feed from across the street. In today's age, someone easily could video record your theft and put the video online for all to see. And then you must lie about where you got the money, if anyone asks, or at least be careful not to disclose the source of funds. So, for example, if you buy a nice gift for your spouse or drinks for your friends, you must not let slip that you got the funds by taking the wallet, lest your friends think ill of you. (By contrast, if you brag about taking the wallet, you will have only friends likely to rob and otherwise abuse you.) It is in this sense that you have made reality your enemy; if your respectable friends learn what you did, they will no longer be your friends. In this way, violating rights undercuts the joyous and undisturbed peace of mind and self-esteem that for a virtuous person is normal.

Further, violating others' rights degrades one's moral psychology and character. As Tara Smith puts the point in the context of honesty, "[L]ying is likely to carry destructive effects on the liar's own psyche and ability to the honest in the future. Engaging in dishonesty encourages a habit of deceit, weakening one's inclination to truthfulness and nurturing an inclination to faking things."[150]

Consider the role of moral character in the case of the dropped wallet. A good person—a person who has habituated the virtues—will automatically, almost without thinking, call out to the shopper about the wallet. If the shopper leaves without the wallet, the person of high character will note the license plate if possible and check the wallet for identification, then return it. If for some reason identification is not provided, the person will turn in the wallet to

150 Tara Smith, *Viable Values* (Lanham, MD: Rowman & Littlefield, 2000), p. 167.

the store's managers, post about the wallet on social media, or take some other comparable action in an effort to find the shopper. By contrast, the sort of person who regularly entertains the possibility of abusing others and taking their wealth will immediately recognize an "opportunity" to take the wallet and keep the cash. True, in that case the person likely will get away with it. But consider the mindset that allows the petty theft. Rather than consistently spend his energy thinking about how to produce wealth and trade consensually with others, the person spends considerable energy looking for ways to unscrupulously take advantage of others. Such a person is far less likely to advance in a productive career and far more likely to engage in criminal behavior more broadly, eventually leading to devastating consequences. Moral character matters to a person's life, profoundly.

Degrading one's moral character brings profound psychological costs, Rand holds; self-esteem depends on virtue. As Darryl Wright puts the point, Rand's egoist "*wants* to treat others as ends. His self-esteem and sense of purpose derive from the creative use of his mind. . . . He therefore has no reason to want to exploit others."[151]

The final main argument for respecting rights pertains to the maintenance of a culture that embraces rights. In a 1967 talk, Rand says, "The only 'obligation' involved in individual rights is an obligation imposed, not by the state, but by the nature of reality (i.e., by the law of identity): *consistency*, which, in this case, means the obligation to respect the rights of others, if one wishes one's own rights to be recognized and protected."[152]

Picking up on Rand's argument, Craig Biddle writes that "what obligates a person to respect the rights of others is his own

---

151 Darryl Wright, "A *Human* Society: Rand's Social Philosophy," in *A Companion to Ayn Rand*, p. 167. Wright also discusses arguments about consistency that we consider below; see pp. 166–167, 174–175 of the same work.

152 Ayn Rand, "The Wreckage of the Consensus," in *Capitalism: The Unknown Ideal* (New York: Signet, 1967), p. 227 (some emphasis omitted). Rand makes similar remarks elsewhere—see her April 29, 1961 letter to John Hospers in Michael S. Berliner, ed., *Letters of Ayn Rand* (New York: Dutton, 1995), p. 556; and her extemporaneous remarks on the matter from 1961 and 1962 in *Ayn Rand Answers*, ed. Robert Mayhew (New York: New American Library, 2005), pp. 110, 115.

self-interest," which depends, in part, on "the social conditions that make peaceful human coexistence possible (e.g., individual rights, freedom, the rule of law)."[153]

Here Rand seems to invoke a sort of social contract theory of rights, in the sense not of a literal contract but of a widespread agreement to respect and protect rights. If I want to live in the sort of society in which people respect my rights, the claim seems to go, then I need to help create such a society by respecting the rights of others. This line of argument is interesting, but it has some weaknesses to which we will return later.

Reconsidering Huemer's Objection

Now that we have reviewed Rand's case for respecting rights, let us see whether it answers Huemer's hypothetical example about the egoist disintegrating homeless people.

The epistemological problem comes into play when we consider the impossibility of knowing the full and long-range implications of disintegrating a person. As Huemer grants, "it is almost impossible to assess the probabilities of all [relevant] possibilities in any definitive manner."[154] Rand would say that it is absolutely impossible and that the impossibility counts as a reason to instead guide one's actions by the principles embodied in the virtues and in individual rights.

What about practical concerns? Huemer wants to remove the practical problem of getting caught by saying that in the sort of society he describes no one cares whether you disintegrate homeless people (except, of course, homeless people, who are not in a position to do anything about it). But many other practical problems immediately arise. For starters, how do you as the egoist tell a homeless person

---

153   Craig Biddle, "Ayn Rand's Theory of Rights," *Objective Standard*, Fall 2011, vol. 6, no. 3, https://www.theobjectivestandard.com/issues/2011-fall/ayn-rand -theory-rights/.

154   Michael Huemer, "Why I Am Not an Objectivist" (sec. 5.3.2), http://www .owl232.net/rand.htm (accessed October 23, 2017). All subsequent quotes by Huemer in this section come from the same essay (sec. 5.3.1, 5.3.2, or 5.3.3), unless otherwise noted.

from a bad dresser? You would not want to accidentally zap a wealthy CEO such as Mark Zuckerberg or a famous actor such as Nick Nolte. If you look for people lying in the streets, you would not want to confuse a recent victim of a violent assault or of a health emergency with a homeless person.

Consider various other practical problems. What if you accidentally zap a bystander? Governments already ban discharge of firearms in crowded areas except (sometimes) in cases of self-defense, and such a ban would apply to the disintegrator ray if only to protect bystanders. Governments also ban the possession of certain types of weapons. The alleged "benefit" of murdering even many thousands of homeless people would not be worth the damage of killing even one bystander, especially considering that you might become such a bystander.

The assumption that no one would care about any homeless person is wildly implausible. Many people who are homeless over a prolonged period have family or friends who care about them and who hope for them to get back on their feet.

And of course many homeless people contribute to the welfare of others. Some people hold down a job even though they are homeless. Some homeless people do amazing things, such as rescue children from a burning building or aid someone stranded on the road.[155] And obviously homelessness is not necessarily a lifelong condition. Many people fall into homelessness for a period of time and then become more successful. For example, the film *The Pursuit of Happyness* (2006) is inspired by the real story of Chris Gardner, a father who was homeless for a time before becoming a successful Wall Street broker and motivational speaker.

---

155   Derek Hawkins, "Homeless Man Saw Smoke Coming from an Apartment—Then Heard Children Scream," *Washington Post*, December 4, 2017, https://www.washingtonpost.com/news/morning-mix/wp/2017/12/04/homeless-man-saw-smoke-coming-from-an-apartment-then-heard-children-scream/; Julia Jacobo, "Homeless Man Who Helped Stranded Woman Buys Home after Nearly $400K Raised," ABC News, December 5, 2017, http://abcnews.go.com/US/homeless-man-gave-20-stranded-woman-buy-gas/story?id=51593887.

This raises another point: Even if a person thinks that he is extremely unlikely to fall into the plight of homelessness, for many people there is probably an outside chance, due to bad decisions or bad luck, of falling into destitution at least for a time. There is some reason, however slight, to sympathize with the homeless with the attitude, "There, but for the grace of God, go I."

Consider too the role of moral psychology. If you are the sort of person who spends time and mental energy figuring out which people to disintegrate, you are probably not the sort of person who is preoccupied with a productive enterprise. Rather, you are likely the sort of person who spends a great deal of energy trying to figure out what you can get away with in terms of abusing others and taking their stuff—exactly the sort of bad moral character that puts a person on the road to self-destruction. By contrast, if you are the sort of person who focuses consistently on work and on other positive values, you probably will not think much if at all about which people on the street may be homeless, and you probably will not even notice the "cost" of spending an extra second to walk around someone in the way, homeless or not.

Huemer objects to the sort of reply I have offered on grounds that hypothetical scenarios are intended to draw out the essential implications of a view, and they can be tightened to rule out contingencies. Huemer grants that "the egoist could argue that for some reason, it was really not in my interests to destroy the homeless person. . . . But even if the egoist is able to think of some very plausible harm that I would be likely to suffer from killing another person, I will just modify the example to remove it."

Arguments about the self-interest of the actor fail to get to the crux of the matter, in Huemer's view:

> [W]hat needs to be kept in mind is that, on the egoist's view, the fact that the other person is a sentient being, with a life of his own, is not what counts. All that counts is that he has a potential to serve my life, or to hamper it if I destroy him.

Therefore, how I treat him need not be, in principle, any different from the way I treat inanimate objects.[156]

Huemer is right that, for Rand, rights-respecting behavior for the actor comes down to the interests of that actor, not fundamentally the interests of the person whose rights are respected. Yet the fact that the other person is a sentient being "with a life of his own" certainly does count, because that is the salient fact relevant to the actor's interests. Later we will see that Rand endorses broad benevolence, so there is a real sense in which the egoist on Rand's conception cares about the interests of others.

Huemer wants to show that self-interest does not consistently sanction rights-respecting behavior and that the reason for this is that egoism cannot actually recognize rights. In Huemer's view, egoism as a consequentialist position cannot accommodate rights, because, contra egoism, the "principles of individual rights are side constraints" that function to set boundaries on self-interested action. Self-interest may be compatible with respecting others' rights, on Huemer's view, but if the two conflict the rights of others trump the interests of the actor.

Rand simply disagrees with Huemer about the nature of rights. Rights function (for Rand) not to restrain self-interest, but to enable a person to pursue his self-interest (in terms of long-term survival) in a social setting.

To Huemer, egoistic arguments that respecting others' rights is really always in one's self-interest are just-so stories. The purpose of hypothetical examples is to reveal the position in stark clarity: Egoism means abusing others if that serves one's interests.

But Huemer risks going too far with his hypotheticals. By way of background, Huemer is a notable moral intuitionist.[157] If he can create hypothetical examples in which abusing the rights of others is really in a person's interests, then I can create hypotheticals in

---

156 Stephen E. Taylor offers similar criticisms in "Is Ayn Rand Really Selfish . . . Or Only Confused?," *Journal of Thought*, January 1969, vol. 4, no. 1, p. 18.

157 See Michael Huemer, *Ethical Intuitionism* (Basingstoke, UK: Palgrave MacMillan, 2005).

which moral intuitions "really" tell us that it is perfectly fine to disintegrate people. Presumably Huemer would reply that intuitions do not really do that, and anyway there is no logical way out of moral intuitionism; it's intuitions all the way down. But Rand would reply that self-interest does not really work the way that Huemer fears and that it's self-interest all the way down (in terms of moral theory). Rand does not fear hypothetical cases of egoistic rights abusers any more than Huemer fears hypothetical cases of murder-promoting intuitions. (We will consider emergency situations later.) What I think we should look for, then, are plausible hypotheticals and, better yet, real-life examples.

A side point: Let us return briefly to Jason Brennan's claim that it might be in an egoist's interests to "rape, dismember, and murder" someone. We've dealt with these issues already in broad terms. It is also worth noting that in Rand's view healthy sex is possible "only in the confidence of being desired and being worthy of desire" (AS 490). Romantic love, which entails sex, is a person's "response to his own highest values in the person of another."[158] So Rand's view of sex offers an additional answer to Brennan's concern about rape.[159]

The upshot is that Rand offers a much more robust theory of rights than what her critics typically presume. Still, we should be slow to dismiss Huemer's concerns. It seems too good to be true that an egoist can never (barring unlikely emergencies) further his own survival by harming others or taking their things. Further, it seems

---

158 Ayn Rand, "Of Living Death," in *The Voice of Reason*, ed. Leonard Peikoff (New York: NAL Books, 1989), p. 54.

159 Some critics will point to the "rape scene" in Ayn Rand, *The Fountainhead*, centennial edition (New York: Penguin Group, 2005), pp. 219–221. Certainly Howard Roark could have been prosecuted for rape had Dominique Francon pressed charges—Roark knew that she would not want to. This scene serves to dramatize the very unusual character of Francon, a person who fears the pursuit of any value before, finally, she makes peace with herself and the world and marries Roark. For further analysis, see Andrew Bernstein, "Understanding the 'Rape' Scene in *The Fountainhead*," in *Essays on Ayn Rand's* The Fountainhead, ed. Robert Mayhew (Lanham, MD: Lexington Books, 2007), pp. 201–208; and Greg Salmieri, "How Should Philosophy Professors Approach Ayn Rand?," *Check Your Premises*, June 25, 2018, http://www.checkyourpremises.org/2018/06/25/therightapproach/.

implausible that the point of respecting others' rights is to further one's own survival; Huemer seems to be on to something in claiming that rights are fundamentally about concern with the interests of others. So it is worth pushing harder on Rand's theory of rights.

The Weakness of Rand's Case for Rights

Rand offers an excellent case that, in a society in which people generally respect rights, it is in an egoist's rational interests to conscientiously respect rights. Much of Rand's case turns on the problems of deceiving people about swindles and the like. But what if society is broken into classes, and people in your class are able to violate the rights of people in other classes openly and with impunity?

Michael Huemer's hypothetical case, in which murdering homeless people is socially accepted, involves such a class-divided society. A limitation to his example is that the class of homeless people is hard to identify and in flux—people drop in and out of homelessness. But what if society were clearly divided into stable classes? We need look no further than our own history for such an example.

Slavery existed in most large-scale human societies for thousands of years. It arose in the colonies that were to form the United States in the early 1600s and continued in large parts of the United States until the ratification of the Thirteenth Amendment in 1865—a longer period than the United States has existed without slavery. Slavery in this time and place involved, with few exceptions, people of European origin and their descendants claiming ownership of people forcibly transported from Africa and their descendants. Slavers bought and sold slaves, including children, forced them to work, and often treated them brutally. A slave could not escape his position unless his "owner" granted him freedom, someone purchased it for him, or he fled at great peril to a region without slavery.

An egoist behind a Rawlsian veil, not knowing if he would be a slave or a free person, undoubtedly would advocate a system of individual rights, not a system of slavery. An egoist in slavery undoubtedly would advocate freedom and equal rights for the enslaved.

But what about someone born into a slave-holding household in a culture and polity where slavery is deeply entrenched, who grows up to inherit his family's estate, complete with all its slaves and all its debts? Would such a person, as an egoist, find it in his interests to free the slaves and pay them restitution? If so, the rationale for doing so was lost on those men who, while owning slaves, signed the document declaring that "all men are created equal" and endowed with "unalienable rights" to "life, liberty, and the pursuit of happiness." Andrew Bernstein, a philosopher who advocates Rand's ideas, argues persuasively that slavery was a great obstacle to economic prosperity generally, yet he grants that "slavery was often profitable for plantation owners and slave traders."[160]

In this context, a great part of Rand's argument for respecting others' rights falls away. The epistemological argument seems turned on its head, as potential gains from freeing one's slaves would be uncertain and hard to trace. Keeping the slaves would seem the safest course, while setting them free would court financial ruin.[161]

Slave holders did not need to skulk about or lie about their behavior; they operated openly and did not need to maintain some pretense. And the system was stable for a long period of time. Sure, a few slaves revolted, but such revolts were infrequent and quickly put down.

Perhaps the egoist should have been concerned about the possibility of a war over slavery. But the egoist could not have prevented war by freeing his slaves unilaterally. If the egoist were convinced of the coming of war and in a position of political power, perhaps he would then advocate the universal freeing of slaves, on grounds that a war would be worse. But such a concern is not grounded in the rights of the slaves.

---

160 Andrew Bernstein, *The Capitalist Manifesto* (Lanham, MD: University Press of America, 2005), p. 280. Neera K. Badhwar has a good discussion of slavery in the context of Socrates and Jefferson in her "Living Long and Living Well: Reflections on Survival, Happiness, and Virtue," in "Is Virtue Only a Means to Happiness?," *Objectivist Studies* 4, ed. William Thomas (Poughkeepsie, NY: Objectivist Center, 2001), pp. 82–83.

161 Neera K. Badhwar reminds us that many Southern states effectively outlawed the freeing of slaves; see her "An Objectivist Case for Libertarianism," Libertarianism .org (Cato Institute), August 30, 2017, https://www.libertarianism.org/publications/ essays/objectivist-case-libertarianism.

Did the slave holder suffer degradation of his moral character? Apparently slave holders had little problem treating slaves one way and everyone else another way. For Rand, the entire point of building moral character is to further one's survival, so it is hard to see how a slave holder in the conditions described could be deemed guilty of having a bad character by that standard.

That leaves the consistency argument. A slave holder was not, due to his position as such, in danger of himself becoming a slave or in any other way suffering an abuse of his rights. So it is hard to see how Rand's argument about consistency would be relevant here. Rand also is concerned about intellectual consistency. It is rationally inconsistent to claim that my rights should be upheld even as I grossly violate the rights of others. Perhaps Rand also would say that the slave holder is dishonest when he leaves this inconsistency unresolved. But there are a couple of problems with this sort of argument. First, it is not really a contradiction to say, "I advance my life by forcing slaves to work for me and by insisting that everyone respect my rights." Second, it is not clear how such an argument about rational consistency can be tied to a survivalist ethic; it seems more Kantian in nature.

Yet I think important parts of Rand's arguments about moral character and consistency carry through. Conceptually, rights turn on the moral propriety of each individual pursuing his own life and values. Slavery involves denying certain individuals their rights based on arbitrary features such as a person's place of birth and skin color. A slave holder who is at all self-aware must at some level realize that he is asking others to respect rights for himself that he refuses to respect for slaves. He must realize that, but for accident of birth, he could as easily have been a slave as a slave holder. Thus, we would expect slave holders to tend to disguise these uncomfortable facts through pervasive self-deception, and that is precisely what we find in the historical record, with all the pseudo-science about Africans allegedly being inferior, inherently subservient, incapable of self-governance, and the like.

Further, we would expect a society of such slave holders generally to move further away over time from the principle of individual rights toward oppression and tyranny. Again, this is what we find in the historical record, as with the South's turn to censorship, repression, and explicitly collectivist ideologies. As historian Alexander V. Marriott summarizes, in the era of slavery the "South not only abandoned the Enlightenment ideals of the founding; it regressed into a closed society infused with tremendous paranoia."[162]

Yet would these concerns prompt a self-aware egoist to free his slaves? Probably not. Plausibly the egoist might treat "his" slaves more humanely, perhaps even pay them, and arrange for them to be freed after his death (as George Washington did). Such an egoist could recognize the injustice of slavery and yet conclude that the personal cost of freeing "his" slaves would leave him destitute and hence undermine his long-term survival. And anyway freeing his own slaves hardly would help to eliminate the scourge of slavery more broadly. So the example of slavery shows that Rand's case for respecting others' rights is not as strong as she supposes.

Rights under Emergencies and Institutional Force

As the example of slavery illustrates, Rand's egoism cannot robustly support rights-respecting behavior within a class-based society. The problem is far broader than slavery (which, after all, has been abolished). In any social system in which some parties routinely use force against others in an institutionalized way, the egoist would not always, by the logic of his position, be bound to respect others' rights. The trouble for Rand is that every human society that has ever existed and that exists today involves some greater or lesser level of institutionalized force. So Rand's case for rights applies fully only within an "unknown ideal" social-political system. Meanwhile, what are people living in the real world to do?

To understand the limitations of Rand's theory of rights, we need to first look at where Rand intentionally carves out exceptions— emergency situations—then see how those cases relate to cases of institutionalized force.

---

162 Alexander V. Marriott, "Getting Lincoln Right," *Objective Standard*, Summer 2014, vol. 9, no. 2, https://www.theobjectivestandard.com/issues/2014-summer /getting-lincoln-right/.

In "The Ethics of Emergencies," Rand argues that it is improper to try to develop a moral theory based on emergency situations that a person is "not likely ever to encounter." Instead, moral principles apply in the normal ways only in "metaphysically normal" conditions. As we've seen, Rand holds that, in an emergency, it may be morally appropriate for an egoist to risk his life for a loved one (or even a stranger, although her case on that point is shaky).[163]

Eyal Mozes argues that, by the logic of Rand's position, "it is not wrong to initiate force" in such life-threatening emergencies.[164] Rand agrees:

> [S]uppose someone lives in a dictatorship, and needs a disguise to escape. If he doesn't get one, the Gestapo or GPU will arrest him. So he must kill an innocent bystander to get a coat. In such a case, morality cannot say what to do.
>
> Under a dictatorship—under force—there is no such thing as morality. Morality ends where a gun begins. Personally, I would say that man is immoral if he takes an innocent life. But formally, as a moral philosopher, I'd say that in such emergency situations, no one could prescribe what action is appropriate. That's my answer to all lifeboat questions. . . . Two men could make opposite choices. I don't think I could

---

163   Ayn Rand, "The Ethics of Emergencies," in *The Virtue of Selfishness* (New York: Signet, 1964), pp. 43, 45–47.

164   Eyal Mozes, "Flourishing and Survival in Ayn Rand: A Reply to Roderick Long," commentary on Roderick T. Long, "Reason and Value: Aristotle versus Rand," in *Objectivist Studies* 3, ed. William Thomas (Poughkeepsie, NY: Objectivist Center, 2000), https://atlassociety.org/sites/default/files/Reason_Value.pdf, p. 94 (emphasis omitted). On this point, see also Tara Smith, *Moral Rights & Political Freedom* (Lanham, MD: Rowman & Littlefield, 1995), pp. 112–113.

kill an innocent bystander if my life was in danger; I think I could kill ten if my husband's life was in danger.[165]

In these extemporaneous remarks, Rand exaggerates by saying "there is no such thing as morality" in emergency situations. She means only that not all normal moral considerations apply. In "The Ethics of Emergencies," Rand writes that, even in emergencies, a person should consider his life and values and practice certain virtues. A person who does not continue to act for his values is "morally guilty."[166] Still, obviously Rand means that not all moral considerations apply in emergencies; killing an innocent person normally would be morally abhorrent, but it might be permissible in an emergency. By the same logic, other sorts of initiating force and of using others' property without permission might be justified in an emergency.

Rand is hardly unique in thinking that there are situations in which normal rights theory does not apply. For example, Huemer grants that coercion might be justified if it is necessary "to prevent the deaths of a million innocent persons."[167] (He does not try to set a lower boundary of harm that might justify force.) Rand and Huemer differ in what they think might justify harmful coercion. For Rand, only self-interest might justify it; for Huemer, usually some consideration other than self-interest might. So Huemer's complaint is not that egoism uniquely permits the initiation of force

---

165   These remarks, given extemporaneously in 1968, are reproduced in Ayn Rand, *Ayn Rand Answers*, ed. Robert Mayhew (New York: New American Library, 2005), p. 114. Given this remark, Roderick T. Long's suggestion that Rand's fictional heroes never would toss someone off of an overfull lifeboat seems off-base; see his "Foundations and Flourishing: A Reply to Miller and Mozes," in "Reason and Value: Aristotle versus Rand," *Objectivist Studies* 3, ed. William Thomas (Poughkeepsie, NY: Objectivist Center, 2000), https://atlassociety.org/sites/default/files/Reason_Value.pdf, p. 109.

166   Ayn Rand, "The Ethics of Emergencies," in *The Virtue of Selfishness* (New York: Signet, 1964), p. 46.

167   Michael Huemer, "Is There a Right to Immigrate?," *Social Theory and Practice*, July 2010, vol. 36, no. 3, p. 433.

in certain atypical situations—his theory permits it too—but that egoism sometimes permits it for inadequate reasons.

In a true lifeboat scenario, in which the boat is overfull and may sink, killing everyone aboard, different moralists would offer different solutions, but few would advocate letting everyone die. Altruists would advocate jumping out yourself, assuming that were sufficient to save everyone else. A utilitarian might advocate throwing out the heaviest, the oldest, or the least accomplished person. Rand would favor herself and her loved ones over strangers.

Regardless of how one comes down on Rand's position on true emergencies, we need to distinguish transient emergencies from cases of institutionalized force and oppression, a distinction that Rand does not make.

Rand offers no good reason to think that emergencies are the only conditions in which various moral principles—particularly the principle of rights—do not apply. In the comments considered above, Rand oddly counts dictatorship as a sort of "lifeboat" case—even though billions of people have lived under dictatorships for long periods of time. So we either have to say that the relevant circumstances extend beyond transient emergencies or else adopt a very broad sense of "emergency." And there is no logical way to draw the line at dictatorship: To whatever degree institutionalized force exists, that would create situations in which rights go out the window, on Rand's premises.[168]

We have considered slavery as an extreme case of oppression; what about less-extreme forms of force that, today, are far more common? Most relevant here are the forced wealth transfers of modern welfare states. My goal here is not to demonstrate that welfare statism is inherently rights-violating (I think it is, but that is a complex conversation for another day), but to show that there is no strong reason for an egoist not to seek wealth via a welfare state, even though doing so violates rights in Rand's view.

---

168 Tara Smith argues that only in emergencies do rights do not apply; she does not consider cases of dictatorship or of other instances of institutionalized force. See her *Moral Rights & Political Freedom* (Lanham, MD: Rowman & Littlefield, 1995), pp. 112–116.

(We should note here that Rand approves of taking welfare benefits only as a sort of restitution for having been made to finance welfare programs.)[169] Robert Nozick points out that, practically speaking, in some contexts a person "can be a parasite and survive; even over a whole lifetime and many generations."[170] Will Wilkinson points out:

[I]n Washington, DC there are hundreds of thousands of people who, basically, earn their living through a system of political predation. But many of them live a very long time. Many of them are happy. And there is no reason to believe that the US is going to collapse *Atlas Shrugged*-style any time soon. These people aren't really risking much by choosing to work for HUD instead of Google. It is just a plain fact about the world that systemic parasitism can be and often is stable.[171]

Obviously people can and do often live, apparently successfully, partially or wholly as parasites (as Rand would call them). If the Objectivist replies that the welfare transfers might dry up, or that the person seeking them would not develop marketable skills, the parasitic egoist would answer that he'd be on the lookout for future problems and develop other skills concurrently with "working" to maximize wealth transfers.

If the problem is that other decent people would despise the recipient of wealth transfers, the parasitic egoist would reply that the

---

169 Ayn Rand, "The Question of Scholarships," in *The Voice of Reason* (New York: NAL Books, 1989), pp. 40–45. See also Ari Armstrong, "The Moral Integrity of Condemning Social Security While Collecting It," *Objective Standard*, November 3, 2012, https://www.theobjectivestandard.com/2012/11/the-moral-integrity-of -condemning-social-security-while-collecting-it/.

170 Robert Nozick, "On the Randian Argument," in *Reading Nozick*, ed. Jeffrey Paul (Totowa, NJ: Rowman and Littlefield, 1981), p. 214.

171 Will Wilkinson, "Third Letter to a Young Objectivist: Ethics," *Fly Bottle*, March 2, 2005, http://www.willwilkinson.net/flybottle/2005/03/02/third-letter -to-a-young-objectivist-ethics/. Michael Huemer makes a comparable point in his "Critique of 'The Objectivist Ethics,'" http://www.owl232.net/rand5.htm (accessed February 8, 2018).

indecency of taking them has to be demonstrated, not presumed, and that, if there is no good argument (on survivalist grounds) against seeking wealth transfers, then other people's attitudes on the matter are not his concern.

If the claim is that living as a parasite is not as fulfilling or meaningful as creating values, then I quite agree—but why this is so is hard to explain on strictly survivalist grounds. An egoist could "work" creatively to gain wealth transfers and also engage in other creative activities. I do not doubt that Objectivists can endlessly explain away criticisms along these lines, but, as in other areas, claims that seeking wealth transfers can never serve a person's survival begin to look like just-so stories.

The Context of Principles

Am I somehow missing the force of Objectivist principles outside of emergency conditions? Let us further consider Leonard Peikoff's reasoning on the matter.

Peikoff begins a discussion of principles by asking why people need to be honest "all the time." Principles are crucial, he says; "if man wants to fulfill the objective requirements that life requires, he has to do it by acting on principle." Although we need to act long-range, Peikoff argues, we have no automatic means of survival, so we need a "deliberate study of the results of what" we do. We can anticipate the future only by means of concepts. "Principled action is action based on man's means of coping with reality, conceptual means," Peikoff says.[172]

The alternative, as Peikoff states it, is to live by principles or else to enter "the short-range, blind state of having no guidance." "When you take a course of action," Peikoff says, "you always have to ask . . . , 'What does this course of action do to my whole life?' not, 'What does this concrete out of context do?' as though this concrete implies nothing else." He continues, "The whole purpose of ethics is to

---

172   Leonard Peikoff, *Understanding Objectivism*, ed. Michael S. Berliner (New York: New American Library, 2012), pp. 90–93.

discuss what principles man should live by"; to throw out principles is to deny "the very nature of ethical action."[173]

How do principles apply to force? A student suggested to Peikoff that it is "more difficult" to show that someone should not initiate force against others than to show that a person is harmed by force. Peikoff denies this: "If man has to live by principle, and if he has to survive by his mind, that, in itself, is sufficient to establish, just as much for the perpetrator as for the victim, that he is violating the essential principle" by initiating force. Peikoff continues:

> Do you grasp the necessity of functioning by principle, coupled with the necessity for rationality to be the principle? If you grasp those two, then as soon as you see that force is a violation of rationality, it's wiped out for everybody, the perpetrator or the victim; it's no more difficult [to show] for one than for the other.[174]

Yet does a person necessarily act against his survival-oriented interests by initiating force against others? Peikoff also holds that "moral principles are absolutes within their conditions. They are absolutes—*contextually*." So, for example, the virtue of productiveness is consistent with a college student being "supported by his parents." Similarly, "Lying is absolutely wrong—under certain conditions," Peikoff writes; it's fine to lie to criminals and the like.[175] Principles, Peikoff generalizes, "are defined by reference to a standard of value, a goal, and they can be applied only within the circumstances where they lead to that goal."[176]

My point about the case of slavery is that it seems to be outside the context in which Objectivists derive the principle not to initiate

173 Leonard Peikoff, *Understanding Objectivism*, ed. Michael S. Berliner (New York: New American Library, 2012), pp. 94–95 (emphasis omitted).

174 Ibid., pp. 120, 127–128 (emphasis omitted).

175 Leonard Peikoff, *Objectivism: The Philosophy of Ayn Rand* (New York: Dutton, 1991), p. 275.

176 Leonard Peikoff, *Understanding Objectivism*, ed. Michael S. Berliner (New York: New American Library, 2012), p. 106.

force. As I've argued, a survival-oriented egoist has good reason not to initiate force, and to respect people's rights, within the context of a generally rights-respecting society. But such an egoist sometimes has no good reason not to exploit others when a system of institutionalized force allows it.

I'm sure that various Objectivists will try to argue that I'm wrong, that egoists should not initiate force even in cases of institutionalized force. But Peikoff actually agrees with my interpretation of Objectivism, at least on one narrow issue. He argues that, under laissez-faire capitalism, government should not restrict the immigration of peaceable and non-contagious people. But in "today's society" of an "advanced welfare state," Peikoff argues, in which many immigrants seek government handouts, join leftist movements, and commit crimes, citizens may rightly call for immigration restrictions. "This is where selfishness comes in; it's our lives versus theirs," he says, however lamentable that may be.[177]

Here Peikoff clearly argues that people, via their government, may forcibly prevent immigrants—including hard-working and peaceable ones—from coming into the United States, even at the invitation of other citizens, because of the institutionalization of elements of force. (Granting that the cases are quite different, "it's our lives versus theirs" also summarizes the attitude of slave holders with respect to "their" slaves. Undoubtedly slave holders argued that, if freed, slaves would seek government handouts, join unsavory causes, and commit crimes.)

Other Objectivists disagree with Peikoff about immigration, and I think that just on immediately practical grounds an egoist normally

---

177 Leonard Peikoff, "What Is the Proper Government Attitude Toward Immigration?," July 5, 2010, http://www.peikoff.com/2010/07/05/what-is-the-proper-government-attitude-toward-immigration/. (Peikoff's remarks are recorded as an audio file.)

should endorse open immigration of peaceable people.[178] But here the point is that there is no reason to think that an egoist necessarily best serves his interests by never initiating force in the context of the institutionalization of force, and on that point Peikoff agrees at least by logical implication of his views on immigration.

Of course there is a big difference between initiating force against Person A to prevent Person B from using force against you (as with immigration in the context of a welfare state) and initiating force against someone just to extract the person's labor (as with slavery). Objectivists would recoil at the idea that a consistent egoist might hold slaves. Yet I think they will be hard pressed to make a convincing case that a survival-oriented egoist should never use force against others—even to the point of keeping them enslaved—when a system of institutionalized force permits it.

To summarize, Rand offers strong reasons for individuals to respect others' rights within a generally rights-respecting society. She also explains why egoists would on the whole do better in a rights-respecting society. But she does not offer strong survivalist reasons why an egoist, finding himself in the privileged class of a class-based society of systematic rights abuses, never should initiate force or violate the rights of others. That Rand's moral theory does not support the respecting of individuals' rights as strongly as Rand hopes points to a weakness in her moral theory.

---

178 For one good account of the benefits of immigration, see Alex Nowrasteh, "The 14 Most Common Arguments against Immigration and Why They're Wrong," Cato Institute, May 2, 2018, https://www.cato.org/blog/14-most-common-arguments -against-immigration-why-theyre-wrong. It is worth noting here that there is some indication that Ayn Rand herself was an "illegal immigrant"; see Shikha Dalmia, "Ayn Rand Was an Illegal Immigrant," *Reason*, February 14, 2012, https://reason .com/archives/2012/02/14/ayn-rand-was-an-illegal-immigrant.

8. Egoists, Free Riders, and Charity

RAND'S EGOISM HAS OTHER PROBLEMS. In important contexts, it offers little reason for egoists not to free ride on the efforts of others, and it undervalues charitable efforts.

The Problem of Free Riders

For an illustration of the problem of free riding, return to the slave example. We have seen why an egoist who is not a slave holder (especially a slave!) would want an end to slavery. A self-aware egoist who is a slave holder would wish that he were not stuck in the moral quandary of holding slaves, and he might contemplate pathways to abolition. But would a consistent egoist actively struggle toward the cause of abolition? It is hard to see why given the problem of free riding.

The free rider problem (developed as a matter of study largely in economics) arises when everyone in a given group may freely enjoy some created good, regardless of whether a particular individual contributes to the creation or financing of that good.[179] Free

---

179 For a brief technical treatment of public goods and free riders, see Tyler Cowen, "Public Goods," Library of Economics and Liberty, http://www.econlib.org/library/Enc/PublicGoods.html (accessed October 29, 2017).

riders are those who enjoy or hope to enjoy such a good without supporting its creation.

Charity is a public good of this sort; among those potential donors who would value some charitable program, every individual could enjoy the existence of the charity program without helping to fund it, so long as everyone else contributed to it. So the question is whether the egoist, who after all is concerned fundamentally with his own interests (for Rand, his interests in terms of long-term survival), has any reason to contribute to the creation of goods when he could free ride.

Notably, a free society is also an achievement that invites free riding. Everyone would benefit by living in a consistently rights-respecting society (goes our argument), yet every individual would enjoy the fruits of a free society if he spent his time earning wealth while everyone else worked toward the establishment and maintenance of a free society. (If someone complains that not everyone would benefit from a shift from a rights-violating society to a rights-respecting society, we can dispute the presumption of what constitutes a benefit, exclude those people from consideration, or think of ways in which the stipulated losers could be compensated through the net gains of reform.)

On the whole, the people of the United States are dramatically better off without slavery than they were with it. (They would have been even better off had people been able to peacefully abolish slavery, without the need for a horrifically bloody civil war.) Yet, aside from slaves, what reason did the individual egoist have to divert resources from the direct furtherance of his life to the fight for abolition? The abolitionist cause was precarious, and the practical benefits of abolition went mostly to people other than the hardest working abolitionists. Indeed, the major abolitionists, such as William Wilberforce and William Lloyd Garrison, were driven not by egoistic self-interest but by righteous religious zeal (albeit religious zeal infused with Enlightenment ideas). The suggestion that the abolitionists actually were working for their own survivalist self-interest seems fantastic.

Before turning to the Objectivist treatment of free riding, we need to delimit the problem. We are not talking about getting any possible benefit for which one does not pay. So-called "external" benefits are ubiquitous; they include such things as a well-kept house (which other people enjoy looking at), sharp dressing, and politeness. The children's book *Sanji and the Baker* offers the great example of a baker who sues a person for enjoying the pleasant aromas of his bakery without paying for the experience; the clever judge awards the baker the sound of tinkling silver coins—not the coins themselves, just the enjoyable sounds they make when they are dropped into a dish.[180] We are focused not on the broader matter of external benefits but on cases when a project or good depends on sufficient support, when every individual who would benefit has an economic incentive to free ride on the efforts of others.

We are also not talking about cases of people who would suffer hardship by supporting projects that they cannot reasonably afford to support, even if they benefit from those projects. There is no need to draw firm lines here, but roughly we are talking about cases in which a person would benefit substantially by a project and can afford to support it without substantially harming his broader life and values, but who chooses not to just because others might pick up the slack.

Objectivists and the Free-Rider Problem

Objectivists might reply to the free-rider problem in a number of ways.

One approach is to deny there is a problem. Eyal Mozes argues "there is no basis, on Objectivist premises, for seeing free-riding as a problem at all. Nor is there any basis for distinguishing between good and bad forms of free-riding." Mozes grants that an egoist might engage in charitable and generous behavior, but only if it brings selfish rewards and does not stem from "a desire not to be a free-rider." For example, charity might be "a form of investment" in potentially fruitful social relationships.[181]

---

180   Robin Tzannes, *Sanji and the Baker*, illustrated by Korky Paul (Oxford University Press, 1993).

181   Eyal Mozes, "The Free Rider Issue: An Objectivist View," https://sites.google .com/site/eyalmozesonobjectivism/fr (accessed October 29, 2017). Mozes originally presented the piece as a paper in 1997.

An extension of the claim that the free-rider problem is not really a problem (or not much of one) is that free markets often can solve the problem. We see examples all around us. Television broadcasts are free to the user; they are funded by packaging the content that people want to watch with paid advertisements that businesses want people to watch. Some types of broadcasts are scrambled, and people must pay for descrambling to access the content. Rather than publish content freely on the internet, various publishers require a paid subscription for access. Charities can offer bonuses for donations (National Public Radio often does this) or offer a sense of community (the Ayn Rand Institute, which survives through private donations, offers bonuses such as newsletters, creates a shared sense of mission, and publicly recognizes large donors). Brian Simpson, an economist who writes from an Objectivist perspective, points out (as do many other economists) that things like lighthouses can be funded by large enterprises willing to bear the full costs and by contingent contracts that guarantee delivery once a certain funding threshold is met.[182]

The division of labor often lowers the costs of achieving some project and so eases the free-rider problem somewhat. Most people involved with a given charitable or social project do not spend much of their own time directly working on it; rather, they contribute a small portion of their funds to pay the salaries of professional organizers or advocates.

I agree that markets often solve problems of external benefits and free riders. But there are a couple of problems with egoists resting their case on that fact.

First, charities often succeed by appealing to people's altruistic impulses (altruistic in the sense that donors reasonably believe that donating is not the best way to further their survival). By and large, people do not give money to African charities (and the like) to further their own survival; they do it to further the survival of impoverished people in Africa. Consistent survivalist egoists would fund charities only if doing so directly furthered their lives.

---

182   Brian P. Simpson, *Markets Don't Fail!* (Lanham, MD: Lexington Books, 2005), p. 92.

Second, market actors cannot, with appeals only to people's survival-oriented self-interest, plausibly solve certain important cases of potential free-rider problems. The abolition of slavery is a case in point; abolition succeeded as an ideological crusade, not as some effort to monetize the freedom of slaves. Generally, the creation and maintenance of a free, rights-respecting society takes enormous effort by people who do not bear most of the benefits of the existence of that society. Consider, for example, the extreme risk that came with signing the Declaration of Independence. We could say that fighting for a free society is deeply spiritually rewarding (and I think it is), but casting such spiritual reward fundamentally as a means to survival is implausible.

Note here that I am not claiming that Rand opposed such things as joining ideological causes and fighting for a free society. Rather, my claim is that often a person who does such things does not thereby further his survival in the most robust way; he typically trades off efforts to further his survival for the sake of other values. In my view, such a trade-off can be perfectly reasonable, but it is not logically consistent with Rand's metaethics. Many self-professed egoists I know do a lot of things (donate to charities, advocate ideas) that others regard as altruistic; here I am suggesting that in such cases usually those people are not actually acting solely for the sake of their own survival.

Another way that Objectivists might reply is to claim that it is always in one's self-interests not to be a free rider (in the relevant cases). Craig Biddle argues that, in a system of voluntary government financing (which he advocates), a person (of sufficient wealth) would be "irrational" for not contributing, because he would thereby ignore "obvious causal connections and the basic principle of justice that he could have learned from *The Little Red Hen*." Biddle continues:

> [T]hose who choose to support a rights-protecting government are not committing a sacrifice by indirectly protecting the rights of free riders, so long as the value the contributors receive—that is, the protection of their own rights plus all the benefits that flow from a rights-respecting

society—is of equal or greater value to them than the funds they contribute.[183]

Presumably we can generalize Biddle's argument to other types of potential free-rider problems, but the case cannot be sustained. In *The Little Red Hen*, the hen declines to share her bread with those who decline to help produce it; the bread is not a "public good." The question is whether the duck, the goose, the cat, and the pig should help to produce the bread, if for some reason they could not be denied a portion of it once produced.[184]

Biddle suggests that it is sufficient for the egoist to get a benefit of equal or greater value than the cost. But surely that is not the case; a consistent egoist would seek to get the most value for the least cost. Very often a person would be willing to pay more for a particular good or service than what it costs (hence the attempt by some businesses to price discriminate—charge different customers different prices for the same thing), yet obviously an egoist should not typically pay more than the asking price. By Rand's metaethics, egoism entails taking actions that best further one's life. If an egoist can get a benefit by paying less (or nothing) rather than by paying more, then the egoist can spend the residual on some other life-furthering value.

Objectivists also could attempt a sort of contractarian argument for not free riding. The Objectivist philosopher David Kelley points out that it "is to the benefit of each of us to live in a society where people extend help" in emergencies, but "there cannot be a society in which such help is available unless people extend help when

---

183   Craig Biddle, "How Would Government Be Funded in a Free Society?," *Objective Standard*, Summer 2012, vol. 7, no. 2, https://www.theobjectivestandard.com/issues/2012-summer/how-would-govt/.

184   I refer to the uncredited text of *The Little Red Hen*, illustrated by J. P. Miller (New York, Golden Book: 1982).

they can."[185] If we generalize the argument, why should it move the egoist to contribute to goods that he could enjoy for free? Anyway, it is far from clear that Objectivism can play nicely with any sort of contractarianism.[186]

Biddle offers another possible solution to the free-rider problem: He suggests that people often "shun and ostracize" free riders, something that could be facilitated in the case of voluntary government financing by receipts that people could publicly display.[187]

The problem with Biddle's sort of argument here is that efforts to ostracize free riders (and to reward those who do not free ride) also are "public goods" in the relevant sense—everyone benefits— meaning that people may be tempted to free ride on the efforts of others to ostracize the initial free riders. So, to support the sort of contractarian arrangement that Biddle seems to have in mind, people at some point need to decide not to free ride for reasons that do not pertain just to their survival.

A more mundane problem is detecting free riders. In Biddle's case of voluntarily funded government, at least there would be a total bill and a good estimate of each individual's due. But what is the appropriate funding level for a program to feed the hungry, to educate needy children, to promote Ayn Rand's ideas, or to research cancer treatments? Moreover, there are so many possible such projects that individuals necessarily specialize in what they want to support. So we cannot say that, because a person does not support Cause X, therefore the person is free riding; perhaps he disproportionately funds Cause Y. Another problem: People reasonably disagree about which projects merit support and how much support they need.

---

185   David Kelley, *Unrugged Individualism* (Poughkeepsie, NY: Institute for Objectivist Studies, 1996), p. 46. Kelley grants that in certain societies people do not trust or help strangers, and in such a society an egoist probably would not offer aid to others.

186   See, for example, Tara Smith, *Viable Values* (Lanham, MD: Rowman & Littlefield, 2000), pp. 31–37, 110.

187   Craig Biddle, "How Would Government Be Funded in a Free Society?," *Objective Standard*, Summer 2012, vol. 7, no. 2, https://www.theobjectivestandard .com/issues/2012-summer/how-would-govt/.

Another: It can be hard to know whether a person is free riding, facing financial troubles, or curbing current spending to invest in future gains. (A person who contributes nothing now and a lot ten years hence is not free riding.) Another: People can partially free ride by ostentatiously giving just a little. For these reasons, effectively ostracizing free riders in most cases seems impossible, even if people were motivated to do it.

Yet another way that Objectivists might reply to the free rider problem is to say that the moral principles embodied in the virtues preclude free riding. This seems to be David Kelley's main argument:

> Someone who would accept help in an emergency but would not provide it to others is acting on the premise of seeking something for nothing. He is seeking a benefit without the effort of producing that benefit; he wants to obtain an end without pursuing the necessary means. His action is therefore incompatible with independence and responsibility, which require that we make our own actions the causes of the benefits we enjoy, rather than depending on others to provide those benefits for us.[188]

One problem with Kelley's argument about independence is that Objectivists do not think that a person must be absolutely independent in producing the values that sustain his life. There is nothing wrong, in Objectivist terms, with inheriting money, receiving a gift, or winning the lottery, as examples. Rand says that when you trade in a free and rational society you receive a "bonus: the material value of your work is determined not only by your effort, but by the effort of the best productive minds who exist in the world around you." Moreover, a person gains values from the "productive genius" of people who came before, and a menial worker earns far more "in proportion to the mental effort that his job requires" than a productive genius receives in proportion to the mental effort that his job requires (AS 1064–1065). So it is not clear why, given that an

---

188   David Kelley, *Unrugged Individualism* (Poughkeepsie, NY: Institute for Objectivist Studies, 1996), p. 46.

egoist can rightly receive those other benefits from others, he cannot (on Objectivist premises) also morally receive the benefits of free riding. (If a person avoids free riding to avoid the censure of others, then that is a different motive than what Kelley discusses.)

Objectivist philosopher Darryl Wright asks whether "a person has a reason to be virtuous rather than to free-ride on the virtue of others." He says yes: "Reasons of psychological survival militate against free-riding."[189] However, the argument about psychological survival turns on doing what one knows to be right. We cannot just assume, without argument, that the right thing for an egoist to do is to refrain from free riding. If a consistent egoist (reasonably) concludes that free riding (in some or all cases) aids his survival (or at least does not harm it), then he will rest easy at night thinking his virtue is intact.

Rand suggests an additional way that Objectivists might deal with the free-rider problem. She writes, "[A]nyone who fights for the future, lives in it today."[190] She makes this remark in the context of a potential artistic renaissance, but presumably we can generalize the sentiment. The idea seems to be that, by taking action to help bring about an ideal society, we enjoy imagining and anticipating such a society, and we more fully enjoy the incremental steps taken in that direction.

We can apply Rand's insight to a rights-respecting society and to a society without extensive free riding. I agree that there is something like an esthetic experience in anticipating an ideal (or even a substantially better) world. But why would a survival-oriented

---

189 Darryl F. Wright, "Evaluative Concepts and Objective Values: Rand and Moral Objectivity," in *Objectivism, Subjectivism, and Relativism in Ethics*, ed. Ellen Frankel Paul, Fred D. Miller, Jr., and Jeffrey Paul (Cambridge University Press, 2008), p. 172, n. 77. Tara Smith also raises this point in her *Ayn Rand's Normative Ethics* (New York: Cambridge University Press, 2006), p. 37, n. 44. Although Wright apparently uses the term "free rider" to mean something different than what is at issue here—he describes a free rider as one who imitates or exploits others in his "Reasoning about Ends," in Allan Gotthelf and James G. Lennox, eds., *Metaethics, Egoism, and Virtue* (University of Pittsburgh Press, 2011), p. 21—presumably he would want to extend his analysis to the sort of free ridership at issue here.

190 Ayn Rand, "Introduction," in *The Romantic Manifesto*, revised edition (New York: Signet, 1975), p. viii.

egoist spend more than a perfunctory effort to achieve a better world for all, when he could free ride on the efforts of others to achieve that world while directly furthering his own survival?

Most Objectivists, like most everyone else, seem to be afflicted with a nagging sense that free riders are jerks for not doing their part. Yet Rand's egoism does not seem to have much to say against free riding, except insofar as it provokes costly responses from others.

Rand's Underwhelming Compassion

Rand, then, definitely sees some noncommercial projects as important (including the creation and maintenance of a free society), but she does not adequately address the egoist's temptation to free ride on the efforts of others to achieve those projects.

Another issue is that Rand sees some projects as not worthwhile, when most people think that they are morally worthwhile. So we should pause to consider whether Rand is missing something. The main issue at hand is that of charity.

Here we move away from the free-rider problem. The discussion about free riders presumes that the relevant individuals in fact regard the project in question as beneficial. Someone who does not regard a given charity or social cause as beneficial does not free ride by declining to contribute to it. That leaves open the question of whether an individual should regard the project as worthwhile.

As we've seen, Rand does not reject charity. Yet she hardly endorses robust charity to help the poor. I have suggested that, in the global capitalist system that Rand envisions, few people would be poor, or at least Rand reasonably believes. But we do not live in that world. In the world that we inhabit, billions of people remain impoverished due to no fault of their own.[191] Even in the most prosperous world that we can reasonably hope for, a few people, due to bad decisions

---

191   As of 2015, over 700 million people lived in "extreme poverty," defined as having less than $1.90 (as adjusted to account for international differences and inflation) per day. Far more lived in moderate poverty. See Max Roser and Esteban Ortiz-Ospina, "Global Extreme Poverty," *Our World in Data*, March 27, 2017, https://ourworldindata.org/extreme-poverty/.

or poor health or mental health problems or bad luck, would, absent assistance, find themselves in life-threatening poverty.

Previously we saw that, in Rand's view, charity might be appropriate if the recipient is "worthy of the help." Rand also says:

> The proper method of judging when or whether one should help another person is by reference to one's own rational self-interest and one's own hierarchy of values: the time, money or effort one gives or the risk one takes should be proportionate to the value of the person in relation to one's own happiness.[192]

So Rand suggests a two-part test for charity. First, the recipient must be worthy of it. I take this to mean that a basically bad person, including one who has long refused to work, does not deserve charity and should not receive it. Second, the charity must further the life of the person giving it. (Remember here that for Rand happiness is the emotional result of pursuing one's survival as an egoist.) Leonard Peikoff similarly says that a recipient of charity must in a sense deserve it, in that appropriate charity benefits the giver according to the giver's hierarchy of values.[193]

If someone is unworthy, or if a given act of charity does not aid the survival of the person offering it, then, according to the logic of Rand's argument, the egoist really should let someone starve rather than help the person. Objectivists tend not to state that conclusion bluntly, but it does follow from Rand's premises.

Objectivists sometimes try to soften their position on charity by tightly restricting the category of the unworthy. For example, Craig Biddle writes that "a truly selfish person would not offer 'help' to bums who are in fact *not* 'helpless' but rather *choose* to be

---

192   Ayn Rand, "The Ethics of Emergencies," in *The Virtue of Selfishness* (New York: Signet, 1964), p. 45.

193   Leonard Peikoff, *Objectivism: The Philosophy of Ayn Rand* (New York: Dutton, 1991), p. 238.

parasites. Only a fool or an altruist would do that."[194] I agree that people who could work for a living, and just choose not to, do not deserve charity. Hopefully such a person finally will break down and get a job and then begin to develop a productive mindset. Yet Biddle dodges the hard issues. What if a person, through a long train of bad decisions, becomes unable to work, due either to physical incapacity or mental health problems? How could a consistent egoist justify offering charity to such a person, even if the person otherwise dies of starvation in the gutter?

Biddle continues, suggesting that an egoist often would want to "help people who genuinely cannot support themselves." The unstated qualifier seems to be that the egoist might help a person who cannot support himself only if the would-be recipient of aid did not put himself in that condition. Biddle asks, "Which environment do I think is in my best interest: one in which genuinely helpless people suffer and die in the streets, or one in which I voluntarily contribute some small fraction of my time, effort, or money to give them a hand?" Biddle suggests that it would typically be in an egoist's interests to lend a hand, yet he leaves the reasons for this unexplained.

In the case of a person who became incapacitated through his own bad choices, perhaps the egoist would simply want to avoid the stench and ugliness of someone dying in the streets. That's plausible. But then it is unclear why the egoist would not just support carting the person out of town to let him die in the wilderness and be eaten by vultures or coyotes. That would be far cheaper than providing the person with food, shelter, clothing, health care, and counseling.

In the case of strangers who have fallen on hard times through no fault of their own, it is unclear why a consistent egoist would help such people, even though Objectivists routinely say it would be in an egoist's interests to do so.

Peikoff says that helping a stranger in an emergency might be justified because of "the potential value of a fellow human being about

---

194 Craig Biddle, "The Poor, Disabled, and Helpless Under Capitalism," *Objective Standard*, April 26, 2017, https://www.theobjectivestandard.com/2017/04/the-poor-disabled-and-helpless-under-capitalism/.

whom nothing evil is known";[195] presumably such considerations apply to some cases of charity. Along similar lines, Tara Smith offers the following egoistic case for offering aid to strangers:

> Even aid to strangers can sometimes be rational for an egoist, since strangers represent potential value, as experience abundantly teaches. . . . [Consider] the vast riches of knowledge and trade that a person can gain from other people. Beyond the myriad material and spiritual ways in which anonymous individuals can add such value to one's life . . . others' very existence can offer value. Knowing the endless variety of specific values that other persons make possible and their capacity to experience in all the ways that we do, we sometimes derive a welcome sense of camaraderie from the sheer awareness of similar beings' existence.[196]

The case by Peikoff and Smith is implausible for any but the most trivial sort of aid. Any aid involving a nontrivial expense of time or resources necessarily detracts from a person's survival (looking only at the cost for now), on the premise that any action a person takes either furthers his life or fails to do so. Rand's moral theory allows no rational room for partial egoism; a consistent Objectivist cannot further his survival, say, eighty percent of the time and fail do so the other twenty.

So then the question becomes whether the benefits that Smith describes possibly can offset the expense of the aid. If a person is lost in the wilderness or stranded on an island, saving a stranger might indeed bring enormous benefits to one's life. But in our normal world, in which we trade, directly or indirectly, with literally millions of people, and in which we must take pains to block out most of the "endless variety of specific values that other persons make possible" lest we lose our minds in an avalanche of information (a person

---

195   Leonard Peikoff, *Objectivism: The Philosophy of Ayn Rand* (New York: Dutton, 1991), p. 239.

196   Tara Smith, *Ayn Rand's Normative Ethics* (New York: Cambridge University Press, 2006), pp. 253–254.

could spend every waking minute just following a Twitter feed, for instance), it is almost impossible that the selfish gains of aiding a random stranger would offset the expense.

Perhaps the egoist should consider other factors, such as the gratitude of the person helped, the increased possibility of striking up a worthwhile relationship with a person he aids, the praise of bystanders, and the avoidance of censure by bystanders. But none of these considerations seems to offer much in the way of an incentive for an egoist in normal conditions. A desire for gratitude from beneficiaries of charity seems alien to Rand's theory of egoistic motivation. An egoist would probably have just as good of luck striking up a beneficial relationship with a random stranger not in need of aid. As for the potential praise and censure of others, other egoists would offer such feedback based on whether the aid furthered the donor's life (and whether the feedback furthered their own lives). We cannot take for granted that praise or censure from non-egoists should matter to an egoist, unless we say that an egoist should pander to what he must see as the irrationality of others, which is contrary to Objectivist virtues.

Perhaps the egoist can find a reason to aid strangers (and maybe even moderately unworthy people) somewhere else. Consider Nathaniel Branden's claims (which Rand references):

> Men of self-esteem, uncorrupted by the altruist morality, are the only men who can and do value human life—because they value their own life, because they are secure in the knowledge of their right to it, and because, to them, *"human being"* is a designation of honor. It is one's view of *oneself* that determines one's view of man and of human stature. The respect and good will that men of self-esteem feel toward other human beings is profoundly egoistic; they feel, in effect: "Other men are of value because they are of the same species as myself." In revering living entities, they are revering their *own* life. This is the psychological base

of any emotion of sympathy and any feeling of "species solidarity."[197]

Branden goes on to say that an egoist might help "an abandoned baby in the street" or an "accident victim" but not someone guilty of a "major evil" such as mass-murder. Although Branden does not address more usual forms of charity, plausibly his arguments extend even to some types of non-emergency charity and to people guilty only of a minor evil. (Despite the reference to humans, the logic of Branden's claims here would even seem to extend to some sort of concern for animal welfare. Interestingly, Rand once noted that a person "should value human life as such" and even "animal life.")[198]

Branden's argument is interesting, but it is hard to see how it justifies the egoist undertaking any sort of nontrivial expense of time or resources, or risks to personal safety, for the sake of strangers or for anyone of suspect character. Perhaps the egoist would help the baby because it would be very easy to call a charity that facilitated the adoption of children (and perhaps people who wanted children would finance the adoptions). Perhaps the egoist would help the accident victim if doing so were not dangerous.

Yet even Branden's line of thinking, in the context of Rand's metaethics, would exclude most of what people usually regard as heroic acts, at least outside the context of professionals who are paid to perform such acts. For example, in 2016, the actor Jamie Foxx saw a truck crash and roll near his home and then catch fire. Foxx helped the passenger get out of the truck, and within a minute of

---

197 Nathaniel Branden, "Benevolence Versus Altruism," *Objectivist Newsletter*, July 1962, vol. 1, no. 7, p. 27, in the bound *Volumes 1–4: 1962–1965* (Gaylordsville, CT: Second Renaissance, 1990). Rand quotes part of this in "The Ethics of Emergencies," in *The Virtue of Selfishness* (New York: Signet, 1964), p. 47. Darryl Wright also discusses this passage in "Rand's Social Philosophy," in *A Companion to Ayn Rand*, p. 161.

198 *Ayn Rand Answers*, ed. Robert Mayhew (New York: New American Library, 2005), p. 113.

the escape the vehicle was engulfed in flames.[199] To most people, Foxx's actions seem praiseworthy. From the perspective of an egoist concerned fundamentally with the furtherance of his own survival, Foxx's actions seem foolish, even profoundly immoral. Foxx easily could have died or become seriously injured. (If we say that Foxx's career stood to benefit because of the publicity, we can also observe that most people's careers are not tightly tied to such publicity. Anyway, the reason most people praise Foxx is not that he got good PR out of the incident.)

Branden's remarks motivate a consistent egoist less as the costs increase and the chances for tangible rewards decrease. In usual cases, even if an egoist revered the lives of others, it is hard to see why the egoist would therefore suffer a nontrivial cost to his own life for the sake of strangers. Wouldn't the reverential egoist instead bow his head in silence for a moment and then move on with his life?

In "The Ethics of Emergencies," Rand writes that some people who conflate sacrifice with benevolence become psychopaths who "are totally indifferent to anything living and would not lift a finger to help a man or a dog left mangled by a hit-and-run driver."[200] Granting that the egoist would feel sorry for such a victim, the question remains why an egoist might do much more than lift a finger to help.

If we push Branden's remarks very far, if we say literally that a person reveres his own life by revering and aiding the lives of others, even random strangers and moderately unworthy people, if we claim that a person should trade off gains to his own survival for the sake of the survival of others, then that just is not egoism any longer, at least not the survivalist sort endorsed by Rand.

Let us step back and see the bigger picture here. Most plausibly, a survival-oriented egoist will help others only when doing so brings a payoff to his life to more than offset the cost (considering the

199   Katia Hetter and Ed Payne, "Jamie Foxx Helps Rescue Man from Burning Truck," CNN, January 20, 2016, http://www.cnn.com/2016/01/19/entertainmen t/jamie-foxx-rescue-man-burning-truck-feat/index.html.

200   Ayn Rand, "The Ethics of Emergencies," in *The Virtue of Selfishness* (New York: Signet, 1964), pp. 43–44.

relevant probabilities), which excludes all nontrivial aid to strangers (except perhaps when one is stranded or the like) and all aid to the unworthy. Basically, the egoist can help strangers only if the cost is trivial, and he can help people he personally knows and likes only if the cost to his own life is modest. But that position seems callous and at odds with what most people regard as the reasonable offering of aid. Rather than follow the logical lines of argument in this regard, Objectivists typically "discover" various subtle reasons why the egoist "really" should accept significant costs to his own life for the sake of others.

What is more likely: That these subtle and intangible benefits of aid to others really do outweigh the obvious and straightforward costs, or that Objectivists are backfilling their theory with just-so stories to make it seem more plausible?

In Chapters 5–8, we have mainly considered reasons to doubt the plausibility of Rand's moral case in terms of how it handles normal human values. Next we revisit the topic of a person's ultimate value, and I propose the essentials of an alternate metaethics to what Rand offers.

9. Rethinking the Ultimate Value

CONTRASTED WITH SUCH COMPETITORS AS supernaturalism, subjectivism, Kantian imperatives, utilitarianism, and the idea that values transcend valuers, Rand's theory seems quite reasonable and grounded in observation-based evidence. Yet a theory is not validated by the flaws of other theories.

In the same essay in which Rand claims that "Kant is the most evil man in mankind's history," she advises: "It is useless to be against anything, unless one knows what one is for. A merely negative stand is always futile. . . . One cannot start with or build on a negative."[201] This advice may serve to warn Objectivists that they cannot save their moral theory just by attacking the inadequacies of other theories.

201   Ayn Rand, "Brief Summary," *Objectivist*, September 1971, vol. 10, no. 9, in the bound *Volumes 5–10: 1966–1971* (New Milford, CT: Second Renaissance Books, 1971) on pp. 1091–1092 (emphasis omitted). If Rand's conclusion about Kant is overstrung, there is more substance behind Rand's surprising claim than many of her critics recognize. Rand introduces another essay in the same publication, Leonard Peikoff's "Kant and Self-Sacrifice," pp. 1092–1103. Peikoff developed this material for his book *The Ominous Parallels* (Briarcliff Manor, NY: Stein and Day, 1982), which includes a chapter, "Kant Versus America." For a more sympathetic treatment of Kant in the context of Rand's criticisms, see George H. Smith, "A Few Kind Words about the Most Evil Man in Mankind's History," Libertarianism.org (Cato Institute), April 8, 2016, https://www.libertarianism.org/columns/few-kind-words-about-most-evil-man-mankinds-history.

Rand's remarks also serve notice to me that I am not likely to convince advocates of Rand's ideas that the Objectivist moral theory is false unless I can point to a more promising alternative. In this chapter, I present what I think are the most promising leads toward a truly reasonable, reality-based, objective moral theory. My main goal is to help people loosen their grip on Rand's theory by considering that a path toward another theory is possible. I hope to shine some light on the right path, but even if I end up needing to retrace some of my steps, hopefully my efforts will encourage others to look for alternatives to what Rand offers.

Ends in Themselves, Revisited

As we saw in Chapter 5, Rand and her advocates regard various experiences—happiness, the enjoyment of art, productive achievements, sex, even the pleasure of hobbies—as ends in themselves. By this Rand means that these experiences are inherently enjoyable and have no direct "practical, material end."[202] Yet, for Rand, things experienced as ends in themselves cannot be moral primaries; by Rand's theory, it is moral to pursue something only if it ultimately furthers (robust, long-term) survival. So, for example, if the pleasure of sex helps a person pursue other, more directly survival-oriented values with more vigor, then sex is a means to survival. And happiness for Rand, recall, is the "reward and concomitant" of "the activity of maintaining one's life" (TOE 29). For Rand, what we experience as an end in itself is fundamentally a means to survival or a reflection of it. Life (as opposed to death) remains the ultimate goal "to which all lesser goals are the means" (TOE 17).

We can see why Rand wants to avoid saying that we can build morality from that which we experience as ends in themselves. If we tried to do that, it seems, we'd quickly slip into moral subjectivism, and say that morality is just a matter of preference, or else into moral intrinsicism, and think that certain experiences are inherently good, apart from their impact on life.

---

202 Ayn Rand, "The Pscyho-Epistemology of Art," in *The Romantic Manifesto*, revised edition (New York: Signet, 1975), p. 16.

In linking happiness to the pursuit of survival, Rand is especially concerned to root out subjectivism. Rand believes that "the achievement of his own happiness is man's highest moral purpose" (TOE 27). (Rand here shifts her use of term purpose; earlier she writes that "his own life [is] the ethical purpose of every individual man"—TOE 25.) But we need to keep in mind what Rand means by this. She continues: "It is only by accepting 'man's life' as one's primary and by pursuing the rational values it requires that one can achieve happiness. . . . To take 'whatever makes one happy' as a guide to action means: to be guided by nothing but one's emotional whims" (TOE 29).

Here we see the same tension in Rand that we see in various other accounts of ethics: Happiness seems to be important—a person should on Rand's account strive to be happy—yet happiness does not seem to be the sort of thing that a person can attain by pursuing it directly or that is good as a primary. Rand does not want to say that survival is valuable fundamentally as a means to happiness, but she does want to say that the rational pursuit of survival normally results in happiness.

Rand's account of ethics is dualistic in a certain way: The moral goal is both life and happiness, and Rand makes sense of this by saying that happiness (normally) flows from pursuing survival, which is morally primary. Yet there is no plausible way to explain this fortunate convergence except as biological coincidence. We happen to be the sort of creatures that experience happiness only by pursuing survival.

If, because of biological development or purposeful design, a conscious creature could experience consistent happiness only by acting partly for ends unrelated to its survival, then this would not affect Rand's survivalist ethics. But if a person could not experience happiness (or the richest possible happiness) only by pursuing his survival, would not then Rand's moral system in effect create for this person something like a moral duty to survive as his ultimate end, assuming that he chooses to live?

As I have argued, I think that people normally do not achieve consistent happiness by acting only (ultimately) to survive. Instead, full happiness requires the pursuit of various values that are fundamentally unrelated to survival—such as raising children (for people who have them) and listening to music. So, in fact, there is a schism between happiness and Rand's survivalism. But even if Rand were right about the relationship between pursuing survival and experiencing happiness (that the two normally perfectly converge), that would not be very satisfying as a moral theory, because it would seem to depend on a coincidence. A moral theory that explained how happiness is inherently related to the moral end, without slipping into subjectivism, would seem a lot more compelling, at least in that regard. Of course I suggest that just such a moral theory is possible.

I suggest that we experience some things as genuine ends in themselves, as things worth experiencing for their own sake, and that these things are morally primary and not valuable fundamentally because they further or reflect survival. I am not talking about mysterious things here but normal aspects of the human experience, such as love for one's child, the joy of sex with one's partner, the pleasure of a good meal, the pride of a productive achievement, the uplift of art. I further suggest that such ends in themselves can become the basis of a viable and objective moral theory and in turn a viable theory of happiness. To begin to see how that is possible, let us revisit the interrelation of values.

Values as Means and Constituents

As Rand recognizes, some values are means to an end. We see examples of this among our many everyday values. I value a toothbrush for clean teeth and healthy gums; I value a clean mouth for general oral health; I value oral health for better overall health as well as for improved social relations.

Rand sees all values ultimately as means to the single, overarching value of one's life, which is in a sense a means to itself (life is "self-sustaining action"). Even when Objectivists talk about a value being an end in itself or helping to constitute a person's life, still the value must also be a means to literal survival, to fit within Rand's metaethics. Here is where Rand goes wrong. Not all values ultimately are means to other values; some values are fundamentally ends in themselves and, as such, constituents of other values.

Consider a simple example of the relationship among values. A telephone is a means to (among other things) conversing with a friend. In a sense a conversation with a friend is a means to sustaining the friendship. But the conversation is not just a means. If we can communicate face-to-face, we don't need the telephone. But it is not as though a friendship can do without friendly conversations; friendship partly consists of such conversations. So the conversation is a means to the friendship and also a constituent of the friendship.

What is friendship for? In part it is a means to mental health, professional networking, mutual aid, and a host of other benefits. Friendship also is valuable for our very survival; people without social contact tend to develop severe psychological problems, as studies on solitary confinement indicate.[203] But friendship is not only a means to other values; it is also valuable for its own sake.

So if by asking what a value is for (as Rand asks) we imply that it must ultimately be a means to some other value, then we are missing something. We also have to consider that some values, such as friendship, are ends in themselves and also constituents of some broader value.

In his review of Aristotle's ethics, J. O. Urmson clarifies the interrelationships among values. He draws our attention to the "distinction between an activity undertaken for its own sake and one undertaken as a means to some end." Urmson continues:

> [W]e must now make a further distinction and recognize a class of actions that are both ends in themselves and also constituents in (not means to) some wider end. We might imagine a person who is dancing and who is doing so for its own sake and not, say, purely for health reasons. Let us now consider each individual step in the dance and ask whether it is being performed for its own sake. If we were to say that each step was being taken simply as a means to dancing, it would seem to follow that none of the dance was being done

203   For a popular account, see Jason M. Breslow, "What Does Solitary Confinement Do To Your Mind?," PBS, April 22, 2014, http://www.pbs.org/wgbh /frontline/article/what-does-solitary-confinement-do-to-your-mind/.

for its own sake. It seems more plausible to say that, just because the dancer is dancing for the sake of dancing, each element in the dance is performed for its own sake. As he performs each motion it will be equally true to say that he is doing it for its own sake or for the sake of dancing. Each movement is an end in itself and a constituent in the dance, which is also the end.[204]

Urmson leaves open the possibility that a person's pursuit of values is even more complicated than he suggests here. A dancer might, for example, dance for the pure joy of dancing (for its own sake) and at the same time as a means to improved health. So a dance step could be an end in itself, a constituent of the dance, and a means to exercise, which is in turn a means to better health.

To extend our analysis, good health can be said to be an end in itself, in that generally good health is enjoyable while poor health is painful and distressing. Good health also is a means to our other values that a healthy body helps us achieve—such as dancing.

Once we begin to trace the interrelationships of human values, we see that a normal adult holds an enormously complex web of values, with some values serving mainly as means to others, some values being valuable in themselves and also means to other values, and some values helping to constitute broader values.

An Ultimate Value

An obvious question emerges from our discussion of values: Does a person have an ultimate value, in the sense that every other value either is a means to that value or else a constituent of (in) it?

I suggest that the answer is straightforward: A person's ultimate value is his life, not in the sense that all of his other values serve his survival, as Rand has it, but in the sense that all of his other values help support or partly constitute his life. In this sense, a person's life

---

204   J. O. Urmson, *Aristotle's Ethics* (Oxford: Blackwell Publishers, 1988), p. 11.

just is the total package of his values. In Aristotelian terms, a person's life is his complete end; none of his values is missing from it.[205]

At first glance it should seem plausible that people often think of their lives as their ultimate values in this sense. People routinely say things such as "My life is going well" (or "not well"), "You have one life, so make the most of it," "It's my life," "My life is going so quickly," and so on. Notably, human beings are uniquely able to think about their hierarchy of values abstractly in this way. We can say that a lion's values add up to its life (or that a tree's values add up to its life), but a lion cannot contemplate its life as an integrated whole of its values pursued over time.

Consider the broad values that compose a person's life. The bulk of a typical person's time goes toward the pursuit of a relative few broad (and overlapping) things: health and survival, career, recreation, physical pleasure (including sex), sociality (including friendship and romance), civic participation, and contemplation (or spiritual awareness, if we concede a secular place for the term).[206] The exercise of one's faculties normally is valuable in itself, and that goes a long way toward explaining why we often enjoy work, recreation, and so on. I won't promise that my list is all-inclusive, but it is hard to think of a value that is not a means to or an aspect of one or more of the items on this short list. A person's complete end, then, is his life of which these major values (and anything I might have missed) are constituents.

Rand, then, is wrong that all values ultimately are means to survival. Instead, our values are either means to other values or

---

205 See J. O. Urmson, *Aristotle's Ethics* (Oxford: Blackwell Publishers, 1988), pp. 13–14. It is worth noting here that the human flourishing described by Douglas J. Den Uyl and Douglas B. Rasmussen serves as a person's complete or inclusive end; see their book, *The Perfectionist Turn* (Edinburgh University Press, 2017), p. 38.

206 Nathaniel Branden lists five broad "areas that allow man to experience the enjoyment of life: productive work, human relationships, recreation, art, sex"; see Branden's "The Psychology of Pleasure," in *The Virtue of Selfishness* (New York: Signet, 1964), p. 62. I consider art as contributing to recreation and contemplation, but I have no problem making it its own category.

ends in themselves, and values that are ends in themselves are also constituents of the broader value of a person's life.

We can ask what ends in themselves (such as friendship) are "for" (to recall Rand's phrasing) only to learn what they help constitute, and that which they ultimately constitute we call an individual's life. If we ask what an individual's life is for, the only coherent answer is that it is for itself and not for anything else. One's life, as I use the term here, is simply that which encompasses all of one's values.

Value Integration as the Basic Moral Standard

What distinguishes certain conscious creatures, such as ourselves, from nonconscious ones is that we care about things. A plant or a bacterium functions and acts in the world, but it does not care about what it is doing or about what happens to it. When a human being or a lion or a deer eats a meal when hungry, it cares about eating in a way that a plant does not care about converting sunlight to energy. We are biologically wired to care via our capacity for pleasure and pain, which has physical and psychological forms. If an artificial being ever becomes a person, it will be partly because he develops (or is given) a capacity to similarly care about what happens to him.

When we talk about the values of caring conscious creatures, generally we mean the things that the organisms pursue because they care about them. We could program a robot to chase and eat a gazelle, and we could even (theoretically) create an artificial digestive system by which the robot converted the food to usable energy. But if the robot lion did not have the capacity to care about eating, it would be, in that respect, more like a plant or a bacterium. We now focus squarely on values in the context of caring conscious creatures and leave other senses of value behind.

What distinguishes human beings from other caring conscious creatures is that people can choose what to pursue based on complex rational calculations about how their values fit together. Other creatures' capacity to do this is either severely restricted or else nonexistent. For example, my cat might decide whether to eat cat food or laze in the sun at a given moment, but her deliberations go little further. People have the capacity to reason—to think abstractly, to understand complex relationships of means and ends and parts and wholes, to plan their lives not just moment to moment but decade to decade. And this capacity is what gives rise to morality in the human sense.

Rand is right that, as humans, we do not pursue our values automatically; our actions are not programmed into us by our genes. We can think, deliberate, choose. That is, we can use our conceptual and logical faculties to guide our actions in the pursuit of values and, to a substantial degree, to decide which values will constitute our lives.

As a consequence of our choices, we fit our values together more or less well. This is often obvious in the case of means and ends. If we plant seeds of a certain sort, water them, and protect the resulting plants from damage, we can eat the produce. Assuming our goal was to get and eat food, we match means to ends. On the other hand, if we plant a pebble or pray to a nonexistent deity to drop bread from Heaven, we do not match means to ends. In the former case our values are integrated; in the latter case they are disintegrated.

We also integrate higher-order values into a whole. Exercise benefits my health, but if I exercise to the exclusion of career and friendship and other major values, I thereby diminish my life and suffer. Granted that normally we need to meet our basic physical needs first, we seek to integrate our major values into our lives as a whole. Indeed, we experience the integration of our lives as an end in itself.

Of course an integrated life can look very different from person to person, as can a disintegrated life. Sam Harris's idea of a moral landscape is a helpful metaphor. Harris asks us to envision "a space of real and potential outcomes whose peaks correspond to the heights of potential well-being and whose valleys represent the deepest possible suffering."[207] Similarly, we can envision many varieties of optimally integrated or maximally disintegrated lives. One person may do well as an unmarried bicycle courier in New York, another as a forest ranger and parent in a large family. The language that Harris uses does not perfectly carry over to our discussion, but it connects

---

207   Sam Harris, *The Moral Landscape* (New York: Free Press, 2010), p. 7. Note that I reject Harris's utilitarianism.

closely. Although the integration of values does not guarantee well-being, which is subject to external forces as well, it largely constitutes well-being and optimizes conditions for success.

Insofar as people reflect on their values, they rely on the integration of values as their standard for pursuing values, at least implicitly. Generally, a person does not set out to fail in a given endeavor or to cause misery in one part of his life by his actions in another part. Rather, generally people seek to fit means to ends and to fit ends together into a functional whole. If they fail it is because they are ignorant of how to integrate their values, due to lack of knowledge, error, or self-deceit (more on this last point later).[208]

The structure of the metaethics in offer is straightforward: Insofar as people consciously pursue values, they implicitly or consciously act to integrate their values, to make them fit into a coherent whole. A person's ultimate value, at least implicitly, is his integrated life. The point of ethics is to help people consciously recognize the standard of value integration and then help them to integrate their values successfully rather than poorly. The integrated life is the moral ideal. We can call the theory at hand value integration theory. It fits nicely with traditional conceptions of flourishing but better explains what flourishing means and how to achieve it.

As for the is-ought problem, there is no bridge to cross. Normativity is built into our value pursuits.

Objectivity with respect to value integration theory arises from the fact that a person can do a better or worse job integrating his values. A person who achieves a happy family, a career he loves, quality friendships, engaging hobbies and interests, and a robust intellectual and emotional life integrates his values better—objectively better—than a person who cheats on his spouse with diseased prostitutes, robs liquor stores, and dies drunk in the gutter. This may not be as pristine a standard as survival, but it has the advantage of fidelity to reality.

Is there a difference between integrating values and integrating values well that undermines value integration theory? Am I slipping

---

208   Obviously people can self-sabotage, something that I attribute to willful ignorance owing to evasion. I cover such phenomena below in the section "A Theory of Evil."

in the "well" without justification? No. The integration of values is inherently something that can be done more or less well, and the standard (implicit or explicit) in our value pursuits is full or complete integration. Once we reflect on what is going on in our value pursuits, and we see that we pursue our values by integrating them, then we see that complete integration is the inherent goal. To integrate our values well means to live successfully and to enjoy the emotional rewards of doing so (happiness). No one honestly looks at his life and longs to live a frustrated existence. (We will deal with dishonesty later.) So Darryl Wright's worry that Aristotle's "living and doing well" (as eudaimonia may be translated) leaves the "well" theoretically hanging does not apply to value integration theory.[209]

Our initial values are due to our biology. We get hungry because we are biologically wired to get hungry. We normally find sex pleasurable because we are biologically wired to do so. We normally enjoy exercising our faculties—all mammalian young play—again because of our biology. Biology helps explain the value we place on sociality. Our biology gives us the capacity for pleasure and pain, happiness and fear and anxiety, love and hate, sympathy and revulsion, and so on.

We need to distinguish (what I'll call) first-order values—those with a direct biological base, such as eating—from second-order or derivative values, which arise largely from our judgments.[210] So biology gives us hunger and makes certain things taste good to us, but we choose whether to value a piece of chocolate cake or a slice of bacon or a cucumber salad. Muslims (among others) rule out bacon on religious grounds; vegans rule it out on moral grounds; some people rule it out because of health; many people love eating it and

209 See Darryl Wright's recorded lecture, *Ayn Rand and the History of Ethics*, available in audio format via the Ayn Rand Institute at https://estore.aynrand.org/p/448/ayn -rand-and-the-history-of-ethics-mp3-download (accessed May 29, 2018).

210 Leonard Peikoff makes this distinction yet downplays the role of biologically-rooted values; see the question period of his sixth lecture of *Modern Philosophy: Kant to the Present*, delivered in 1970, available in audio format via the Ayn Rand Institute at https://estore.aynrand.org/p/96/modern-philosophy-kant-to-the-present-history -of-philosophy-part-2-mp3-download (accessed August 8, 2018).

even think it's healthy. So our diets start with biology but quickly become guided by a complex set of scientific and moral beliefs, as well as by individual characteristics (such as food allergies) and food availability. We find the same pattern elsewhere.

Integrating our values means doing the best we can to pursue them individually and as a whole guided by reasonable beliefs rather than by unreasonable ones. Partly this means recognizing that we are prone to error and blindness and seeking to overcome such problems. We recognize biases and the like as problems precisely because they interfere with our integration of values; if integrating our values did not matter, it would not matter if we were guided by reason.

It is a mistake, then, to think that, because human beings are prone to bias and delusion (as is the fad to emphasize these days), that therefore reason cannot be the animating force of ethics. The fact that people are prone to error hardly is a new insight; it is why Aristotle needed to codify the rules of logic and why scientists needed to refine the scientific method. We know about our tendencies toward bias and delusion only because we have the capacity to reason, to conceptually distinguish bias from objectivity, to tell a good argument from a bad one, to research facts about the mind. The fact that we can go wrong and make bad choices is precisely why we need to actively seek to integrate our values, to guide our interrelated value pursuits by reason. Such is possible. As Daniel Kahneman (himself!) points out, a "focus on error does not denigrate human intelligence, any more than the attention to diseases in medical texts denies good health."[211]

In some ways integrating values might mean sublimating certain biological impulses. Biology seems to have something to do with the way that people tend to like to pick sides and seek status (as examples);[212] regardless of biology's role people often do such things. Competition can manifest as war or politics or a sports match. Status-seeking can

211   Daniel Kahneman, *Thinking, Fast and Slow* (New York: Farrar, Straus and Giroux, 2011), p. 4. More recently, Steven Pinker points out we can overcome biases and become more rational; see his *Enlightenment Now* (New York: Viking, 2018), pp. 383–384.

212   Frans de Waal makes some suggestions along these lines in his *Good Natured* (Harvard University Press, 1996), pp. 39, 93.

manifest as brutal subjugation of others or hard work in a productive career. If we imagine a vampire (to take a striking hypothetical), a person with a literal physiological desire to drink fresh human blood, the person could kill people for blood, turn to blood banks or animal blood, try meditation, or seek to develop a drug to block the urge. Obviously only some paths allow for integrated values. So what we do with our first-order, biologically related potential values depends on how we pursue our values as a whole.

Consider another implication of value integration theory, one that casts what are initially means-only values in a new light. We have seen that some values, such as buying a toothbrush and brushing one's teeth, are means to other values. But, once a person sees all of his values as integrating into his life as a whole, in a sense all of his values, however minor, can become ends in themselves in the moment of their pursuit, as constituents of his life. To draw an analogy based on Urmson's dancer, everything we do, however minor, becomes a step in a person's dance of life, something that we can experience as meaningful and often joyous in itself.

Rethinking Intrinsicism

Does value integration theory treat some things as intrinsically valuable, and, if so, is that a problem?

If an intrinsic value is something that we experience as valuable as an end in itself or for its own sake, then value integration theory arises from intrinsic value; the point is to integrate values that are ends in themselves and values that are means to such values.[213] If nothing is valuable for its own sake, then it is hard to see why we should or how we could do anything. Even in Rand's theory, the only conceivable reason to choose to live is that living is in some way valuable for its own sake. If Rand were to claim that living can never

---

213 The *Stanford Encyclopedia of Philosophy* says that the term intrinsic value typically refers to something valuable "in itself," "for its own sake," "as such," or "in its own right"; see Michael J. Zimmerman, "Intrinsic vs. Extrinsic Value," December 14, 2014, https://plato.stanford.edu/entries/value-intrinsic-extrinsic/.

be valuable for its own sake, then the choice to live would seem an onerous duty rather than a joyous commitment.

But, when Rand criticizes intrinsicism, she does not refer to things that people experience as valuable in themselves or for their own sake. In *Atlas Shrugged* and in "The Objectivist Ethics," Rand focuses on the errors of subjectivism (personal or social) and mysticism (AS 1011, TOE 14), which she (elsewhere) ties to intrinsicism. In "What Is Capitalism?" (1965), Rand discusses intrinsicism as she sees it:

> The intrinsic theory holds that the good is inherent in certain things or actions as such, regardless of their context and consequences, regardless of any benefit or injury they may cause to the actors and subjects involved. It is a theory that divorces the concept of "good" from beneficiaries, and the concept of "value" from valuer and purpose—claiming that the good is good in, by, and of itself. . . . The intrinsic theory holds that the good resides in some sort of reality, independent of man's consciousness.[214]

In "Causality Versus Duty" (1970), Rand critically quotes Kant to the effect that an action to maintain even a horrible life has intrinsic value (as she conceives it), which would preclude committing suicide to end great suffering.[215]

Leonard Peikoff takes Rand's meaning of intrinsicism, saying that "values are not intrinsic features of reality." "Value requires a valuer," he points out, which is what intrinsicism as he understands it denies. "Moral value does not pertain to reality alone or to consciousness alone," he adds, which is what he thinks intrinsicism and subjectivism, respectively, hold.[216]

---

214 Ayn Rand, "What Is Capitalism?," in *Capitalism: The Unknown Ideal* (New York: Signet, 1967), pp. 21–22 (emphasis omitted). Here Rand says that intrinsicism as she conceives it leads logically to totalitarianism.

215 Ayn Rand, "Causality Versus Duty," *Philosophy: Who Needs It* (New York: Signet, 1984), pp. 96–97.

216 Leonard Peikoff, *Objectivism: The Philosophy of Ayn Rand* (New York: Dutton, 1991), pp. 241–242.

Obviously Rand's idea of an intrinsic value has nothing to do with something that a person experiences as valuable for its own sake, as an end in itself. Something experienced as valuable for its own sake involves consequences that matter, entails a benefit to the actor, and is (partly) dependent on a person's consciousness. I have no problem saying that value integration theory relies on intrinsic value, so long as it is clear that such intrinsicism, if it is called that, has nothing to do with what Rand or Peikoff describes.[217]

When I say that something is valuable "in itself," I do not mean that it is valuable apart from human consciousness. It seems obvious that, for something to be experienced as valuable for its own sake, it must be so experienced by a conscious being. For example, a sunset cannot be enjoyed if there is no one around to enjoy it.

Tara Smith, who discusses intrinsicism at length, says that intrinsic values are "things that are good in themselves." Smith points out that different people have attributed intrinsic value to various things, including "states of affairs" and experiences, and that G. E. Moore extends intrinsic value even to some states apart from any conscious valuer.[218] But the fact that different people have proposed wildly different ideas about what is an intrinsic value, some of which are obviously untenable, does not preclude the possibility of people experiencing certain things as good for their own sake or as ends in themselves (roughly as Rand herself uses such terms).

Smith links intrinsic value to spooky intuitionism. She writes, "The absence of objective evidence for intrinsic value, alongside the utterly subjective basis on which people assert it (their feelings or intuitions), leaves us without grounds to credit its existence."[219]

---

217 David Kelley grants that things such as cleaning up one's living area by taking out the trash and exercising virtue can be experienced as "intrinsically enjoyable"; see his "Why Virtue is a Means to Our Ultimate End," commentary on Neera K. Badhwar, "Is Virtue Only a Means to Happiness?," in *Objectivist Studies* 4, ed. William Thomas (Poughkeepsie, NY: Objectivist Center, 2001), pp. 68–69.

218 Tara Smith, *Viable Values* (Lanham, MD: Rowman & Littlefield, 2000), pp. 61, 62, 65.

219 Ibid., p. 69.

If Smith means that there is no reason to think that any value exists apart from a valuer, then I quite agree. But if she means that we have no evidence that we experience certain things as valuable for their own sake, then I would point to the abundance of evidence from our daily lives: happiness, communion with loved ones, the joys of food and sex, the satisfaction of exercising our faculties. As for Smith's charge of subjectivism, obviously things are values to subjects. But we really do value certain things; it is not as if the pleasure of (say) eating tasty food when hungry is just a delusion, the product of a fevered imagination. It is no big mystery why we experience certain things as valuable in themselves; at the level of first-order values, the sciences of biology and neuroscience readily explain such things, at least in broad outline (and potentially in fine detail). And whether and to what degree a person integrates his values is a matter of fact.

One of Smith's criticisms of intrinsicism is that, by the theory, "value is not . . . as mind-free as it pretends to be." Some intrinsicists suggest that value is mind-free in an important sense, because, for example, we prefer "our children's actual success to our deluded misimpression of it" and "genuine accomplishments to the sense of accomplishment that a virtual-reality machine might provide." Smith argues that the distinction between the purely subjective and the completely external is untenable.[220] But this is a problem only for the sort of intrinsicism that holds that values can exist apart from valuers. If instead by intrinsicism we mean simply that we in fact value certain things as ends in themselves, then it is obvious that we value not just certain conscious states apart from external conditions, but certain conscious states in certain relations to external conditions. So, for example, we do not wish merely to experience the pleasure that would result from sex, as a drug might induce; we normally want to experience actual sex with a real human being whom we really love. Our relationship to reality is inseparable from our conscious states.

---

220   Tara Smith, *Viable Values* (Lanham, MD: Rowman & Littlefield, 2000), p. 76. Robert Nozick nicely deals with the matter of pure experience versus experience of reality with his thought experiment of the experience machine; see his *Anarchy, State, and Utopia* (New York: BasicBooks, 1974), pp. 42–45.

One problem that Rand and her defenders recognize is that the things we experience directly as valuable owing to our psychology or biology cannot, by themselves, give us moral standards. Value integration theory explains where moral standards come from. Just because eating is inherently pleasurable (in normal contexts) does not mean we should descend into gluttony. Just because sex is pleasurable for its own sake does not mean we should try to have sex at every opportunity. Besides values related to basic pleasures and pains, we also value our future selves, the continuity of our lives, and the harmony of our values. To achieve value integration we need more than what biology automatically gives us; we need a conceptual understanding of our values and of what it means to integrate them.

Rand says that an objective theory of values "holds that the good is an aspect of reality in relation to man."[221] Rand is right about that. She is just wrong that objectivity derives from the relation of values to an organism's survival. Objectivity actually derives from the facts that we really do experience some things as valuable for their own sake and that we really do integrate our values more or less well. If this be (a version of) intrinsicism, make the most of it.

The Individual in Society

If we consider the individual alone, it is relatively easy to make the case that value integration is what morality is basically about. But can the theory really explain the individual in society? Doesn't it seem odd to say that a person should, say, respect the rights of others because doing so helps the person integrate his values? Isn't respecting the rights of others fundamentally about other people, not yourself?

It is worth noting, as we saw in our review of Rand's discussions of rights, that respecting others' rights normally does bring profound selfish benefits in terms of maintaining relations of friendship and trade, avoiding conflict, and maintaining a virtuous character.

But, unlike Rand's survival-based metaethics, value integration theory does not presume selfish egoism. Rather, it recognizes that

---

221 Ayn Rand, "What Is Capitalism?," in *Capitalism: The Unknown Ideal* (New York: Signet, 1967), p. 22 (emphasis omitted).

a person's interests and values normally encompass the welfare of other people. So part of what integrating one's values means is giving due concern to the well-being of others. Value integration theory is neither selfishly egoistic nor altruistic as Rand defines it, where altruism refers to the sacrifice of one's interests. Rather, value integration theory recognizes that a person often has an interest in the well-being of others and often advances his interests by advancing the interests of others; the two are intertwined.

Rand offers a perfect statement of this convergence of interests: "The practical implementation of friendship, affection and love consists of incorporating the welfare (the *rational* welfare) of the person involved into one's own hierarchy of values, then acting accordingly."[222] The problem for Rand is that ultimately she must trace all of a person's values to that person's survival, so her theory is fundamentally egoistic in a way that value integration theory is not. Within value integration theory, a person can value another person's welfare simply, as an end in itself, and not as a means to some other purely selfish value.

We can turn to biology (again) to help explain why we normally are interested in the well-being of other people. Because the human brain is so large and takes so long to develop, humans are born relatively undeveloped, and human parents spend an unusually long time looking after infants.[223] As Richard Joyce points out, "In modern humans, two-thirds of neural growth has to occur post-natally."[224]

As big-brained mammals, humans are innately social. The mother-infant bond is extraordinarily important to human survival. This strong bond has biological components; for example, Sarah Blaffer Hrdy likens the mother's attachment to breast feeding, promoted

---

222 Ayn Rand, "The Ethics of Emergencies," in *The Virtue of Selfishness* (New York: Signet, 1964), p. 46.

223 Humans "spend almost twice as long in childhood and adolescence as chimps, gibbons, or macaques do"; see Priyanka Pulla, "Why Do Humans Grow Up So Slowly? Blame the Brain," *Science*, August 25, 2014, http://www.sciencemag.org /news/2014/08/why-do-humans-grow-so-slowly-blame-brain.

224 Richard Joyce, *The Evolution of Morality* (Cambridge: MIT Press, 2006), p. 45.

by surges of pleasure-inducing hormones, to an addiction.[225] As Cicero writes, the parent-child bond plausibly is "the source of the mutual and natural sympathy between humans," that by which "we are fitted by nature to form associations, assemblies and states."[226] Biology lends this view some support; oxytocin plays a key role in maternal care and in social trust more broadly.[227] Hrdy argues that evolution promoted communal bonds: "[T]he help of group members in addition to the genetic parents was absolutely essential for the survival of infants (birth to weaning) and children (weaning to nutritional independence) in the Pleistocene." This helps explain why humans are so good at "guessing what others want" and why humans "exhibit spontaneous impulses to share with others and are routinely eager to help."[228]

By biological confluence, the very forces that gave us the capacity for rationality by bestowing us with big brains (by primate standards) also made us especially social.

Once we recognize that the individual sometimes has an interest in advancing the interests of others, our interest-based account of ethics can accommodate the concern of Michael Huemer and others that respecting others' rights is fundamentally about concern for others, not advancing selfish aims. Sometimes your interests *are* my interests.

Yet the idea of universal rights is relatively new. Most people throughout human history have distinguished their social group from outsiders, and the idea that outsiders have rights rarely (if ever) occurred to them. The bridge consists of the facts, as Rand argues, that human beings are able to produce wealth and to collaborate with others by mutual consent. It is possible for human beings to live together peacefully, even in a global economy in which most people

---

225 Sarah Blaffer Hrdy, *Mother Nature* (New York: Pantheon Books, 1999), p. 537.

226 Quoted in Richard Joyce, *The Evolution of Morality* (Cambridge: MIT Press, 2006), p. 46.

227 Matt Ridley, *The Rational Optimist* (New York: HarperCollins Publishers, 2010), p. 94.

228 Sarah Blaffer Hrdy, *Mothers and Others* (Harvard University Press, 2011), pp. 65, 67.

are strangers, and such peaceful coexistence is profoundly good for rational individuals. The point we can add to Rand's analysis is that the sympathy that evolved largely to facilitate the raising of children can also help support the institution of individual rights, for we can see in our mind's eye (or in the news) and feel emotionally the suffering of oppressed people anywhere in the world.

Value integration theory also embraces Rand's point that rights protect the individual's ability to think and act on his own judgment for the betterment of his own life. To pursue and integrate our values we need the freedom to do so.

As we've seen, Rand makes some attempt to justify rights, in part, on grounds of consistency, which brings her (perhaps uncomfortably) close to the views of Kant.[229] Value integration theory permits us to bring in arguments for logical consistency beyond those already considered, arguments rooted in an individual's interests (so we steer clear of Kant's mystifying metaphysics)[230] but that recognize interests broader than survival. Plausibly, we are wired by our biology to care about fairness to others, which a consistent application of moral principles makes possible. Moreover, we recognize that we cannot plausibly advocate fair treatment for ourselves if we do not treat others fairly. What actually constitutes fairness is a thorny debate, but most people agree at least that fairness and intellectual consistency entail recognizing others' rights. Hence, value integration theory allows a role for rational discourse in refining an individual's interests.

What of charity? It is easy to see how value integration theory makes much more room for charity, even for strangers and for those impoverished by their own choices, than does Rand's survivalist ethics. Yet value integration theory also avoids the view, one that flies in the face of common sense, that a well-off person somehow owes

---

229   Rand critiques Kant (among other places) in the title essay of Ayn Rand, *For the New Intellectual* (New York: Signet, 1961), pp. 30–33.

230   Douglas J. Den Uyl and Douglas B. Rasmussen aptly refer to Kant's "mysterious noumenal self"; see their "Life, Teleology, and Eudaimonia in the Ethics of Ayn Rand," in *The Philosophic Thought of Ayn Rand*, ed. Den Uyl and Rasmussen (University of Illinois Press, 1984), p. 71.

others an extreme portion of his wealth, as the logic of Peter Singer's position seems to imply.

With respect to others, the mature value integrator advocates a Society of Ends (to adapt Kant's idea) and a Society of Citizens. As a Society of Ends, we mutually recognize and respect individual rights. Each person is an end in himself, and each person rightly pursues his own values. As a Society of Citizens, we recognize that establishing and maintaining a rights-respecting society is an enormously difficult project, and our interests in contributing to that project extend beyond our own survival. Also as citizens we have an interest in aiding others, insofar as we are economically stable ourselves and able to help others in a way consistent with our broader values. As citizens, we have an interest in the welfare of the human race as a whole (and even in the welfare of members of other species) and in the future of humanity.

A Theory of Evil

How does value integration theory account for evil? If someone believes that, by blowing up a cafe full of strangers, he will help spread God's kingdom on earth and also receive vast rewards in Heaven, he might claim that he pursues his values in the best way possible. Yet his actions are rooted in self-delusion. His imagined deity does not exist, he will receive no rewards in an afterlife, and what he pretends is God's kingdom on earth is really a brutal theocracy. The person has wasted his life and destroyed the lives of others for nothing— less than nothing. If he could bring himself to see clearly what he is really doing—murdering a bunch of innocent people at the behest of nihilistic monsters—he could not go through with it.

Rand's theory of evil is basically correct, and it readily attaches to value integration theory. Evil, as Rand saw, arises essentially from evasion (or a failure to think leading to evasion), purposely turning one's mind away from uncomfortable facts. Rand writes:

Thinking is man's only basic virtue, from which all the others proceed. And his basic vice, the source of all his evils, is that nameless act which all of you practice, but struggle never to admit: the act of blanking out, the willful suspension of one's consciousness, the refusal to think—not blindness, but the refusal to see; not ignorance, but the refusal to know. (AS 1017; see also TOE 20–22)

Often hand-in-hand with evasion comes rationalization, the concoction of a set of false reasons a person gives himself to disguise his bad behavior. "I'm not really robbing this bank; I'm just liberating some of the funds expropriated by the greedy bankers," goes the pattern. Often criminals say they are not "really" guilty, if only we understood the situation. "He deserved it," goes the typical rationalization for brutalizing someone else.

Sometimes a person rationalizes bad behavior in the pursuit of wealth, sex, or some other perceived value. Sometimes a person's motives are darker still. Some people are motivated by a misdirected hatred, even a universalized hatred. Such hatred, coupled with rationalizations, is, I think, what allows some people to commit atrocities such as the mass murder of strangers.

Such universalized hatred is related to what Rand calls "hatred of the good for being the good."[231] Rand describes the motives of people with such hatred:

> They do not want to own your fortune, they want you to lose it; they do not want to succeed, they want you to fail; they do not want to live, they want you to die; they desire nothing, they hate existence, and they keep running, each trying not to learn that the object of his hatred is himself. (AS 1046)

In value integration theory (as in Rand's moral theory) the crown virtue is reason, by which one can come to see the world clearly; the main sin is evasion, the abdication of one's reason and embrace of self-delusion. Evasion disintegrates values.

Here we must distinguish honest error from evasion. It is not a moral failing for a person (say) to eat wheat when he has coeliac disease, if he has no knowledge of the problem. It becomes a moral problem if the person ignores the disease or fails to deal with

---

231 Ayn Rand, "The Age of Envy," in *The Return of the Primitive* (New York, Meridian, 1999), p. 130 (emphasis omitted).

symptoms out of some desire to hide the truth from himself. The general progression of human knowledge means that people now have less excuse for certain offenses against self and others than perhaps they once did.

A person who tends to evade and rationalize will tend to develop a bad character. The person will habituate not only evasion and rationalization but various other bad practices they lead to.

Self-honesty, which is essentially a commitment to reason, relates to what we often call authentic living. The authentic person does his best to understand relevant features of himself and the world around him; the inauthentic person lies to himself about himself and about reality.

Rand and Value Integration

Contrast Rand's metaethics with value integration theory. Rand would say that she advocates the integration of all of a person's values as oriented to his long-term survival. But, as I've argued, it is not the case that all of our values so integrate; our values are about more than survival. Rand thinks that we need to locate a final end to which all other values ultimately serve as means; this misses the possibility that a person's life is his ultimate value as *constituted* by various other values that are genuinely ends in themselves. Rand looks for moral standards in that to which (she believes) values point, survival; this misses the fact that value integration itself can both point to an ultimate value (the integrated life) and provide moral standards for achieving it.

So Rand's moral theory is quite different from value integration theory. Yet it is helpful to point out how close Rand sometimes comes to value integration theory. For example, the ideal "new intellectual," for Rand, is "an integrated man."[232] Elsewhere Rand writes, "In choosing a goal, [a rational person] considers the means required to achieve it, he weighs the value of the goal against the difficulties of

---

232 Ayn Rand, *For the New Intellectual* (New York: Signet, 1961), p. 51 (emphasis omitted).

the means and against the full, hierarchical context of all his other values and goals."[233]

In her earlier writings, Rand seems to start down the path to value integration theory. Drawing on Leonard Peikoff's 1997 lectures *Objectivism Through Induction*, Gregory Salmieri writes that, after a person grasps that he chooses his values, he can proceed to consciously integrate them:

> Peikoff argues that an intelligent, first-handed [independent] thinker would [at a relatively early stage] be able to grasp that all of his values contribute to his life and his enjoyment of it. . . . In her later writings Rand advocates Man's Life [as] the standard of value. The joyous life standard which Peikoff discusses in his lectures is considerably more primitive, but it is not subjective like "whatever makes one happy." Instead of judging goals in isolation by the feelings they evoke, it judges them by how they would fit into a holistic, if imprecise, conception of a happy life.[234]

Salmieri points out that Prometheus, the protagonist of Rand's *Anthem*, essentially embraces such a standard. Certainly Prometheus regards happiness as important: "I know what happiness is possible to me on earth. And my happiness needs no higher aim to vindicate it. My happiness is not the means to any end. It is the end. It is its own goal. It is its own purpose."[235] Yet, as Salmieri notes, happiness for Prometheus is not hedonism; rather, at the end of the story Prometheus describes a world of prosperity and reason that he intends to help build.

Even in her early twenties, Rand saw the importance of value integration. She held that thoughts and feelings properly come

---

233 Ayn Rand, "Causality Versus Duty," *Philosophy: Who Needs It* (New York: Signet, 1984), p. 99.

234 Gregory Salmieri, "Prometheus' Discovery: Individualism and the Meaning of the Concept 'I' in *Anthem*," in *Essays on Ayn Rand's* Anthem, ed. Robert Mayhew (Lanham, MD: Lexington Books, 2005), p. 277.

235 Ayn Rand, *Anthem*, fiftieth anniversary edition (New York: Dutton, 1995), p. 95

together when a person logically "connect[s] together the things [he] observes." Rand expressed her ideal: "Every thought should be part of yourself, your body, your nature, and every part of your nature should be a thought." The opposite sort of existence, a disintegrated life, involves "stumbling helplessly in a chaos of inconsistent ideas, actions, and feelings that can't be put together."[236]

Around this time, Rand also seemed to endorse the idea that what matters is life of a certain quality beyond survival; this too is similar to value integration theory. She writes, "Achievement is the aim of life. Life is achievement."[237] Rand describes a person as truly alive who feels "strong, high emotion" that accompanies "tense, exalted" action. A person is not truly living who does "not hold anything to be very serious or profound," who does "not know how to value or desire."[238] In *We the Living*, Kira says, "Why do you think I'm alive? Because I have a stomach and eat and digest the food? Because I breathe and work and produce more food to digest? Or because I know what I want, and that something which knows how to want— isn't that life itself?"[239] In a 1936 letter, Rand writes that "any form of swift physical annihilation is preferable to the inconceivable horror of a living death," such as a life "devoid of the pride and joy of a man's right to his own spirit."[240]

Gregory Salmieri and Darryl Wright, in commenting on such passages, see continuity between Rand's early views and her mature metaethical views.[241] But the more natural reading of Rand's early

---

236   David Harriman, ed., *Journals of Ayn Rand* (New York: Plume, 1999), p. 24.

237   Ibid., p. 8 (emphasis omitted).

238   Ibid., p. 28.

239   Ayn Rand, *We the Living* (New York: Random House, 1959), p. 376.

240   Michael S. Berliner, ed., *Letters of Ayn Rand* (New York: Dutton, 1995), pp. 33–34.

241   Darryl Wright, "Needs of the *Psyche* in Ayn Rand's Early Ethical Thought," in *Essays on Ayn Rand's* Anthem, ed. Robert Mayhew (Lanham, MD: Lexington Books, 2005), pp. 190, 191, 194; and Gregory Salmieri, "The Act of Valuing (and the Objectivity of Values)," in *A Companion to Ayn Rand*, pp. 49–50. Salmieri indicates that the text from *We the Living* quoted above appears in both the 1936 and 1959 versions of the novel.

remarks is that she endorsed life of a certain quality, not life as survival, and that value integration was central to her vision of life. Rand's later metaethical views can best be seen, I think, as an after-the-fact attempt to justify her earlier views, not a logical extension of them. Rand just did not know how else to account for normal human values without slipping into subjectivism.

To speculate, perhaps Rand was unable to develop a self-sufficient theory of value integration because she did not see how to deal with happiness absent a solid, directly observable phenomenon such as survival to anchor values. She feared that Aristotle's eudaimonia falls prey to subjectivism, and she likely would have had similar concerns about value integration theory. But value integration theory not only offers objective moral standards, it reflects the reality of human values, as Rand's survivalism does not.

An Expanded View of Life

Some years before starting this book, I reached the view that Rand's moral theory is correct, given a certain interpretation of it. A person's life is his ultimate value, I agreed, but a person's life entails all of the values and actions that constitute his life—even if those values and actions do not always promote survival. The idea is that we act to preserve the sort of life we have. So, for example, if I value my child so much that I'd risk or surrender my life to save his, then such is the nature of the life that is my ultimate value. We might call this the inclusive life standard.

This interpretation seems to dissolve all of the problems associated with a survival-oriented metaethics. For example, we can sensibly talk about an egoist risking his life for others, committing suicide to avoid horrible suffering, and enthusiastically participating in charity work to help even strangers.

But this inclusive life standard ultimately is unstable. Rand's metaethics rests on the fundamental alternative of life as opposed to death, of life in terms of survival. Once we incorporate values that are not strictly tied to one's survival, we float away from Rand's metaethical base, and we have to come up with some other justification for holding values. If we have such a justification, Rand's metaethics no longer is necessary.

Interestingly, a number of people inspired by Rand's moral theory—and Rand herself—have hinted at some sort of inclusive life standard and even something like value integration theory. This is a very natural position to take given the duel importance of survival and happiness in Rand's moral theory.

As we have seen, Rand holds that a person can experience a "kind of pure happiness that is an end in itself" (TOE 29). Similarly, Nathaniel Branden writes, "Through the state of enjoyment, man experiences the value of life, the sense that life is worth living, worth struggling to maintain."[242]

Tara Smith writes that the choice to live "depends on what kind of experience a given individual finds satisfactory."[243] Elsewhere she argues: "[I]ndividuals value their lives for the sake of satisfying experiences: pleasures of varying depth and resonance, a sense of the importance of some of their activities, accomplishing goals that they consider valuable."[244] Darryl Wright puts the point, "To find one's life worth living . . . must be to experience the process of living—the activities that define and give substance to one's life—as intrinsically motivating, as a source of pleasure and fulfillment."[245]

Such is interesting language coming from philosophers who explicitly reject any theory of intrinsic value. As Ole Martin Moen notes, such remarks seem "to allow for the possibility that we can judge whether or not a life is worth living by reference to a further standard." Moen points out that we recognize "that happiness is

---

242 Nathaniel Branden, "The Psychology of Pleasure," in *The Virtue of Selfishness* (New York: Signet, 1964), p. 61.

243 Tara Smith, *Viable Values* (Lanham, MD: Rowman & Littlefield, 2000), p. 107.

244 Tara Smith, *Moral Rights & Political Freedom* (Lanham, MD: Rowman & Littlefield, 1995), p. 43. Smith seems to have refined her views on this point between the publication of this book and her next. In the 1995 work, Smith also says that people who "choose to maintain their lives . . . do so for the sake of having lives of a desirable character" (p. 44). She adds that "the quality-quantity of life distinction is untenable" (p. 45).

245 Darryl F. Wright, "Evaluative Concepts and Objective Values: Rand on Moral Objectivity," in *Objectivism, Subjectivism, and Relativism in Ethics*, ed. Ellen Frankel Paul, Fred D. Miller, Jr., and Jeffrey Paul (Cambridge University Press, 2008), p. 174.

better than suffering" and that quality of life matters above and beyond staying alive.[246] David Kelley, following Rand, states that "the maintenance of [a person's] life is his ultimate goal." But, he adds, "If the commitment is not there, if I do not actually value my life, then my life cannot be a value for me." The value we place on our lives "lies in the things that make life seem worth living, the things that give meaning to our lives as individuals," Kelley continues; "Meaning is connected with things we find intrinsically satisfying and not merely means to an end." Kelley endorses value integration at some level: "If what you want collides with the facts, of course, you have to take the collision into account, and adjust your commitments accordingly."[247] What Kelley does not seem to realize is that the logic of his remarks shows the superfluity of Rand's survivalist metaethics.

Robert Bidinotto (who was long associated with Kelley's Objectivist organization) advocates something like an inclusive life standard coupled with a nascent value integration theory. He suggests that "the 'self' and 'life' Rand alluded to was something much more than one's mere physical survival." He explains: "For a Roark, 'self-preservation' could well include the terms and conditions that would enable him to build a Stoddard Temple—because if he couldn't, the entity we call 'Roark' would no longer exist, or find his life worth living." But this expansive view of self does not mean that anything goes: "Irrational ideas and values are those which collide with reality. They lead to destruction—not to some 'alternative' kind of life." Bidinotto continues: "An 'irrational self' is . . . precisely the absence of a self—or at best, a self in chaotic disintegration."[248] But, again,

---

246   Ole Martin Moen, "Is Life the Ultimate Value? A Reassessment of Ayn Rand's Ethics," *Reason Papers*, October 2012, vol. 34, no. 2, https://reasonpapers.com /pdf/342/rp_342_9.pdf, pp. 108, 111, 116. Moen also discusses the passages by Rand and Branden quoted a couple paragraphs above.

247   David Kelley, "Choosing Life," Atlas Society, June 22, 2010, https:// atlassociety.org/commentary/commentary-blog/3705-choosing-life.

248   Robert Bidinotto, "Survive or Flourish? A Reconciliation," April 19, 2016, http://bidinotto.blogspot.com/p/archives.html (emphasis omitted); originally published by *Full Context* in February and April, 1994.

once we grant that life properly includes values that are not means to survival, we leave Rand's metaethics behind.

Various people inspired by Rand haltingly step down the path toward value integration theory before leaping back to Rand's metaethical base. I suggest they walk a little farther.

Conclusion

Ayn Rand rightly feared the twin errors in ethics of intrinsicism (the sort that severs values from interests) and subjectivism (which severs interests from facts). She proposed an elegant standard of value that, she thought, rescued Aristotelian flourishing from subjectivism. With her life-based standard of value, Rand thought, finally ethics takes its place among the sciences.

But, for reasons we've seen, Rand's metaethics does not hold up. That we face an alternative of life versus death does not imply that all of a person's values should orient to his survival.

At the biological level, it is not the case that organisms generally function and act to further their own survival, as Rand claims; rather, organisms normally advance the reproduction of their genes, which can involve self-sacrifice in terms of survival.

At the human level, people normally do not organize their values only around personal survival, although usually many of a person's values help support survival. We can see this in such choices as to have children, to commit suicide to prevent unrelenting suffering, and to risk one's own safety or life for the sake of others. Because of its problems, Rand's theory falls into various theoretical bogs, as with its peculiar premoral "choice to live" and its apparent dependence on death, as seen with Rand's example of the indestructible robot.

Further, although Rand offers more powerful arguments for respecting others' rights than what many critics recognize, her survivalist metaethics cannot sustain robust rights-respecting behavior in important contexts, as the example of slavery illustrates. And, although Rand's ethics offers some reasons for people not to free ride and to help others charitably, those reasons are insufficient.

I have outlined a different Aristotle-inspired metaethics, value integration theory, that avoids all of the problems of Rand's theory while keeping intact Rand's valid findings. Value integration theory shares with Rand's metaethics the agent relativity of values (everything that is valuable is so because it is valued by an actor, at least potentially), a focus on biology as the starting point of values, an individualist ultimate value that provides objective moral standards, an emphasis on reason and related virtues, a social theory based on mutual consent, and a theory of evil that sees evasion as the key problem.

Value integration theory sees a person's ultimate value as his life in terms of integrated values, a life that makes more room for the interests of others than what Rand's theory logically allows. Value integration theory takes seriously the interests of individuals, and it clearly recognizes that an individual's interests normally entail the interests of others in important ways.

So value integration theory has no problem explaining, for example, why a person might want to have children, or risk his safety or life for others (in certain contexts), or respect the rights even of the severely disempowered, or advance social causes such as a free society or prosperity for future generations, or give charitably even to strangers and the self-destructive (again in certain contexts). Such acts are not self-sacrificial, by the lights of value integration theory, but neither are they always purely egoistic in terms of personal survival or the like. A consistent value integrator is self-interested— and keenly aware that the values of which he composes his self often encompass the interests of others.

Will value integration theory hold up under criticism? Is it true? I think so, but I acknowledge that turning it into a full-fledged theory will require a great deal of work. My goal here was to briefly sketch what I regard as the most plausible alternative to Rand's moral theory. I wanted to indicate both to critics and to adherents of Rand's philosophy that one can abandon Rand's survivalist metaethics while retaining many of Rand's insights. If my theory is wrong, that does not prove that Rand's theory is correct; it proves that we need to again check our premises.

Rand makes a valiant effort to stuff human life into her metaethics, but life bursts from the suit and splits its seams. The sort of human life that reflective and clear-eyed people normally aspire to (once they shed their dogmas) fits comfortably into value integration theory, because the suit takes the full measure of the person.

Appendix:
The Literature on Rand's Moral Theory

SCHOLARLY TREATMENT OF AYN RAND'S PHILOSOPHY, focused mostly on her moral and political theories, got rolling around a decade after the 1957 publication of *Atlas Shrugged*. Scholars and commentators continue to produce a steady stream of articles and books about Rand's ideas. Here I very briefly discuss many of the works pertaining to Rand's moral theory. Sometimes I interject my own views; other times I quote or summarize an author's view without reply, whether or not I agree with the view expressed. I use parenthetical notes to indicate page numbers of the work under discussion. In all cases I omit emphasis in quotes, except for titles.

Initially, philosophic discussion of Rand's ideas came mostly from Rand and from Nathaniel Branden, Rand's close associate at the time. In *Atlas Shrugged* (1957),[249] primarily through the lengthy speech of John Galt, Rand lays out her most systematic account of her philosophy.

In 1958, Nathaniel Branden founded the Nathaniel Branden Institute (NBI), which offered "lecture courses . . . on Ayn Rand's

---

249 Ayn Rand, *Atlas Shrugged* (New York: Dutton, 1992).

philosophy, Objectivism, and its application to the social sciences."[250] In 1962 Rand and Branden began publishing the *Objectivist Newsletter*. During this time, Rand attended some sessions of NBI to take questions from participants and met with her group of friends ironically dubbed the Collective.[251]

In **"For the New Intellectual"** (1961),[252] an essay in the book of the same title, Rand critiques contemporary society and modern philosophy. She discusses the archetypes of "Attila," the person of force, and the "Witch Doctor," the mystic (14). She also pens one of her most well-known lines: "[A] free mind and a free market are corollaries" (25). Rand claims that "during the nineteenth century, the world came close to economic freedom, for the first and only time in history" (25)—a claim disputed by some libertarians.[253]

"The Objectivist Ethics" (1961)[254] is Rand's fullest statement of her moral theory. Rand delivered the paper for a symposium at the University of Wisconsin to some "twelve hundred students, faculty members and visitors," Nathaniel Branden recounts.[255] The paper was published as the lead essay in *The Virtue of Selfishness* (1964), a volume that contains a number of other important essays about Rand's moral philosophy, including Rand's introduction (vii–xi), her

---

250   Nathaniel Branden, "About the Authors," in *Who Is Ayn Rand?* (New York: Paperback Library, 1964).

251   Jennifer Burns, *Goddess of the Market: Ayn Rand and the American Right* (Oxford University Press, 2009), pp. 181–182.

252   Ayn Rand, "For the New Intellectual," in the book of the same title (New York: Signet, 1968), pp. 10–57. The main copyright is from 1961; Rand dates her preface October 1960.

253   See, for example, Steven Horwitz, "The Errors of Nostalgi-tarianism," Libertarianism.org (Cato Institute), July 13, 2018, https://www.libertarianism.org /columns/errors-nostalgi-tarianism; and Neera K. Badhwar, "An Objectivist Case for Libertarianism," Libertarianism.org (Cato Institute), August 30, 2017, https:// www.libertarianism.org/publications/essays/objectivist-case-libertarianism.

254   Ayn Rand, "The Objectivist Ethics," in *The Virtue of Selfishness* (New York: Signet, 1964), pp. 13–35.

255   See Nathaniel Branden's preface in *Who Is Ayn Rand?* (New York: Paperback Library, 1964), p. 5.

"The Ethics of Emergencies" (43–49), and Nathaniel Branden's "Isn't Everyone Selfish?" (57–60).

Nathaniel Branden's **"The Moral Revolution in *Atlas Shrugged*"** (1962)[256] is the first major published work (not counting Branden's lecture courses) by someone other than Rand to explain Rand's moral theory. Among the topics Branden covers are the choice to live and the competing theories of Aristotle, Epicurus, and Spinoza. The book containing Branden's essay, *Who Is Ayn Rand?*, appeared several years before Branden's acrimonious break with Rand. Later Branden "repudiate[d]" the book, "primarily" because of its biographical essay by Barbara Branden.[257]

Nathaniel Branden's *The Vision of Ayn Rand: The Basic Principles of Objectivism* (1958–1968)[258] began as a set of lectures that Branden developed starting in 1958. Branden delivered the lectures live, then recorded and distributed them. The transcripts of the lectures were published as a book in 2009. (I'm not sure what date the taped lectures on which the book is based were recorded—see vii). The lectures represent the first presentation of Rand's philosophic system following *Atlas Shrugged*—and they remain an excellent resource for understanding Rand's ideas.

In **"What Is Capitalism?"** (1965),[259] Rand offers her fullest critique of moral intrinsicism. Rand uses the terms intrinsicism and subjectivism very broadly to encompass every moral theory other than

---

256 Nathaniel Branden, "The Moral Revolution in *Atlas Shrugged*," in *Who Is Ayn Rand?* (New York: Paperback Library, 1964), pp. 7–56. The book is copyright 1962.

257 Michael Etchison, "Break Free! An Interview with Nathaniel Branden," *Reason*, October 1971, http://reason.com/archives/1971/10/01/break-free/8.

258 Nathaniel Branden, *The Vision of Ayn Rand: The Basic Principles of Objectivism* (Gilbert, AZ: Cobden Press, 2009).

259 Ayn Rand, "What Is Capitalism?," in *Capitalism: The Unknown Ideal* (New York: Signet, 1967), pp. 11–34. The essay originally was published in *Objectivist Newsletter*, November 1965, vol. 4, no. 11, pp. 51–52, 54, and December 1965, vol. 4, no. 12, pp. 55–56, 59–61, in the bound *Volumes 1–4: 1962–1965* (Gaylordsville, CT: Second Renaissance, 1990).

her own.[260] Ultimately, she argues, because there is no intrinsic value, intrinsicist moral theories amount to or devolve to subjectivism (23).

Arguably, philosopher John Hospers is the single most important figure in gaining for Rand some measure of credibility within academic philosophy, at least until the currently active crop of Objectivist philosophers gained university positions.

Hospers, also the 1972 Libertarian Party candidate for president, had a longstanding interest in the philosophic foundations of liberty. *Letters of Ayn Rand* contains some sixty pages of Rand's letters to Hospers from 1960 and 1961 (his letters to her are not included),[261] indicating Hospers's keen interest in Rand's ideas.[262] Yet, as Jennifer Burns relates, Hospers also wrote Rand a letter in 1960 complaining of a culture of conformity at Nathaniel Branden's events at the time (when Branden worked actively with Rand), and in 1962 Rand ended her friendship with Hospers after Hospers invited her to a meeting

---

260   Rand would interpret every moral theory other than Objectivism as some variant or "mixture" of intrinsicism or subjectivism—see p. 22—hence, she would not concede to Jason Brennan that Objectivists oversimplify the moral landscape. See Jason Brennan, "Craig Biddle's Chart on Essential Moral Theories; Objectivist Strawmen," *Bleeding Heart Libertarians*, July 16, 2014, http:// bleedingheartlibertarians.com/2014/07/craig-biddles-chart-on-essential-moral -theories-objectivist-strawmen/.

261   Michael S. Berliner, ed., *Letters of Ayn Rand* (New York: Dutton, 1995), pp. 502–563.

262   Hospers includes several passages from Rand's works in his *Human Conduct* (New York: Harcourt, Brace, & World, 1961); see pp. 258–259, 274, 410, 448. Objectivist scholar Gregory Salmieri believes that Hospers's 1961 book is "the first ethics textbook to include discussion of [Rand's] views"; see Salmieri's "An Introduction to the Study of Ayn Rand," in *A Companion to Ayn Rand*, p. 16, n. 6.

of the American Society for Aesthetics and then orally critiqued her presentation there.[263]

In the second edition of *An Introduction to Philosophical Analysis* (1967),[264] John Hospers discusses or mentions Ayn Rand on eleven pages (see the index entry), and his treatment of Rand is respectful and even friendly.

The same year, in *An Existentialist Ethics* (1967),[265] Hazel Barnes discusses Rand as a foil to existentialism. In many ways Barnes fails to grapple with (or simply misunderstands) Rand's arguments, and she barely mentions the centrality of life to Rand's ethics. Barnes does get in some good licks. For example, regarding the problem of John Galt "selfishly" threatening to kill himself to save Dagny Taggart, Barnes writes, "It is amusing to see Galt defending himself against the suspicion of altruism with the same sort of rationalizing that most people employ to convince themselves that they are not really selfish" (139).

Stephen Taylor wonders, **"Is Ayn Rand Really Selfish . . . Or Only Confused?"** (1969).[266] Unfortunately, Taylor is himself often confused about Rand's positions. Taylor anticipates criticisms

---

263 Jennifer Burns, *Goddess of the Market: Ayn Rand and the American Right* (Oxford University Press, 2009), pp. 187–188, 233. Harry Binswanger, who attended the event in question, disputes Burns's claim (elsewhere) that Rand "lashed out" at Hospers. Instead, as Binswanger recalls, Hospers was "hostile" toward Rand and Rand was "gentle and earnest" in her response; see Binswanger's "John Hospers' Betrayal of Ayn Rand—An Eyewitness Report," November 21, 2017, https://www.hbletter.com/10354-2/. Burns also mentions that Hospers thought he lost some career opportunities because of his association with Rand. Incidentally, Libertarianism.org hosts a half-hour video of Hospers discussing his relationship with Rand at https://www.youtube.com/watch?v=wLO4yttQet4; the event was filmed in 1996 and the video was posted on May 9, 2012.

264 John Hospers, *An Introduction to Philosophical Analysis*, second edition (Englewood Cliffs, NJ: Prentice-Hall, 1967). Hospers continues to discuss Rand in the fourth edition of the book (London: Routledge, 1997); the contents vary between the editions.

265 Hazel E. Barnes, "Egoistic Humanism: Ayn Rand's Objectivism," in *An Existentialist Ethics* (New York: Alfred A. Knopf, 1967), pp. 124–149.

266 Stephen E. Taylor, "Is Ayn Rand Really Selfish . . . Or Only Confused?," *Journal of Thought*, January 1969, vol. 4, no. 1, pp. 12–29.

of Michael Huemer and others when he characterizes egoism as "regarding others only as a means to one's own good," a position that implies that "there can be no categorical obligation to respect the rights of others" (18).

In **"Refuting the Egoist"** (1969),[267] Donald Emmons does not address Rand's ideas specifically; his essay is of interest here because of the chain of discussion it set off. During this period, John Hospers edited the *Personalist*, in which Emmons's essay appears, and Hospers actively sought to bring Rand's point of view to the journal. Contra Rand, Emmons claims that there are "irreducible conflicts of interest" that egoism cannot handle (311).

With his **"Ethical Egoism: Introduction to Nathaniel Branden's Essay"** (1970),[268] John Hospers brings Rand's ideas into an academic journal. He challenges Branden to explain "that egoism is right even in cases where virtually all men would give a reason other than self-interest in an attempt to justify the act," as with abstaining from robbing a bank when the risks seem minimal (193).

In **"Rational Egoism: A Reply to Professor Emmons"** (1970),[269] Nathaniel Branden presents the Objectivist ethics to an academic audience. Although Branden wrote the essay after his break with Rand, the piece is true to Rand's ideas and heavily reliant on Rand's texts.[270]

---

267 Donald Emmons, "Refuting the Egoist," *Personalist*, Summer 1969, vol. 50, no. 3, pp. 309–319.

268 John Hospers, "Ethical Egoism: Introduction to Nathaniel Branden's Essay," *Personalist*, Spring 1970, vol. 51, no. 2, pp. 190–195.

269 Nathaniel Branden, "Rational Egoism: A Reply to Professor Emmons," *Personalist*, Spring 1970, vol. 51, no. 2, pp. 196–211.

270 Other articles in the journal on the topic include Donald Emmons, "Rational Egoism: Random Observations," *Personalist*, Winter 1971, vol. 52, no. 1, pp. 95–98; Tibor R. Machan, "A Note on Emmons' Random Observations," *Personalist*, Winter 1971, vol. 52, no. 1, pp. 99–106; Donald C. Emmons, "Professor Machan's Objections: A Rejoinder," *Personalist*, Winter 1972, vol. 53, no. 1, pp. 71–73; John Hospers, "Rule-Egoism," *Personalist*, Fall 1973, vol. 54, no. 4, pp. 391–395; and William Dwyer, "The Argument against 'An Objective Standard of Value'," *Personalist*, Spring 1974, vol. 55, no. 2, pp. 165–181.

In **"Causality Versus Duty"** (1970),[271] Ayn Rand clearly articulates the view that morality hinges on a premoral choice to live. Some of Rand's critics suggest that this relatively late essay clashes with some of the assumptions of her earlier work. (I discuss my views on the matter in the main text.) William F. O'Neill's *With Charity Toward None: An Analysis of Ayn Rand's Philosophy* (1971)[272] is a mean-spirited and dishonest discussion of Rand's ideas. As examples, O'Neill wrongly attributes to Rand the views that "[p]leasure is intrinsically good" (150), that value means "pleasure derived by means of wealth" (177), and that "the poor are bad" (227). The very title of the book is a lie; O'Neill quotes Rand's support for some voluntary charity (226–227).

Several years before Harvard philosopher Robert Nozick became famous for his *Anarchy, State, and Utopia* (New York: Basic Books, 1974), Nozick read and analyzed Rand's philosophic ideas. In his **"On the Randian Argument"** (1971)[273] for the *Personalist*, Nozick is interested in the "moral foundations of capitalism." He seeks a "natural rights ethics" that is neither utilitarian nor based on social contract. Because Rand was interested in something similar, here Nozick follows Rand's argument to see how it holds up (206). Although Nozick frequently fails to track Rand's arguments, he makes some insightful criticisms. For example, he points to the implausibility of an immortal being not being able to have values (208–209). It is worth noting that, although Nozick finds Rand's arguments wanting, he holds that "Rand is an interesting thinker,

---

271   Ayn Rand, "Causality Versus Duty," in *Philosophy: Who Needs It* (New York: Signet, 1984), pp. 95–101. The essay originally was published in the *Objectivist*, July 1970, vol. 9, no. 7, in the bound *Volumes 5–10: 1966–1971* (New Milford, CT: Second Renaissance Books, 1971) on pp. 865–870.

272   William F. O'Neill, *With Charity Toward None: An Analysis of Ayn Rand's Philosophy* (New York, Philosophical Library, 1971).

273   Robert Nozick, "On the Randian Argument," in *Reading Nozick*, ed. Jeffrey Paul (Totowa, NJ: Rowman and Littlefield, 1981), pp. 206–231. This essay originally was published in the *Personalist*, Spring 1971, vol. 52, no. 2, pp. 282–304, and also appears in Nozick's *Socratic Puzzles* (Harvard University Press, 1997), pp. 249–264.

worthy of attention." He points this out partly because Rand "has been given a largely vituperative and abusive hearing" (222, n. 1). I discuss Harry Binswanger's *The Biological Basis of Teleological Concepts* (1976)[274] at some length in the main text. Although this book often is cited in passing by Objectivist scholars, it gets surprisingly little attention among either defenders or critics of Rand's moral theory.

"**Harry Binswanger's 1977 Letter to Robert Nozick**"[275] replies to Nozick's 1971 article; unfortunately, the letter was not published until 2016. Binswanger criticizes Nozick for approaching Rand's philosophy from the perspective of "contemporary analytic philosophy." "Science-fictional counterexamples, borderline cases, and the analytic-synthetic dichotomy can buzz-saw through any positive position," Binswanger writes; no position can offer a "knock-down deductive argument" by such standards. But Binswanger dismisses too much—Rand herself uses the science-fiction example of the immortal robot, and she addresses borderline cases of emergencies. Binswanger's remarks are notable for their endorsement of the views that life in terms of survival is the ultimate end, that moral principles function as Rand describes, and that the choice to live is premoral. That the Ayn Rand Society of the American Philosophical Association's Eastern Division published the letter in 2016, via its *Check Your Premises* blog, is itself a sign of Rand's continued influence.

Douglas Den Uyl and Douglas Rasmussen also reply to Nozick in "**Nozick on the Randian Argument**" (1978).[276] They argue that "Nozick's criticisms of Rand fail completely" (233). Although they

---

274   Harry Binswanger, *The Biological Basis of Teleological Concepts* (Los Angeles, CA: Ayn Rand Institute Press, 1990). The original copyright is 1976.

275   Harry Binswanger, "Harry Binswanger's 1977 Letter to Robert Nozick," *Check Your Premises*, January 31, 2016, http://www.checkyourpremises.org/harry-binswangers -1977-letter-to-robert-nozick/. Binswanger dated his letter August 25, 1977.

276   Douglas Den Uyl and Douglas Rasmussen, "Nozick on the Randian Argument," in *Reading Nozick*, ed. Jeffrey Paul (Totowa, NJ: Rowman and Littlefield, 1981), pp. 232–269. This essay originally was published in the *Personalist*, Spring 1978, vol. 59, no. 2, pp. 184–205.

successfully argue that Nozick often misses Rand's point, they in turn sometimes miss the force of Nozick's criticisms, as with his remarks about the immortal robot and about parasitic egoism.

In **Understanding Objectivism** (1983),[277] originally a set of lectures, Leonard Peikoff aims to help students of Rand's philosophy remain oriented to reality and to avoid rationalism, the error of using "concepts detached from reality" (54). The work is helpfully seen as a companion to Peikoff's later and more formal and systematic *Objectivism: the Philosophy of Ayn Rand.*

The first important book-length treatment of Rand's philosophy is *The Philosophic Thought of Ayn Rand* (1984),[278] edited by Douglas Den Uyl and Douglas Rasmussen. Here I mention the essays in the book most related to Rand's moral theory.

In "Life, Teleology, and Eudaimonia in the Ethics of Ayn Rand" (63–80), Den Uyl and Rasmussen wonder whether and in what respect Rand's ethics can properly be called survivalist; they are unclear in their answer (at least I think they're unclear). Jack Wheeler offers "Rand and Aristotle: A Comparison of Objectivist and Aristotelian Ethics" (81–101).

The best essay in the set, in my view, is J. Charles King's "Life and the Theory of Value" (102–121).[279] King points out that a (hypothetical) immortal being still could have "a whole range of the interests or desires of ordinary human life" (109). He writes, "What a being must have to have values is . . . the capacity for desire or preference or interest or caring" (110). King then argues that survival often is a means to other values and not just the end goal of values

---

277 Leonard Peikoff, *Understanding Objectivism*, ed. Michael S. Berliner (New York: New American Library, 2012). The book is based on a set of lectures that Peikoff delivered in 1983 and that were "offered on tape to audiences in more than a hundred cities" starting in 1984 (see p. vii).

278 Douglas J. Den Uyl and Douglas B. Rasmussen, ed., *The Philosophic Thought of Ayn Rand* (University of Illinois Press, 1984).

279 King, a philosophy professor before he took a job with Liberty Fund (see p. 229), seems to have gone on to become an Anglican priest in 2002; see https://st-edward-the-confessor.com/the-very-reverend-j-charles-king-dean-and-rector/ (accessed May 16, 2018).

(111). He also writes that, on Rand's premises, "I can see no reason why each of us must regard the other as an end in himself or herself" (119).[280]

In "The Fundamental Moral Elements of Rand's Theory of Rights" (122–161), Eric Mack wonders whether Rand's ethics truly can be said to be concerned with life in terms of survival as the ultimate end. Mack points out (among other things) that people in welfare states such as Sweden have long life expectancies, which is hard to explain if Rand is right that parasitism always harms survival (139). Mack argues that our "desires and interests" can be unified under a broader "life and happiness" standard (147). In his last few pages, Mack discusses the problem for Rand of providing an egoistic justification of rights-respecting behavior.

In "Selfishness and the Unintended Consequences of Intended Action" (183–205), Antony Flew argues that Adam Smith largely supports Rand's case for capitalism. Yet Flew largely fails to engage Rand's main positions and best arguments. For example, he offers the example of two people competing for a job to counter Rand's claims that there are no fundamental conflicts of interest among rational people (189), yet Rand easily can handle such cases.

In **"Why Should One Act on Principle?"** (1988),[281] originally a talk, Leonard Peikoff discusses how people can handle the complexity of life by forming concepts and rational principles. "If moral principles are to function successfully in human life . . . they must be accepted as absolutes . . . ; you cannot compromise them," Peikoff says (243). Unfortunately, here Peikoff does not explain his idea of contextual absolutes, meaning that principles apply in certain

---

280   For a reply to King, see Paul St. F. Blair, "The Randian Argument Reconsidered: A Reply to Charles King," *Reason Papers*, Spring 1985, no. 10, pp. 91–100, https://reasonpapers.com/pdf/10/rp_10_7.pdf.

281   Leonard Peikoff, "Why Should One Act on Principle?," in *Why Businessmen Need Philosophy*, ed. Debi Ghate and Richard E. Ralston (New York: New American Library, 2011), pp. 233–248. The work is a transcript of a talk that Peikoff delivered in 1988. The Ayn Rand Institute publishes the work online (with different pagination) at https://campus.aynrand.org/works/1988/01/01/why-should-one-act-on-principle.

contexts. Still, the piece is excellent, and Peikoff's take-down of pragmatism is effective (and very funny).

Leonard Peikoff's *Objectivism: The Philosophy of Ayn Rand* (1991)[282] remains the best systematized account of Rand's philosophy. The book is based on Rand's works, Peikoff's lectures as authorized by Rand (see xiv–xv), and countless hours of discussion between Peikoff and Rand. Here I'll mention but one important quote: "[T]he course of action that survival demands is continuous, full-time, all embracing. No action an organism takes is irrelevant to its existence. Every such action is either in accordance with what self-preservation requires or it is not; it is for the entity's life or against it" (215).

Ronald Merrill's *The Ideas of Ayn Rand* (1991),[283] derided by Allan Gotthelf as an "amateurish work by a non-philosopher,"[284] nevertheless raises some good questions about Rand's moral theory. Merrill asks: "Do humans never regard life as a means to an end" (102)? "Do humans never seek any other value for its own sake?" He notes, "Rand's chain of reasoning will not hold unless she can show that, as a matter of metaphysical fact, there is no 'end in itself' other than life" (103). Merrill believes that he has solved the puzzle, but his answer will not do: "Life is an ordered collection of activities, which are means to achieving an end, which is—simply those activities." Merrill tries to rule out certain actions because it would be a "contradiction" to do anything to undermine life given that life is a necessary means to values (104), but of course people sometimes trade off the robustness or longevity of their survival for other values, such as the well-being of their children, and that is no contradiction.

---

282 Leonard Peikoff, *Objectivism: The Philosophy of Ayn Rand* (New York: Dutton, 1991). Peikoff's *Advanced Seminars* on the book, delivered in 1990 and 1991, are available in audio format from the Ayn Rand Institute via http://www.peikoff.com/courses_and _lectures/objectivism-the-philosophy-of-ayn-rand/ (accessed May 30, 2018).

283 Ronald E. Merrill, *The Ideas of Ayn Rand* (La Salle, IL, Open Court, 1991). The book was revised and updated by Marsha Familaro Enright as *Ayn Rand Explained*, part of the Ideas Explained series (Chicago: Open Court, 2013).

284 "Gotthelf Craig Letter," *Check Your Premises*, http://www.checkyourpremises. org/gotthelf-craig-letter/ (accessed August 29, 2018). The letter originally is dated August 12, 1998.

Harry Binswanger's **"Life-Based Teleology and the Foundations of Ethics"** (1992)[285] serves as a condensed version of his 1990 (1976) book. He makes now-familiar arguments such that "in relation to its survival-needs, the vegetative actions of an organism have an inherent value-significance: they aid or hinder the organism's struggle to survive." He summarizes: "[E]thics is teleological, not deontological, and . . . survival needs are the necessary basis of teleology (of the concept of 'value')." Binswanger recapitulates Rand's position: "If values depend on having something at stake in the action, the question arises: what is the fundamental thing an entity can have at stake in its actions? . . . Rand answers: the entity's existence. To benefit an entity means to preserve it; for it to be harmed, to suffer a loss, means to threaten its existence." Although the basic alternative is to live or to die, Binswanger argues, a person can adopt "an inconsistent mixture of life-enhancing and life-defeating actions."

In **"Post-Randian Aristotelianism"** (1992),[286] David Kelley pushes back against the suggestion of Douglas Rasmussen and Douglas Den Uyl that flourishing is something district from robust, long-term survival.[287] Kelley emphasizes, "In Ayn Rand's approach, every value and every virtue that goes to make up a good life must be shown to have a bearing on survival; in one way or another, it must enhance the prospects for self-preservation" (58).

Some background: Kelley founded the Institute for Objectivist Studies in 1990 as an alternative to the Peikoff-associated Ayn Rand Institute. Kelley's organization became the Objectivist Center in 1999 and the Atlas Society in 2006. The debate between Kelley and

---

285   Harry Binswanger, "Life-Based Teleology and the Foundations of Ethics," *Monist*, January 1992, vol. 75, no. 1. (The digital version that I accessed does not show page numbers.)

286   David Kelley, "Post-Randian Aristotelianism," *Liberty*, July 1992, vol. 5, no. 6, http://www.libertyunbound.com/sites/files/printarchive/Liberty_Magazine_July_1992.pdf, pp. 54–55, 57–59.

287   See Douglas B. Rasmussen and Douglas J. Den Uyl, *Liberty and Nature: An Aristotelian Defense of Liberal Order* (La Salle, IL, Open Court, 1991).

Peikoff is captured largely in Kelley's *The Contested Legacy of Ayn Rand* and in Peikoff's "Fact and Value."[288]

In **"Survive or Flourish? A Reconciliation"** (1994),[289] Robert Bidinotto, a writer once associated with David Kelley's organization, argues that "self-preservation" entails preserving the values that make a person's life "worth living." Rand would agree in the abstract, but only insofar as what makes life worth living ties back to survival.

In **Ayn Rand: *The Russian Radical*** (1995),[290] Chris Matthew Sciabarra argues that Rand was strongly influenced by Russian dialectical thinking. Gregory Salmieri, on the other hand, argues that Sciabarra overemphasizes the impact of Russian intellectuals on Rand's thought.[291] Sciabarra suggests that "the 'survivalist' interpretation of Rand's ethics is fundamentally flawed" because Rand recognizes a "reciprocal connection" between virtue and survival and sees virtues as constituents of life (260). But virtue, for Rand, does have to tie back to survival.

In **Moral Rights & Political Freedom** (1995),[292] Tara Smith devotes a book to developing Rand's theory of rights. "[R]ecognition

---

288   David Kelley, *The Contested Legacy of Ayn Rand: Truth and Toleration in Objectivism*, second revised edition (Poughkeepsie, NY: Objectivist Center, 2000), originally published in 1990 as *Truth and Toleration*, https://atlassociety.org/sites /default/files/The_Contested_Legacy_of_Ayn_Rand.pdf (Kelley distributed his paper prior to formally publishing it); Leonard Peikoff, "Fact and Value," originally published by *Intellectual Activist*, May 18, 1989, vol. 5, no. 1, and republished by the Ayn Rand Institute at https://ari.aynrand.org/issues/culture-and-society /religion-and-morality/Fact-and-Value.

289   Robert Bidinotto, "Survive or Flourish? A Reconciliation," April 19, 2016, http://bidinotto.blogspot.com/p/archives.html; originally published by *Full Context* in February and April, 1994.

290   Chris Matthew Sciabarra, *Ayn Rand: The Russian Radical* (Pennsylvania State University Press, 1995). Penn State published the second edition of the work in 2013. Sciabarra summarizes differences between the editions in "Russian Radical 2.0: 1995 vs. 2013: What's Different," August 14, 2013, http://www.nyu.edu /projects/sciabarra/notablog/archives/001853.html.

291   Gregory Salmieri, "The Objectivist Epistemology," in *A Companion to Ayn Rand*, pp. 313–314, n. 104.

292   Tara Smith, *Moral Rights & Political Freedom* (Lanham, MD: Rowman & Littlefield, 1995).

of individual rights depends on the belief that it is morally proper for individuals to act to promote their own interest," she writes, following Rand (66). Smith addresses (among many other topics) the matter of welfare "rights" (194–195, 199–206). Unfortunately, Smith punts on the important question of "how a person originally acquires property" (189).

In **"Why I Am Not an Objectivist"** (1996),[293] Michael Huemer argues that egoism entails treating people instrumentally, as "means to promoting your own" life. "Egoism is inconsistent with the idea that individuals are ends in themselves," Huemer writes. Rand's egoist can have a genuine interest in the well-being of others and so treat them as ends in themselves, but I agree that egoists do not always pay sufficient attention to the interests of others. Huemer agrees with G. E. Moore that egoism is inherently contradictory because it holds that "each man's happiness is the sole good—that a number of different things are each of them the only good thing there is—an absolute contradiction!"[294] But the egoist holds that his own good is the only ultimate good thing that there is for him, not the only good thing in some transcendent sense.

In his lectures **"Objectivism Through Induction"** (1997),[295] Leonard Peikoff argues that "self-sustaining activities are automatically built into living organisms," but egoism is a matter of choice (third lecture). He says that a person just beginning to understand ethics will not grasp Rand's metaethical arguments about value and life, but that such a person can grasp a "unique common denominator uniting all values and constituting the standard by which they're defined." To reach egoism, a person needs to grasp that individuals achieve their

---

293   Michael Huemer, "Why I Am Not an Objectivist," http://www.owl232.net /rand.htm (accessed at different times in 2017 and 2018). Huemer reports that he originally posted the essay to Usenet in 1996.

294   See G. E. Moore, *Principia Ethica* (Cambridge University Press, 1965), sec. 59, p. 99.

295   Peikoff's *Objectivism through Induction* is available in audio format via the Ayn Rand Institute at https://campus.aynrand.org/campus-courses/objectivism -through-induction and for sale at https://estore.aynrand.org/p/107/objectivism -through-induction-mp3-download (accessed May 29, 2018).

values, Peikoff argues; the view that God or society creates values will lead to a contrary conclusion. A nascent standard of value, Peikoff says, is something like "a full, rich, happy life," "a successful, fulfilled life," "life and happiness," or "life plus the enjoyment of life." Peikoff also discusses the evil of initiating force, the objectivity of values, and other topics.

In **"What's Wrong with Libertarianism"** (1997),[296] Jeffrey Friedman makes various criticisms of Rand's political views in the context of a broader discussion of libertarianism (a camp in which Friedman places Rand). "Every legal system throws a net of coercion over the entire society it covers," Friedman argues (428), so the libertarian presumption of property rights rooted in Lockean acquisition is arbitrary. Rand would reply (and I would agree) that there is nothing arbitrary about tying property rights to productive achievements, however difficult it may be to properly recognize specific property claims. Friedman thinks that Rand's central claim regarding rights is that people "think and act individually" (437), but that is only an aspect of Rand's case. And Rand's individualism hardly precludes learning from others and acting in groups, as Friedman suggests it does. Friedman argues that libertarians typically offer inadequate reasons to reject the view that "government interventions" might "sometimes be better at meeting human needs than laissez faire" (438). I agree that Rand's case for laissez faire is relatively weak and undeveloped. Friedman argues that, if Rand succeeded in showing that rights derive "from the nature of man" (450), then her claims about the destructive force of intervention— the sort of destruction central to the plot of *Atlas Shrugged*—would be irrelevant in terms of evaluating proper policy. If rights trump all, then consequences don't matter. But, I think Rand would reply, what is bad for individuals is bad for groups of individuals. The question is whether (initiated) force is always bad for individuals and, therefore, for a society of individuals. I think that Friedman is largely right to say

---

296   Jeffrey Friedman, "What's Wrong with Libertarianism?," *Critical Review*, Summer 1997, vol. 11, no. 3, pp. 407–467. A disclosure: Years ago I attended a conference led by Friedman and funded by Friedman's supporters.

that Rand psychologizes the advocates and agents of welfare statism (451), seeing herself as a participant "in a Manichean struggle against unscrupulous wrongdoers with impure motives" (452). I think the motives that Rand discusses sometimes but not always pertain. Friedman, who has been influential among libertarians over the past couple of decades, calls for a research program into the consequences of politics, focusing on such phenomena as mass public ignorance. Eric Mack critiques Rand's theory of rights in his **"On the Fit between Egoism and Rights"** (1998).[297] Mack advocates (what he calls) a coordinate view of rights, by which "egoism is not the root of rights," but rather "the doctrine of egoism and the doctrine of rights are complementary principles within an ethic" (5). Mack argues that egoism simply cannot explain rights as treating others as ends in themselves (6–9). I agree that egoism cannot always do so, even though Rand has a much richer conception of egoistic interests and of moral principles than what Mack recognizes. Mack holds that people being ends in themselves is "more fundamental than either the doctrine of egoism or the doctrine of rights" (12). Mack argues that self-interest "will be rendered nugatory" without "moral restrictions against interferences with the exercise of" self-interest (16), but Rand would recognize that argument as thoroughly egoistic. Beyond that, Mack offers few hints as to the nature and justification of the "more fundamental" moral obligations.

In a condescending article that basically fails to grapple with Rand's ideas, Jan Narveson, in **"Ayn Rand as Moral & Political Philosopher"** (1998),[298] misleadingly summarizes Rand's view as "life is necessarily an end in itself." But he makes some of the obvious criticisms, such that Rand's theory has trouble with rational suicide (96).

---

297   Eric Mack, "On the Fit between Egoism and Rights," *Reason Papers*, Fall 1998, no. 23, https://reasonpapers.com/pdf/23/rp_23_1.pdf, pp. 3–21.

298   Jan Narveson, "Ayn Rand as Moral & Political Philosopher," *Reason Papers*, Fall 1998, no. 23, https://reasonpapers.com/pdf/23/rp_23_12.pdf, pp. 96–100. The same issue includes several other articles about Rand; see https://reasonpapers.com/archives/ (accessed May 22, 2018).

In their "working draft" of *The Logical Structure of Objectivism* (1999), available online via the Atlas Society,[299] William Thomas and David Kelley present Rand's philosophy as an integrated system of axioms, induced premises, and deduced conclusions. In their preface, they write that "this 'beta' version is not for . . . scholarly citation." I mention it here anyway for sake of completeness, with the authors' caveat, given that the work is available to the public.

In his **"Critique of 'The Objectivist Ethics'"** (2000),[300] Michael Huemer makes some powerful criticisms (even though he sometimes misses the subtlety of Rand's arguments). For example, he points out that people often pursue values for reasons other than to prolong their lives, that the actions of living things generally "result in the reproduction of their genes" and not always their personal survival, and that parasites in certain contexts seem to do quite well for themselves.

In *On Ayn Rand* (2000),[301] Allan Gotthelf offers a brief introduction to Rand's life and works. Gotthelf reminds us that, for Rand, life is the "fundamental alternative that every value-pursuer faces, to which every value makes a difference. . . . Life is thus the end for which values exist" (80–81).

In **"Reason and Value: Aristotle versus Rand"** (2000),[302] Roderick Long argues that Rand's premoral choice to live is reminiscent of Hume's subjectivism. Long also argues that Rand's politics is essentially Hobbesian: "According to the Hobbesian approach, justice (that is, respect for the rights of others) is valuable as an instrumental means to one's own well-being" (35). Long suggests that Rand wavers between the goals of "bare survival" and flourishing (39). Rand, of course, would recognize no such split; she

---

299   William Thomas and David Kelley, *The Logical Structure of Objectivism* (Atlas Society, 1999), https://atlassociety.org/sites/default/files/LSO%20Binder.pdf.

300   Michael Huemer, "Critique of 'The Objectivist Ethics,'" http://www.owl232 .net/rand5.htm (accessed at different times in 2017 and 2018). Huemer reports that the essay was first published in 2000 and edited as recently as 2014.

301   Allan Gotthelf, *On Ayn Rand* (Belmont, CA: Wadsworth, 2000).

302   Roderick T. Long, "Reason and Value: Aristotle versus Rand," in *Objectivist Studies* 3, ed. William Thomas (Poughkeepsie, NY: Objectivist Center, 2000), https://atlassociety.org/sites/default/files/Reason_Value.pdf, pp. 5–64.

is after robust, long-term survival, which (she holds) requires virtue and results in happiness. Long also makes some common objections such that Rand's immortal robot might still have values (41) and that suicide does not square with Rand's metaethics (44–45).

In his reply to Long in the same publication, "Flourishing and Survival in Ayn Rand: A Reply to Roderick Long" (85–100), Eyal Mozes argues that flourishing for Rand must be understood in the context of survival as the ultimate end. Mozes argues that people normally should respect the rights of others because of the "psychological role" of principles (95). By committing to principles, we preclude cheating on them lest we do damage to our character and psyche.[303] Mozes has an interesting take on self-risking behavior for the sake of loved ones (as discussed in the main text).

In his rebuttal, "Foundations and Flourishing: A Reply to Miller and Mozes" (101–122), Long suggests that Mozes's position is not coherent; it amounts to "offering egoistic reasons for renouncing egoism" (109). As Long writes, the position "seems to make self-interest a mere ladder that one kicks away once one has climbed up it" (111). (Long also addresses comments by Fred D. Miller, Jr.)

The publication of Tara Smith's *Viable Values: A Study of Life as the Root and Reward of Morality* (2000)[304] marks an important milestone in the advance of Rand's ideas in the academy. To my mind, the book remains the single best defense of Rand's ethics. Smith quickly makes clear that she follows Leonard Peikoff in (what I think of as) the standard interpretation of Rand's moral theory: "It is only in relation to the goal of living that we can distinguish objects as good or bad, Rand argues. All genuine values are such by virtue to their contribution to this end" (2). Incidentally, Smith also sits on the board

---

303   See also Mozes's discussion of principles in his "Deriving Rights from Egoism: Machan vs. Rand," *Reason Papers*, Summer 1992, no. 17, https://reasonpapers.com /pdf/17/rp_17_6.pdf, pp. 87–93.

304   Tara Smith, *Viable Values* (Lanham, MD: Rowman & Littlefield, 2000). Reviews of the work include Mark LeBar, *Journal of Value Inquiry*, December 2001, vol. 35, no. 4, pp. 575–579; and Irfan Khawaja, *Reason Papers*, Summer 2003, vol. 26, https://reasonpapers.com/pdf/26/rp_26_5.pdf, pp. 63–88.

of the Ayn Rand Institute,[305] and she holds the BB&T Chair for the Study of Objectivism at the University of Texas at Austin.[306]

Louis Pojman, in **"Egoism and Altruism: A Critique of Ayn Rand"** (2000),[307] criticizes Rand's moral theory without bothering to mention what Rand's main arguments are. Not surprisingly, then, he distorts Rand's views, as by claiming that Rand thinks we "have a moral duty" to perfect our abilities and to attain happiness (483). Pojman's sloppy treatment of the concepts of self-interest and of altruism leaves his criticisms mostly unconnected to Rand's positions. Pojman presumes that a "moral conflict of interests" is inevitable between people (484), but he does not mention Rand's detailed arguments to the contrary. Pojman does offer an interesting account of reciprocal altruism (486), which has nothing to do with what Rand means by altruism but which opens important questions about free riding and mutual aid.

In his lecture **"Reason and Selfishness"** (2001),[308] Darryl Wright contrasts egoism and altruism, arguing that "selfishness is inherent in the commitment to guide one's actions by reason."

In **"Is Virtue Only a Means to Happiness?"** (2001),[309] Neera Badhwar argues that neither happiness nor virtue is as tightly tied to

---

305 See https://ari.aynrand.org/experts/tara-smith (accessed May 17, 2018).

306 Smith's university was awarded $2 million in 2008 for Smith's work on Rand; see "BB&T Donates $2 Million for Ayn Rand Research at The University of Texas at Austin," *UT News*, March 20, 2008, https://news.utexas.edu/2008/03/20/lib_arts_ayn _rand. See also "BB&T Chair for the Study of Objectivism," University of Texas at Austin, https://liberalarts.utexas.edu/bbtobjectivism/index.php (accessed May 17, 2018).

307 Louis P. Pojman, "Egoism and Altruism: A Critique of Ayn Rand," in *Philosophy: The Quest for Truth*, ninth edition (New York: Oxford University Press, 2014), pp. 482–487. The essay is copyright 2000 (see p. 483).

308 Wright's lecture, *Reason and Selfishness*, is available in audio format via the Ayn Rand Institute at https://estore.aynrand.org/p/447/reason-and-selfishness-mp3 -download (accessed May 30, 2018).

309 Neera K. Badhwar, "Is Virtue Only a Means to Happiness?," in *Objectivist Studies* 4, ed. William Thomas (Poughkeepsie, NY: Objectivist Center, 2001), pp. 5–36. For an earlier version of this work, see Badhwar's "Is Virtue Only a Means to Happiness? An Analysis of Virtue and Happiness in Ayn Rand's Writings," *Reason Papers*, Fall 1999, no. 24, https://reasonpapers.com/pdf/24/rp_24_2.pdf, pp. 27–44.

survival as Rand thinks, and I agree. But Badhwar does not sufficiently account for Rand's subtle arguments that such things even as literature and philosophy contribute to survival, that happiness results from the achievement of rational values, and that virtue both supports and helps constitute a person's life. In the same work, David Kelley (61–71) and Badhwar (73–90) continue the discussion. In her reply ("Living Long and Living Well: Reflections on Survival, Happiness, and Virtue"), Badhwar recounts some good reasons to doubt Rand's survivalist metaethics. People generally care about quality of life even at the cost of length of life (74–75), organisms generally advance the continuation of their genes even over their own survival (76), and we have some values that are not basically about survival (76). Some of our values are "independent of . . . our survival needs," and "loving life means knowing what makes life worth living," she writes (76–77).

In **"Is Benevolent Egoism Coherent?"** (2002),[310] Huemer restates some of the criticisms of his earlier works. He also responds in detail to Lester Hunt's idea that, for the egoist, "the good of others might literally be part of my own good" (273, Huemer's terms).[311] Hunt's claim accounts only (or at least most strongly) for the good of one's friends, not for strangers, Huemer argues (274). And it seems not to be able to explain an absolute prohibition against violating rights—would not the consistent egoist violate rights if the rewards were sufficiently great (275–276)?

In **"Rand on Obligation and Value"** (2002),[312] Douglas Rasmussen pushes back against the standard Objectivist view that "ethics depends upon a 'premoral' choice to live" (69). That view, Rasmussen argues, implies that, because "moral obligation is hypothetical" (depending on the choice to live), "one can . . . choose to opt out of the 'moral game'" (71). The standard view, he

---

310   Michael Huemer, "Is Benevolent Egoism Coherent?," *Journal of Ayn Rand Studies*, Spring 2002, vol. 3, no. 2, pp. 259–288.

311   See Hunt's "Flourishing Egoism," *Social Philosophy and Policy*, Winter 1999, vol. 16, no. 1, pp. 72–95, also available at http://philosophy.wisc.edu/hunt /webtext.15.htm.

312   Douglas B. Rasmussen, "Rand on Obligation and Value," *Journal of Ayn Rand Studies*, Fall 2002, vol. 4, no. 1, pp. 69–86. Rasmussen adapted a 1990 talk for this paper.

continues, implies that "the choice to live is ultimately optional or arbitrary. There is no reason why one should choose to live or choose not to live" (73).

In *Loving Life: The Morality of Self-Interest and the Facts that Support It* (2002),[313] Craig Biddle offers a popular account of Rand's ethics. Biddle writes, "If [a person] chooses to continue living, reality . . . dictates what he ought to do: He ought to pursue the values necessary to sustain and further his life" (47). But this deals inadequately with whether people should sometimes pursue values that do not further their survival and should in some circumstances risk or surrender their lives.

In his lecture **"Aristotle as Ethicist"** (2003),[314] Gregory Salmieri discusses Aristotle's ethics and compares and contrasts the views of Aristotle and Rand. Salmieri casts Rand as Aristotle's philosophic "heiress."

Eric Mack, in **"Problematic Arguments in Randian Ethics"** (2003),[315] writes that "line-by-line many of Rand's ethical arguments are just awful" (4) and that Rand displays "enormous ignorance" of thinkers and ideas she dismisses (6). Despite such problems, Mack holds, Rand makes an "important contribution to moral thought" with her theory that "the phenomenon of valuing exists for the sake of the life of the valuing being" (7). But, he writes, "In human beings, it is obvious that an individual's ultimate good or well-being does not consist entirely in her survival" (12). Moreover, Mack argues, Rand equivocates between claiming that virtues are "part of man's ultimate good" and claiming that "virtues are the causally required means for the attainment of survival" (13). This apparent equivocation Mack calls the Shuffle. Although something can be both a means to and a constituent of life, I do think that Rand and her supporters

313   Craig Biddle, *Loving Life: The Morality of Self-Interest and the Facts that Support It* (Richmond, VA: Glen Allen Press, 2002).

314   Salmieri's *Aristotle as Ethicist* is available in audio format via the Ayn Rand Institute at https://estore.aynrand.org/p/436/aristotle-as-ethicist-mp3-download (accessed May 30, 2018).

315   Eric Mack, "Problematic Arguments in Randian Ethics," *Journal of Ayn Rand Studies*, Fall 2003, vol. 5, no. 1, pp. 1–66.

sometimes shuffle in that they embrace virtues that do not in fact always best support survival. Mack points out various other problems with Rand's account, including the implausibility of the claim that parasitism never can advance a person's survival (19–25, 42).

In his **"Second Letter to a Young Objectivist: Human Sociality"** (2004),[316] Will Wilkinson argues that Objectivism fails to recognize "the essentially social nature of human beings." This is not entirely fair; consider how social people are in Galt's Gulch. Still, Wilkinson has a point: "Rand's failure to understand and integrate the evidence of biology and anthropology into her picture of human nature leads to a distorted picture of our psychological constitution." In his follow-up "Third Letter" (2005),[317] Wilkinson argues that a wealthy market order with a "stable liberal welfare state" allows for "benign predation." Wilkinson goes off track at various points, as by confusing the interdependence of our division-of-labor economy with the sort of dependence that Rand (rightly) finds troublesome and by wrongly accusing Rand of a sort of destructive hyper-rationalism. (Rand probably rationalized some things in her personal life, such as her affair.) Wilkinson also brings up the familiar point that, contra Rand, living things tend to maximize the furtherance of their genes, not their personal survival.

In his lecture, **"Ayn Rand and the History of Ethics"** (2005),[318] Darryl Wright discusses the possibility of evaluating ends, rather than only means, by reason. In this context, Wright discusses the philosophic views of Hume, Moore, and Aristotle as well as those of Rand.

---

316   Will Wilkinson, "Second Letter to a Young Objectivist: Human Sociality," *Fly Bottle*, August 17, 2004, http://www.willwilkinson.net/flybottle/2004/08/17/second-letter-to-a-young-objectivist-human-sociality/.

317   Will Wilkinson, "Third Letter to a Young Objectivist: Ethics," *Fly Bottle*, March 2, 2005, http://www.willwilkinson.net/flybottle/2005/03/02/third-letter-to-a-young-objectivist-ethics/.

318   Wright's *Ayn Rand and the History of Ethics* is available in audio format via the Ayn Rand Institute at https://estore.aynrand.org/p/448/ayn-rand-and-the-history-of-ethics-mp3-download (accessed May 29, 2018).

***Essays on Ayn Rand's* Anthem** (2005)[319] contains a couple of essays worth mentioning here. (Generally the volumes on Rand's major novels, all edited by Robert Mayhew, are superb.) In "Needs of the *Psyche* in Ayn Rand's Early Ethical Thought" (190–224), Darryl Wright seeks to show the continuity between Rand's early comments about living a rich and meaningful life and Rand's mature metaethical views. Similarly, in "Prometheus' Discovery: Individualism and the Meaning of the Concept 'I' in *Anthem*" (255–284), Gregory Salmieri argues that the "joyous life standard" that *Anthem*'s Prometheus eventually advances (277) leads to Rand's mature life-based metaethics.

The **Spring 2006** *Journal of Ayn Rand Studies* (vol. 7, no. 2) features a lengthy discussion about Rand's ethics.

Tibor R. Machan ("Rand and Choice," 257–273) replies to Eric Mack's 2003 charge that the Objectivist choice to live is (contra the name of the philosophy) subjectivist. Machan says that the choice to live is not a mere affection but "a fundamental and first act of will or decision to live" (260), but I don't think that he effectively rebuts Mack's criticism. To reject egoistic parasitism, Machan offers a consistency argument: "[I]t is irrational . . . to believe (or act as if one believed) both that other human beings lack human rights while one has them" (264). But this smacks of Kantianism.

Frank Bubb ("Did Ayn Rand Do the Shuffle?," 275–286) implausibly argues that, when Rand claims that looters "may achieve their goals for the range of a moment, at the price of destruction" (285, from TOE 24), she is implying that her conclusion holds "if everyone did that" (285).

Eric Mack ("More Problematic Arguments in Randian Ethics," 287–307) sensibly argues that values are about more than (ultimately) survival (294), but he offers a strange functionalist account for why people should pursue values. Mack also continues to argue that egoism cannot adequately account for the wrongness of violating others' rights (304–305).

---

319   Robert Mayhew, ed., *Essays on Ayn Rand's* Anthem (Lanham, MD: Lexington Books, 2005).

Douglas B. Rasmussen ("Regarding Choice and the Foundation of Morality: Reflections on Rand's Ethics," 309–328) continues to argue that, if the basic choice to live is premoral, a failure to make that choice cannot be blameworthy (310). Rasmussen asserts that Rand "never says or implies that a premoral choice to live is necessary for moral obligations to exist" (319), but I think such is the logic of her position in "Causality Versus Duty."

In *Ayn Rand's Normative Ethics: The Virtuous Egoist* (2006),[320] Tara Smith devotes a chapter to each of the virtues that Rand emphasizes: rationality, honesty, independence, justice, integrity, productiveness, and pride. Even those who reject Rand's metaethics can fruitfully read the book for its insights into virtuous living. The first two chapters, Smith's introduction and abbreviated presentation of Rand's egoism, also serve as an excellent introduction to Rand's ethical thought. Without a survival-based standard, Smith writes, "we would have no basis for pronouncing what a person should value. Values would collapse into a matter of mere taste" (22). Smith helpfully describes flourishing, within the Objectivist framework, as "living in such a manner that one is fit to continue to live, long term" (28).

In *Objectivism in One Lesson* (2008),[321] Andrew Bernstein offers a popular introduction to Rand's thought that is filled with examples from history and from Rand's fiction. Bernstein's book fits with (what I regard as) the standard interpretation of Rand's ethics, which is not

---

320   Tara Smith, *Ayn Rand's Normative Ethics: The Virtuous Egoist* (New York: Cambridge University Press, 2006). Reviews of the book include Helen Cullyer, *Notre Dame Philosophical Reviews*, November 12, 2006, https://ndpr.nd.edu/news /ayn-rand-s-normative-ethics-the-virtuous-egoist/; Stephen R. C. Hicks, *Philosophy in Review*, October 2007, vol. 27, no. 5, pp. 377–379; Diana Brickell (Hsieh), *Objective Standard*, Spring 2007, vol. 2, no. 1, https://www.theobjectivestandard. com/issues/2007-spring/egoism-explained/; and Carrie-Ann Biondi, *Reason Papers*, Fall 2008, no. 30, https://reasonpapers.com/pdf/30/rp_30_5.pdf, pp. 91–105. For a debate on the book, see the essays in *Reason Papers*, July 2013, vol. 35, no. 1, by Eyal Mozes, https://reasonpapers.com/pdf/351/rp_351_10.pdf, pp. 124–131; and Carrie-Ann Biondi and Irfan Khawaja, https://reasonpapers.com/pdf/351 /rp_351_11.pdf, pp. 132–140.

321   Andrew Bernstein, *Objectivism in One Lesson* (Lanham, MD: Hamilton Books, 2008).

surprising given that the book's "primary editor" is Onkar Ghate of the Ayn Rand Institute (see the acknowledgements). Bernstein writes, "[V]alues exist only to promote life. . . . [I]f X does not promote life, it is definitively eliminated from the realm of values" (68). Presumably he means something like "proper values" here.

In **"Evaluative Concepts and Objective Values: Rand on Moral Objectivity"** (2008),[322] following a lengthy discussion of Rand's ideas about objectivity, Darryl Wright turns to the matter of psychological survival in Rand's theory. Unlike animals, Wright explains, people need to actively maintain their psychological "capacity to value." Humans uniquely need what Wright calls "conceptual pleasure," "the need to have one's life mean something or . . . the need for it to be worth living" (174). This line of thought is interesting (and in line with my own views), but Wright is not successful, I think, in tying his discussion of psychological motivation to Rand's survivalist metaethics (179–180).

In **"Ayn Rand's Ethics: From *The Fountainhead* to *Atlas Shrugged*"** (2009),[323] Darryl Wright offers a fascinating and illuminating account of Rand's development of her moral theory between the writing of her two most influential novels. Wright points out that already in *The Fountainhead* we find the view that "the requirements of life are the proper standard for moral evaluation" (259). The following seems to be the clearest statement from the novel supporting Wright's interpretation: "The code of the creator . . .

---

322 Darryl F. Wright, "Evaluative Concepts and Objective Values: Rand on Moral Objectivity," in *Objectivism, Subjectivism, and Relativism in Ethics*, ed. Ellen Frankel Paul, Fred D. Miller, Jr., and Jeffrey Paul (Cambridge University Press, 2008), pp. 149–181. Tara Smith also has an essay in this volume, "The Importance of the Subject in Objective Morality: Distinguishing Objective from Intrinsic Value," pp. 126–148.

323 Darryl Wright, "Ayn Rand's Ethics: From *The Fountainhead* to *Atlas Shrugged*," in *Essays on Ayn Rand's* Atlas Shrugged, ed. Robert Mayhew (Lanham, MD: Lexington Books, 2009), pp. 253–273.

rests upon the alternative of life or death. [It] is built on the needs of the reasoning mind which allows man to survive."[324]

In 2010, the Cato Institute published a lengthy discussion, titled **"What's Living & Dead in Ayn Rand's Moral & Political Thought,"**[325] by contributors who more or less reject Rand's moral theory and who make familiar criticisms. In "The Winnowing of Ayn Rand,"[326] Roderick Long argues that Rand treats "the individual's ultimate good sometimes as a robust human flourishing that has virtue as a component, and sometimes as mere survival to which virtue is only an external means." Long also argues that the heroes of Rand's novels "evidently value quality of life over mere quantity." In "Why Ayn Rand? Some Alternate Answers,"[327] Michael Huemer argues that individuals being ends in themselves is "directly and obviously contrary to ethical egoism." In "Ayn Rand's Significance: A Reply to Douglas Rasmussen,"[328] Neera Badhwar argues, "Rand's reply [to the is-ought problem] that, if you choose (and, thus, desire) to live, then you ought to be moral, in effect grants Hume's point that 'pure reason' cannot ground ethics." Badhwar also continues to erode Rand's position that survival, happiness, and virtue inherently converge, although Badhwar misses elements of Rand's case.

In **"Choosing Life"** (2010),[329] David Kelley states the problem he seeks to address: "A perennial question in Objectivism is whether

---

324 Ayn Rand, *The Fountainhead*, centennial edition, (New York: Penguin Group, 2005), p. 713.

325 Here I discuss only three essays in the exchange published by *Cato Unbound*; the rest are listed at https://www.cato-unbound.org/issues/january-2010/what s-living-dead-ayn-rands-moral-political-thought (accessed May 4, 2018).

326 Roderick T. Long, "The Winnowing of Ayn Rand," *Cato Unbound*, January 20, 2010, https://www.cato-unbound.org/2010/01/20/roderick-t-long/winnowing-ayn-rand.

327 Michael Huemer, "Why Ayn Rand? Some Alternate Answers," *Cato Unbound*, January 22, 2010, https://www.cato-unbound.org/2010/01/22/michael-huemer /why-ayn-rand-some-alternate-answers.

328 Neera K. Badhwar, "Ayn Rand's Significance: A Reply to Douglas Rasmussen," *Cato Unbound*, January 25, 2010, https://www.cato-unbound.org/2010/01/25 /neera-k-badhwar/ayn-rands-significance-reply-douglas-rasmussen.

329 David Kelley, "Choosing Life," Atlas Society, June 22, 2010, https:// atlassociety.org/commentary/commentary-blog/3705-choosing-life.

(1) life is a value because one chooses to live, or (2) one should choose to live because life is a value." Kelley finds "truth in both" propositions, but I don't think that he succeeds in unifying them. Metaethics aside, Kelley offers some good advice for living a life filled with values.

Metaethics, Egoism, and Virtue: Studies in Ayn Rand's Normative Theory (2011)[330] is the first book produced by the Ayn Rand Society, which is organized under the American Philosophical Association, Eastern Division. Here I mention several essays from the volume.

In "Reasoning about Ends: Life as a Value in Ayn Rand's Ethics" (3–32), Darryl Wright points out that, in Rand's view, and contra Hume, it is possible to rationally "desire something as an end" (5). Wright continues, "Rand sees all of a person's major values as helping to constitute his life" (12, n. 7). Wright offers a typical defense of John Galt threatening to commit suicide to save Dagny Taggart from torture, arguing that "there is an intolerable and unsustainable incompleteness in a life that lacks values" (12, n. 7); I don't think he adequately makes sense of this case in a way that squares with Rand's metaethics. Wright also argues that exploitation "hampers and destroys those on whose support" the exploiter depends; undercuts a person's development of pro-survival skills and "intellectual resources"; and causes "psychological suffering, a sense of helplessness, and a sense that life offers him or her nothing worth living for" (21). Wright concludes with a lengthy discussion of the choice to live (23–32).

In "The Choice to Value" (33–46), Allan Gotthelf replies to Douglas Rasmussen's arguments about the choice to live. (The essay is an updated version of one that Gotthelf offered originally in 1990.) Gotthelf convincingly argues that, for Rand, moral obligation flows from a premoral choice to live. Gotthelf argues that it is not the case

---

330   Allan Gotthelf and James G. Lennox, eds., *Metaethics, Egoism, and Virtue: Studies in Ayn Rand's Normative Theory* (University of Pittsburgh Press, 2011). For a list of the titles in the series, see http://aynrandsociety.org/books (accessed May 2, 2018). Mark LeBar critically evaluates the book for *Reason Papers*, July 2014, vol. 36, no. 1, https://reasonpapers.com/wp-content/uploads/2014/09/rp_361_16.pdf, pp. 175–180.

that "a human being's life is somehow inherently an ultimate value for him, regardless of whether he pursues it or not" (39). Gotthelf argues that the opposite of choosing to live "is simply shutting down," and so Rasmussen's distinction between "choosing not to live" and "not choosing to live" is one without a difference (41). But then Gotthelf would be hard-pressed, I think, to distinguish the cases of a person who simply takes no action and dies (which I would take to be not choosing to live) and a person who, like James Taggart, stays alive for many years in active rebellion to life in Rand's sense. Gotthelf seems to grant my point in an updated note (46, n. 14). In the rest of his essay Gotthelf is concerned to show that the choice to live is not arbitrary or optional.

In "Rational Selves, Friends, and the Social Virtues" (113–125), Helen Cullyer, in evaluating the work of Tara Smith, argues that it is not truly egoistic, at least in Rand's sense, to hold others as valuable in ways that people normally do. But Cullyer's call to think of ourselves "as part of a greater whole" (121) is ambiguous—what is this "whole" and in what sense is the individual a "part of" it?—and unnecessary to explain our valuing of others. Cullyer offers the usual critique that egoists have insufficient reason to respect the rights of others (122). Cullyer also argues that Rand offers insufficient reason to help others. The egoist has little incentive to help those unjustly imprisoned—provided the egoist faces no such risk (123)—and the egoist has little reason to risk his life to help Jews escape Nazis (124). Such "heroic conduct . . . seems very hard to explain as egoistic," Cullyer notes (124). Smith (elsewhere) comes close to granting Cullyer's point when she claims that we cannot assume that all those who rescued Jews were sufficiently egoistic in doing so. Smith also argues (implausibly, I think) that risking one's life to save Jews in some cases might have been egoistic in Rand's sense.[331] In the same

---

331 Tara Smith, *Ayn Rand's Normative Ethics* (New York: Cambridge University Press, 2006), pp. 254–255. Cullyer mentions these pages. Smith in turn mentions an essay by Neera K. Badhwar that argues that people who saved Jews did not typically act egoistically and that that was a good thing; see Badhwar's "Altruism Versus Self-Interest: Sometimes a False Dichotomy," *Social Philosophy and Policy*, Winter 1993, vol. 10, no. 1, pp. 90–117.

volume (in "Egoistic Relations with Others," 126–130), Smith ably (if briefly) responds to Cullyer.

In **"Is Life the Ultimate Value? A Reassessment of Ayn Rand's Ethics"** (2012),[332] Ole Martin Moen retraces Rand's metaethical arguments, focusing on their epistemological underpinnings. The problem, Moen argues, comes with the choice to live that sets people on the path to pursuing their lives as the ultimate value. After an excellent discussion of various approaches to dealing with the choice to live, Moen offers his own solution: "It is rational for an agent to choose to live if and only if she has reason to believe that life will bring more happiness than unhappiness" (103). But this approach does not fit with Rand's metaethics, and Moen's treatment of happiness as the ultimate value has its own set of serious problems (as Rand would recognize).

In **"Ayn Rand vs. the Pygmies"** (2012),[333] Eric Michael Johnson attempts to show that Rand's selfishness clashes with human evolutionary history. But, by suggesting that a tribesman's attempt to benefit from the efforts of his fellows is somehow comparable to Rand's approach to ethics, Johnson proves only that he fundamentally misunderstands Rand's ideas. Johnson also ignores the very different senses in which Rand and most evolutionary biologists use the term altruism.[334] In important ways Johnson's follow-up misinterprets Rand and quotes early views of hers that her mature writings

---

332 Ole Martin Moen, "Is Life the Ultimate Value? A Reassessment of Ayn Rand's Ethics," *Reason Papers*, October 2012, vol. 34, no. 2, https://reasonpapers.com /pdf/342/rp_342_9.pdf, pp. 84–116. David Kelley replies in "Happiness or Life, or Both: Reply to Ole Martin Moen," *Reason Papers*, Spring 2015, vol. 37, no. 1, https://reasonpapers.com/wp-content/uploads/2015/04/rp_371_6.pdf, pp. 65–79.

333 Eric Michael Johnson, "Ayn Rand vs. the Pygmies," *Slate*, October 3, 2012, http://www.slate.com/articles/health_and_science/human_evolution/2012/10 /groups_and_gossip_drove_the_evolution_of_human_nature.single.html.

334 For more on this point, see Ross England, "Rand's Ethics Withstand Objections from Evolutionary Anthropologists," *Objective Standard*, October 19, 2012, https:// www.theobjectivestandard.com/2012/10/rands-ethics-withstand-objections-from -evolutionary-anthropologists/.

abrogate.[335] Still, Johnson's main point holds: People have more inborn pro-social tendencies than what Rand recognizes. In **"Ayn Rand and Altruism"** (2012),[336] a five part series, George H. Smith argues that Rand's use of the term altruism, which many people find peculiar, jibes with Auguste Comte's original use of it. Smith summarizes, "[H]owever much critics may dismiss Rand's attacks on altruism as unjustified, her treatment of altruism, as discussed and defended by the man who originated the term and who defended altruism in more detail than any other philosopher, before or since, was remarkably on point." Smith points out, "Comte's altruism went far beyond the conventional moral beliefs that we should exercise benevolence and charity toward our fellow human beings. Altruism, for Comte, was the absolute duty of humans to subordinate all personal interests . . . to the interests of others, and ultimately to 'humanity' as a whole."

In **"A Critique of Ayn Rand's Theory of Rights"** (2014),[337] Matt Zwolinski makes some familiar criticisms, such as this one: "The fact that your life is a value to you does not logically entail that I have an obligation to allow you to live it" (5).

Peter Schwartz, long active with the Ayn Rand Institute, offers a popular account of Rand's moral theory with his *In Defense of Selfishness* (2015).[338] "[E]mbracing reason means embracing principles," Schwartz writes. "To use reason," he continues, "is

---

335 Eric Michael Johnson, "Why Ayn Rand Was Wrong about Altruism, Selfishness, and Human Nature," *Evonomics*, September 21, 2015, http://evonomics.com/ayn-rand-was-wrong-about-selfishness-altruism/.

336 George H. Smith, "Ayn Rand and Altruism, Part 1," October 23, 2012, https://www.libertarianism.org/publications/essays/excursions/ayn-rand-altruism-part-1. Parts 2–5 share the same url save for the last digit; they are dated October 30, November 6, November 13, and November 20, 2012.

337 Matt Zwolinski, "A Critique of the Ayn Rand's Theory of Rights," presented to the Ayn Rand Society in 2014, reproduced at *Bleeding Heart Libertarians* at http://bleedingheartlibertarians.com/wp-content/uploads/2014/04/A-Critique-of-Ayn-Rands-Theory-of-Rights.pdf. Zwolinski posts some related comments in his "Ayn Rand's Theory of Rights—A Critique," *Bleeding Heart Libertarians*, April 15, 2014, http://bleedingheartlibertarians.com/2014/04/ayn-rands-theory-of-rights-a-critique/.

338 Peter Schwartz, *In Defense of Selfishness* (New York: Palgrave MacMillan, 2015).

to integrate all the facts into an ever-expanding, unified body of knowledge" (48). "Unlike the man of principle, who takes into account both the short- and long-term effects of his choices, [the unprincipled individual] focuses on nothing but the immediate moment," Schwartz writes (49).

In a pair of hit pieces, starting with (the ironically titled) **"This Is What Happens When You Take Ayn Rand Seriously"** (2016),[339] psychologist and columnist Denise Cummins makes the following bogus claims or insinuations about Rand's conception of self-interest: It is typified by rape (see my note 159), it opposes cooperation and looking "out for each other," it sanctions actions "without regard to the impact . . . on others," it does not allow "[f]airness [to] enter into it," it promotes destructive competition within firms, it is responsible for poverty and government mismanagement in Honduras, and it holds that there is "more evil than good" in voluntary cooperation. Cummins also ignores the meaning of the term altruism as Rand uses it and ignores the role that virtues play in Rand's moral theory. Cummins does correctly note that, in Rand's view, a person normally "has no moral obligation to offer help to those who are suffering." (Cummins channels Bernie Sanders when ineptly explaining the mortgage meltdown, the relative prosperity of nations, the nature of economic inequality, and the engines of the "wheels of commerce," complex topics for another day.) Objectivist scholars Ben Bayer and Greg Salmieri reply to Cummins in some detail.[340] In yet a third piece, Cummins misrepresents what Rand means by the term "tabula rasa" (although

---

339 Denise Cummins, "This Is What Happens when You Take Ayn Rand Seriously," PBS, February 16, 2016, https://www.pbs.org/newshour/economy/column-this-is -what-happens-when-you-take-ayn-rand-seriously; Denise Cummins, "What Ayn Rand Got Wrong about Human Nature," PBS, March 17, 2016, https://www.pbs .org/newshour/economy/column-what-ayn-rand-got-wrong-about-human-nature.

340 Ben Bayer, "Response to Cummins on Rand at PBS," *Check Your Premises*, February 16, 2016, http://www.checkyourpremises.org/2016/02/16/cummins -on-rand-at-npr/; Greg Salmieri, "Another Critic Who Doesn't Care What Rand Thought or Why She Thought It, Only That She's Wrong," *Check Your Premises*, March 23, 2016, http://www.checkyourpremises.org/2016/03/23/cummins-gets -rand-wrong-again-though-less-so-this-time-around/.

she does point out that people have more inborn dispositions than Rand recognizes) and misconstrues Rand's observation that only humans can continually expand their knowledge over generations (she also repeats some of her other material).[341]

A Companion to Ayn Rand (2016)[342] is a remarkable work of scholarship that carefully presents Rand's ideas and comprehensively discusses the scholarly engagement of those ideas.[343] With 521 large-format pages and extensive endnotes, and written by scholars intimately familiar with Rand's works and sympathetic to them, the *Companion* is the definitive guide to Rand's ideas and probably will remain so into the foreseeable future. Here I discuss several of the essays in the volume.

In "The Act of Valuing (and the Objectivity of Values)" (49–72), Gregory Salmieri, following Rand's lead, approaches ethics from the perspective of the valuing individual. Salmieri sees continuity between Rand's early statements about living robustly and her mature metaethics: "By connecting meaning to work and work to survival as he does, Roark strengthens the connection between living (as opposed to merely existing) and living in the biological sense (in which it is opposed to dying). It is by the spiritual activity of living (i.e., of valuing) that human beings literally survive" (60).

In "The Morality of Life" (73–104), Allan Gotthelf and Gregory Salmieri[344] retrace Rand's metaethical arguments from *Atlas Shrugged* and "The Objectivist Ethics" (76–78). The authors rightly dismiss claims that Rand takes as the moral standard "some particular way of life which is not required for survival." Such an interpretation "would entirely undermine Rand's moral philosophy," they point out (78).

---

341 Denise Cummins, "More on What Ayn Rand Got Wrong About Human Nature," *Psychology Today*, March 17, 2016, https://www.psychologytoday.com/us /blog/good-thinking/201603/more-what-ayn-rand-got-wrong-about-human-nature.

342 Allan Gotthelf and Gregory Salmieri, ed., *A Companion to Ayn Rand*, part of the Blackwell Companions to Philosophy series (Chichester, UK: John Wiley & Sons, 2016).

343 Carrie-Ann Biondi reviews the book for *Reason Papers*, Winter 2017, vol. 39, no. 1, https://reasonpapers.com/wp-content/uploads/2017/09/rp_391_9rev.pdf, pp. 124–136.

344 As noted previously, this chapter was written by Gotthelf and "completed by" Salmieri following Gotthelf's death.

Life in Rand's system must be "understood literally, in terms of the alternative between existence and non-existence" (79). Although proper values and virtues are "essential constituents of a successful and happy life," the authors note, they are values and virtues "only because each plays a crucial role in enabling a human being to survive" (81).

In "Egoism and Altruism: Selfishness and Sacrifice" (130–156), Gregory Salmieri follows Rand in describing an "intrinsic good" as "something that is good in virtue solely of facts independent of human consciousness," whereas an "objective good is something that an individual has chosen as a value for himself in accordance with a rational, fact-based standard" (132). Salmieri argues that virtues are both means to life and an aspect of life. He holds that "Rand was not a consequentialist" because for her "an individual's welfare is not something that can be separated from his actions and evaluated apart from them." At the same time, "traits such as honesty, justice, and integrity are virtues precisely because they are indispensible means to further values" (134). Virtues are not merely instrumental; "the moral values and virtues are essential constituents of the ultimate end that is a person's life, and they owe their status as constituents to the causal contribution they make to the sustenance of this life" (135). Salmieri offers an excellent discussion of Rand's views on altruism (136–150).

In "'A *Human* Society': Rand's Social Philosophy" (159–186), Darryl Wright discusses why and how egoists treat others as ends. "The only possible path to human good in a social context is through independent thought, productive achievement, and trade," Wright remarks. A person needs to have his life recognized as an end in itself "by the culture and institutions of his society" (167). Wright argues that the egoist's "self-esteem and sense of purpose derive from the creative use of his mind," so he "has no reason to want to exploit others." Exploitation "represents an attack on the person—the moral stature—of the producers, and it flows from a sense of inadequacy and self-hatred on the part of the non-producers" (167). Wright's claims that the "sanction of the victim" is necessary for exploitation to continue (166, 181, n. 41) is implausible at least in some contexts, such as that of slavery in America.

In their **entry on Rand for the** *Stanford Encyclopedia of Philosophy* (2016),[345] Neera Badhwar and Roderick Long nicely summarize Rand's approach to ethics as well as some common objections to it. Badhwar and Long grant that Rand "thought that she had only one, consistent metaethical view: the ultimate goal is the individual's own survival," but they spend far more effort trying to show that Rand unintentionally incorporates incompatible views than attempting to follow Rand's case for the harmony of survival, virtue, and happiness. The authors summarize the major objections to Rand's case, including the points about biological self-risk for offspring and about the difficulty for Objectivists of explaining robust mutual aid.

In **"Secular, Objective Morality: Look and See"** (2017),[346] Craig Biddle argues, "If we don't need [morality], then we don't need it, and there is no point in pursuing the subject at all." Biddle inserts a note at this point indicating his position: "If man needs morality or values, then he must need them for some life-serving purpose. What else could 'need' mean?" That is indeed the question; if "need" and other evaluative concepts have meaning only in relation to a person's life in

345   Neera K. Badhwar and Roderick T. Long, "Ayn Rand," *Stanford Encyclopedia of Philosophy*, September 19, 2016, https://plato.stanford.edu/entries/ayn-rand/. This is the most substantive such entry on Rand. Other encyclopedic works include an entry by Stephen R. C. Hicks for the *Internet Encyclopedia of Philosophy*, http://www.iep.utm.edu/rand/; a *Wikipedia* article on Objectivism and Rand, https://en.wikipedia.org/wiki/Objectivism_(Ayn_Rand); an entry by Allan Gotthelf and Gregory Salmieri for *The Dictionary of Modern American Philosophers*, ed. John R. Shook (Bristol, UK: Theommes, 2005), pp. 1995–1999; and an entry by Chandran Kukathas for the *Routledge Encyclopedia of Philosophy*, https://www.rep.routledge.com/articles/biographical/rand-ayn-1905-82/v-1 (web pages accessed May 14, 2018). For a critique of the *Routledge* entry, see Allan Gotthelf, "Gotthelf Craig Letter," *Check Your Premises*, http://www.checkyourpremises.org/gotthelf-craig-letter/ (accessed August 29, 2018). For a friendly review of the piece by Badhwar and Long, see Ben Bayer, "Updates to Stanford Encyclopedia of Philosophy Entry on Ayn Rand," *Check Your Premises*, January 24, 2016, https://checkyourpremises.org/2016/01/24/updates-to-stanford-encyclopedia-of-philosophy-entry-on-ayn-rand/.

346   Craig Biddle, "Secular, Objective Morality: Look and See," *Objective Standard*, April 3, 2017, https://www.theobjectivestandard.com/2017/04/secular-objective-morality-look-and-see/.

terms of survival, then Rand's metaethics holds. But Biddle, following familiar Objectivist terrain, offers no additional reason to think that needs are so bound. For example, I might need to protect my son by using my body to block a bullet, even if that results in my death.

Stephen Hicks and Matt Zwolinski debate Rand's theory of ethics and rights in **"Debate: Is Ayn Rand Right about Rights?"** (2017).[347] Zwolinski begins with a basic question, "If my life is the standard of morality, then why should I refrain from interfering with your freedom if doing so will advance my interests?" Zwolinski thinks there is no good reason. Hicks replies with the standard argument that people need to live by moral principles. Next, Zwolinski rightly points out that Rand does not much develop a theory of property rights, especially regarding the problem of original use of resources. Hicks replies that resources initially are unowned, and people owning and developing them increases rather than decreases the opportunities of others. Finally, Zwolinski points out that defining initiatory force depends on defining property rights. Hicks sensibly replies that the moral propriety of force depends on the context, as Rand recognizes.

In **"An Objectivist Case for Libertarianism"** (2017),[348] Neera Badhwar seeks to answer the question, "[W]hat if advancing our own good requires us to trample over other people?," from the perspective of Rand's philosophy. But Badhwar's approach is to assume that Rand did not understand her own ideas, so as an interpretation of Rand's philosophy Badhwar's account is not very satisfying. Badhwar argues that "Rand is thinking of 'human good,' 'survival qua man,' and 'happiness' in partly moralized terms even though she never acknowledges this point." What Badhwar apparently means here by

---

347 Stephen Hicks and Matt Zwolinski, "Debate: Is Ayn Rand Right about Rights," *Learn Liberty*, April 16, 2017, http://www.learnliberty.org/blog/debate-is-ayn-rand-right-about-rights/.

348 Neera K. Badhwar, "An Objectivist Case for Libertarianism," Libertarianism .org (Cato Institute), August 30, 2017, https://www.libertarianism.org/publications /essays/objectivist-case-libertarianism. Badhwar reports that the essay is a revised version of what appeared in Aaron Ross Powell and Grant Babcock, eds., *Arguments for Liberty* (Washington, D.C.: Cato Institute, 2016).

the term "moralized" is that Rand implicitly advocates a view by which people take into account more than (ultimately) their own survival. (Of course Rand though of human good and the like as fundamentally moral issues.) Badhwar suggests that the correct approach is to hold that "virtue is an end in itself," "partly constitutive of the ultimate end of a good human life" and also of "instrumental value." Rand does not deny that virtue helps to constitute a proper human life; her point is that any constituent of a good human life can be so only because it serves a person's life in terms of survival. So Rand does not float away from her survivalist metaethics, at least in terms of her formal philosophy, as Badhwar implies. Obviously I agree with Badhwar that some particular positions that Rand takes—such that suicide can be rational—do ultimately clash with Rand's metaethics. Rand would agree with Badhwar that "happiness . . . requires a sense of justified pride in oneself, and justified pride requires virtue." But Rand would rebel at the suggestion that justified pride becomes some sort of moral primary apart from life in terms of survival.

In **"Philosophy Shrugged: Ignoring Ayn Rand Won't Make Her Go Away"** (2018),[349] Skye Cleary approaches Rand's ideas by assuming that Rand is dishonest and vicious. "Rand is dangerous precisely because she appeals to the innocent and the ignorant using the trappings of philosophical argument as a rhetorical cloak under which she smuggles in her rather cruel prejudices," Cleary writes. Unsurprisingly, although Cleary suggests that philosophers should take Rand seriously in order to refute her ideas, Cleary grossly distorts Rand's views. For example, Cleary claims that "Rand victim-blames: if someone doesn't have money or power, it's her own fault." Apparently Cleary forgot (or never read), for example, the sections of *The Fountainhead* in which the protagonist, Howard Roark, and his friend Steven Mallory, are reduced to poverty by no fault of their own. The so-called "rape scene" in *The Fountainhead* demonstrates, Cleary imagines, that

---

349 Skye C. Cleary, "Philosophy Shrugged: Ignoring Ayn Rand Won't Make Her Go Away," *Aeon*, June 22, 2018, https://aeon.co/ideas/philosophy-shrugged -ignoring-ayn-rand-wont-make-her-go-away.

Rand thinks that "[m]ight makes right." Cleary ignores the peculiar literary function of that scene (see my note 159) and Rand's vast writings on individual rights. Rand "conveniently ignores the fact that many laws and government regulations promote freedom and flourishing," Cleary claims, ignoring Rand's frequent and forceful calls for rights-respecting government and objective law. Cleary imagines that, because Rand opposes bureaucratic regulations, she thereby endorses free-for-all pollution, ignoring that Rand endorses standard tort actions against polluters. Cleary claims that Rand was a hypocrite because she accepted Social Security and Medicare payments while condemning the programs, and on this point at least Cleary presents part of Rand's rationale for doing so. Yet Cleary does not think through the implications of her critique; as I have pointed out, in a totally socialized system, in which government confiscated all of a person's resources, by Cleary's logic no one could complain about any government action, as everyone would be totally dependent on government for their every morsel.[350] Cleary is generous toward Rand in a couple of lines. "With ideals of happiness, hard work and heroic individualism . . . it's perhaps no wonder that she caught the attention and imagination of the US," Cleary writes. And, Cleary grants, perhaps Rand's ideas, as bad as Cleary thinks they are, "contain some small elements of truth." Unfortunately, until Cleary is willing to take her own advice to read Rand carefully, she is unlikely to discover those elements.[351]

---

350 See my "The Moral Integrity of Condemning Social Security While Collecting It," *Objective Standard*, November 3, 2012, https://www.theobjectivestandard .com/2012/11/the-moral-integrity-of-condemning-social-security-while-collecting-it/.

351 Greg Salmieri pens a detailed and excellent reply to Cleary in his "How Should Philosophy Professors Approach Ayn Rand?," *Check Your Premises*, June 25, 2018, http://www.checkyourpremises.org/2018/06/25/therightapproach/. Ben Bayer also replies to Cleary in his "Real Philosophers Don't Just Reflect the Trendy Consensus," *New Ideal* (Ayn Rand Institute), July 2, 2018, http://newideal.aynrand.org/real -philosophers-dont-just-reflect-the-trendy-consensus/.

In *The Philosophy of Capitalism* (forthcoming),[352] the third book from the Ayn Rand Society, various Objectivist scholars engage Rand's critics in the context of Rand's theories of rights and politics. Here I discuss the works of two contributors to that work, Darryl Wright and Gregory Salmieri.

In "The Place of the Non-Initiation of Force Principle in Ayn Rand's Philosophy," Wright points out that Rand's view of the moral impropriety of initiating force "is shaped by her epistemological views." Wright begins on familiar ground, following Rand in arguing that living things need values "in order to maintain their lives," and this applies (for people) to moral values. In a note, Wright claims that "so-called 'altruistic' aspects of much animal behavior" do not contradict "any of Rand's claims about the way animals function." But Wright's reasons for this amazing claim strike me as opaque; Wright suggests that, "at least for most species of animals, there is no real distinction to be made between the interests of an individual animal and the interests of its kind." Moving on, Wright, following Leonard Peikoff, emphasizes "the role of principles in ethics." Wright argues that "we have no way of evaluating the relation of a given action to the ultimate end independently of secondary principles." Wright further argues that "the self-esteem that one needs in order to live" depends on a realistic "conception of a properly human life." Yet Wright grants, "In formulating moral principles, we must suppose a context in which those principles are substantially reciprocated and set the terms for the functioning of a society." Hopefully in a future work Wright will explain how he thinks this applies to my concerns in Chapter 7. Part of my point is that sometimes we have a moral obligation to respect others' rights even when the principle of rights

---

352   Gregory Salmieri and Robert Mayhew, eds., *The Philosophy of Capitalism: Objectivism and Alternative Approaches* (forthcoming, possibly under a different title). Salmieri anticipates that the book will be published in 2019 (the published text might vary from the drafts that I read). Salmieri and Darryl Wright granted me permission to cite their essays prior to their publication. I read their essays after completing the first full working draft of this book, and, for that reason and because the new essays have not yet been published, I restrict my commentary of them to this appendix. The essays at hand are excellent, but they do not cause me to change my mind on any substantive point.

does not "set the terms for the functioning of a society." Wright also discusses the free rider problem, but, unfortunately, he conflates free riding with expropriation, so he does not effectively address the problems of egoistic free riding that I discuss in Chapter 8. Wright also discusses in considerable detail (both in this chapter and in one titled "Force and the Mind") the nature of force and its impacts on a person's mind and life.

In "The Scope and Justification of Rand's Non-Initiation of Force Principle," Wright "takes up the question of whether there can be a rational justification for initiating force, from the initiator's perspective." Wright follows Leonard Peikoff's view that to live successfully people must act by principle. Wright also invokes a sort of rational consistency argument similar to those considered in the main text.

In "Selfish Regard for the Rights of Others,"[353] Salmieri seeks to answer the question (from the perspective of Rand's philosophy), "Why (if at all) is it in an individual's interest to respect the rights of others?" Salmieri's take on Rand's views is similar to my own: "Rand's understanding of force and the wrongness of initiating it is part of the moral theory that forms the context for her theory of rights. It is because her discussions of rights presuppose this context that they do not focus on why it is selfish to respect the rights of others." For Rand, political deliberation "presupposes . . . [her] straightforwardly egoistic justifications" of moral principles. Salmieri denies that principles, for Rand, are either good strictly instrumentally or good strictly as constituents of a human life apart from consequences. It is a mistake, Salmieri argues, to hold that "values and virtues are instrumentally valuable to an individual as mere means to his survival, without themselves being constituents of the life that they help to sustain." At the same time, it is a mistake to think that values and virtues are detached from survival. As an interpretation of Rand's theory, Salmieri's take is exactly right. But Salmieri does not successfully rescue Rand's theory from the sorts of concerns that

---

353   The complete title is "Selfish Regard for the Rights of Others: Continuing a Discussion with Zwolinski, Miller and Mossoff"; the subtitle refers to Matt Zwolinski, Fred Miller, and Adam Mossoff, whose essays (among others) also will appear in the book.

I raise in my chapter about rights. Salmieri argues that "morality is a fundamental means to a human being's survival and, therefore, an essential constituent of a human life." My point is that there are contexts in which refraining from initiating force does not serve survival (yet it is still the right thing to do). Interestingly, Salmieri notes as an aside the problem of "a comparatively free member of a society in which other members are unfree," but he punts on the related questions. Salmieri comes close to granting my position when he writes, "The further the judicial system departs from this norm [of objectivity], the less applicable the principle of rights-respecting is, since the context for the concept of rights is a society of independent equals, and this does not exist when the law favors some individuals over others." Hopefully in a future work Salmieri can address such matters more fully. In the last part of his essay Salmieri offers an excellent (if cursory) discussion of the derivation of property rights.

Index

The index includes mostly names of people discussed in the work (except for Ayn Rand, whose name appears on almost every page). I sometimes but not always refer to authors of articles listed in notes. I do not include titles of books or articles. To refer to a note, I list the page number with the note in parenthesis; for example, 17(20) refers to page 17, note 20.

Made in the USA
Monee, IL
02 July 2020